Praise for *No Escape*

"*No Escape* puts a human face on the systematic persecution of the Uyghurs in China's Xinjiang region. An accomplished lawyer and activist, Turkel has emerged as one of the most respected voices for Uyghur human rights. In this book, he provides an excellent overview of the Chinese government's brutal detention of perhaps a million Uyghur citizens, many of whom have been subjected to forced labor. The book is also a powerful personal account of Turkel's journey and the costs his activism has exacted on his family and friends. *No Escape* should be required reading for government officials, policy makers, business executives—anyone, really—who cares about the deeply troubling direction China has taken in recent years."

—Michael Posner, director of the NYU Stern Center for Business and Human Rights and former assistant secretary of state for the Bureau of Democracy, Human Rights, and Labor

"Nury Turkel's memoir of life in China as a Uyghur is a chilling reminder of the people left behind in China's Gulag. It is essential reading for anyone interested in understanding the greatest human rights tragedy of the 21st century."

—John Pomfret, author of *The Beautiful Country and the Middle Kingdom: America and China, 1776 to the Present*

"Powerful, inspiring, harrowing and heart-breaking, Nury Turkel has written a deeply moving memoir, a searing exposé of genocide and an essential challenge to the free world to act to stop the Chinese Communist Party's atrocity crimes before it is too late."

—Ben Rogers, cofounder and chief executive of Hong Kong Watch and author of *Burma: A Nation at the Crossroads*

The True
Story of
China's
Genocide
of the
Uyghurs

NO
ESCAPE

NURY TURKEL

HANOVER
SQUARE
PRESS

HANOVER
SQUARE
PRESS™

Recycling programs
for this product may
not exist in your area.

ISBN-13: 978-1-335-46956-4

No Escape

Hanover Square Press
22 Adelaide St. West, 41st Floor
Toronto, Ontario M5H 4E3, Canada
HanoverSqPress.com
BookClubbish.com

Printed in U.S.A.

For my parents, Ayshe and Ablikim, still trapped in China, and my brother Mirsalih, who stayed behind to care for them

TABLE OF CONTENTS

ACKNOWLEDGMENTS

I never expected to write a memoir this early in life. A few years ago, I delivered the opening speech at the Oslo Freedom Forum, calling attention to the horrific crimes that the Chinese regime was committing against my people while the world looked on. It was the first time I'd had a chance to speak out on a global stage. I took the risk of addressing this major human rights event knowing full well the urgency with which I must sound the alarm and call on the international community to act. I am particularly indebted to Garry Kasparov, chair of the Human Rights Foundation, who invited me to speak, for his dedication to raising these issues, and to Thor Halverson and Alex Gladstein for providing me with that incredible platform. Because of this, I had the chance to socialize with authors, including American lawyer Preet Bharara and Stanford University scholar Larry Diamond, who suggested that my speech could be turned into a book.

I consulted with authors in my professional circle on the idea. While I have always believed in the power of storytelling,

I quickly learned that authoring a book is not a solitary effort. I have been incredibly fortunate to undertake this labor of love with the support and camaraderie of many. Of the authors I have been instructed and inspired by, Jim Millward, a history professor at Georgetown University, is one of the top scholars and experts on the Uyghur issues with whom I have had the honor to work closely over the years. This book would not be possible if it were not for Jim's introducing me to my literary agent, Howard Yoon. I could not have asked for a better agent. Howard is a smart, passionate, thoughtful, strategic, and super kind person who understood what I wanted to accomplish with this book. Howard believed in me and has given me this once-in-a-lifetime opportunity to share Uyghur stories. I am also incredibly thankful to Howard for teaming me up with my amazing collaborator, James Hider. This book owes an enormous debt to James, whom I have been so fortunate to work with over the past two years. I have benefited enormously from his historical and cultural knowledge and unique experiences as a journalist. I am eternally grateful to him for serving as the intellectual engine behind this book, helping me to organize my stories, and sitting through countless hours of interviews and editing. I could not be more grateful to my US and UK publishers, Peter Joseph and Shoaib Rokadiya, and their team for the incredible support, keen insights, guidance and diligent efforts. Thank you to Grace Towery for all the heavy lifting and for keeping this project on track. Writing a book about the story of your life is a surreal process, and I am forever indebted to Howard, James, Peter, and Shoaib for their ongoing support in bringing my stories to life.

I was privileged to get to know better and learn more about the painful experience that Uyghur camp survivors and victims suffered. Mihrigul Tursun, Zumrat Dawut, Qelbinur Sidik, Abduweli Ayup and Bahram Sintash deserve special dues for sharing their compelling stories and sitting through long hours of interview sessions. I am also grateful to Tursunay Ziyawudun, Gulbahar Hatiwaji, Gulbahar Jelilova, Omer Bekili, Sayragul Sauytbay and Gulzira Auyelkhan for their courage and personal sacrifice. Your bravery, perseverance and courage compel me each and every day to do more to contribute to the efforts to stop the Uyghur genocide and hold the perpetrators to account. You should know that your sacrifice and bravery have not only exposed China's crimes against our people but also compelled those in power to act.

My special thanks to Rian Thum, Laura Murphy, Kai Stritmatter, Adrian Zenz, Andrea Pitzer, Shawn Zhang and Vicky Xu for their contributions to this project. Thank you for sharing your knowledge, expertise and unique perspective with me. Without your help, I would not be able to adequately address China's digital authoritarianism, the size of the Chinese concentration camps, the enslavement of the Uyghurs in the global supply chain, the enforced sterilization of Uyghur women and the forcible separation of Uyghur children from their families. Your contributions in this endeavor cannot be understated.

I am deeply indebted to House Speaker Nancy Pelosi, not only for her appointing me as a Commissioner to the US Commission on International Religious Freedom (USCIRF) but also for the courage and hope she has given me. Speaker Pelosi has not only given me a platform to advance the Uyghur cause and garner the bipartisan support that we enjoy in the halls of Congress and the executive branch of the US government, but she has also given the Uyghur people both inside and outside China much-needed hope that influential policy makers and people in the free world really do care and are concerned about the suffering of the Uyghurs. I am grateful to my former and current USCIRF commissioners, Gayle Manchin, Gary Bauer, Johnny Moore, Nadine Maenza, Tony Perkins, Anurima Bhargava, Jim Carr, Fred Davies, Khizr Khan and Sharon Kleinbaum for their support and wise counsel. It is fair to say that Beijing's sanctions against several of these colleagues were due to their admirable work to defend Uyghur freedom and dignity alongside me. Finally, my work at USCIRF would be impossible without the support of our executive director, Erin Singshinsuk, and the professional staff. It's been an honor and privilege to be a part of this team to advance and protect religious freedom around the world.

My colleagues at the Hudson Institute have been incredibly supportive of my work. I am particularly grateful to Tim Morrison for bringing me into this excellent policy institute. I feel at home because of the strong emphasis on China studies, my passionate colleagues and their incredible support. Hudson deserves a lot of credit for shining a spotlight on the worsening Uyghur situation in China early on when no other think tanks were paying the same level of attention to the issue. We are all indebted to my good friend Eric Brown for organizing policy forums with the support of Ken Weinstein, former president and distinguished fellow. I am profoundly grateful to Hudson's president, John Walters, and vice presidents Joel Scanlon, Dan McKivergan and Ann Marie Hauser for their ongoing support, guidance and encouragement. I am also particularly grateful to John for being an empowering, inspirational and engaged boss. I would not be able to do my work at Hudson without the support of a professional staff team, including Julia Sibley, Carolyn Stewart, Phil Hegseth and Kirsten Moler.

I have had the fortune and privilege to work with some courageous and inspiring activists over the past two decades. My many colleagues in the human rights community, the A-team at the Uyghur Human Rights Project and too many others to name each personally have served as a constant source of inspiration and motivation. Special appreciation goes to Rebiya Kadeer, Erkin Alptekin, Omer Kanat, Dolkun Isa, Kuzzat Altay, Louisa Greve, Sophie Richardson, Maya Wang, Sarah Cook, Annie Boyajian, Wu'er Kaixi (Örkesh Dölet), Henryk Szadzieski,

Zubayra Shamseden, Rahima Mahmut, Jewher Ilham, Elise Anderson, Mustafa Aksu, Peter Irwin, Julie Millsap, Joey Siu, Badiucao, and Bhuchung Tsering for their devotion to the noble cause of fighting for human rights, democratic freedom and dignity. I am particularly grateful to Louisa for believing in me when I knocked on her door at the National Endowment for Democracy in 2003. She not only opened the door for us but also guided us through the process of establishing the Uyghur Human Rights Project, developing it into becoming a leading organization for Uyghur human rights research and documentation today. I deeply admire Sophie's strength, moral clarity, strategic vision and non-apologetic yet forceful and respectful engagement with policy makers and diplomats pushing for human rights-centric policy. Thank you, Sophie, for being there for me and my family over the years.

Hats off also to the Radio Free Asia Uyghur Service led by my long-time friend and colleague Alim Seytoff and his courageous team for exposing the Chinese Communist regime's crimes at high personal cost. More than half of their reporters' families and loved ones have disappeared into Chinese camps in what appears to be retaliation against them for simply doing their jobs.

I am also appreciative of the US government colleagues in Congress and both the Trump and Biden administrations. They have helped me to advocate and push through a strong policy response to the Uyghur genocide. A special thanks to Matt Pottinger, Sam Brownback, Bob Destro, Kelley Currie, Mary Kissel, Miles Yu, Sarah Makin, Ivan Kanapathy, Elnigar Iltebir, Kurt Campbell, Dan Kritenbrink, Rick Waters, Scott Busby, Julie Turner, Rashad Hussain, Dan Nadel, Mariah Mercer, Tina Mufford, Kevin Miles, Travis Sevy, Brett Hansen, Reva Price, Michael Schiefer, Charlotte Oldham-Moore, Peter Mattis, Bethany Poulos-Morrison, Will Green, Matt Squeri, Todd Stein, Scott Flipse, Jon Stiver, Piero Tozzi, Byran Burack, Megan Reiss, and

Elyse Anderson. Thank you, Reva, Scott, Peter, Bethany and Will, for your efforts and perseverance during the process of passing the Uyghur Human Rights Policy Act and the Uyghur Forced Labor Prevention Act. I am forever grateful to Mary, Peter, Kelley and Julie for their friendship, support and wise counsel, which I treasure.

I would also like to thank my Australian friends, Richard Mc-Gregor and John Garnaut. Richard, thank you for your work educating me about the true nature of the Chinese Communist Party (CCP) and for your assistance during my last advocacy trip down under. John, I am deeply indebted to you for your courage in calling on the global community to wake up to and push back against the danger of CCP influence operations around the world. Australia and the world will be a better place because of your early warnings and advocacy for strong legislative action to address these threats.

I have been encouraged by the work of my British, European and Australian colleagues in parliament who have done the heavy lifting of pushing for policy change in their respective nations, including Nusrat Ghani, Lord David Alton, Sir Iain Duncan Smith, Raphael Glucksmann, Reinhard Butikofer, and Michael Danby. It is truly an honor to be working alongside each of you to push for global policy change.

I have been moved by the efforts of the Notre Dame Religious Liberty Initiative that awarded me the inaugural prize for religious liberty. My special thanks to Dean Marcus Cole, and professors Stephanie Barclay and Diane Desierto. Their leadership on religious freedom issues, and particular dedication to bringing focus to the atrocities suffered by the Uyghur people, has been deeply moving.

Without the love, support and moral courage of my family, none of this would be possible. I wish there was a better way to express my profound appreciation to them, as they have suffered irreparable harm directly as a result of my work. Dad and

Mom, I would not be here if it was not for your financial sacrifice and support early on when I asked for your blessing to go to America. I could not ask for better parents, and I thank you for your unconditional love and moral courage. To my three brothers, Mirkamil, Mamutjan and Mirsalih: you each are amazing friends and confidants. I am blessed to share the same last name with you. Mirkamil is a talented musician, and his beautiful musical performances help me cope with homesickness. My family appreciates Mamutjan's great sense of humor. Even to this day, when our parents feel down, we turn to Mamutjan to cheer them up. He is one of the most sincere and loyal people I know. Mirsalih would sacrifice everything he has for his family. The fact he was willing to give up his steady life and interrupt his PhD studies in Istanbul to look after our parents speaks volumes about his character. We are deeply indebted to Mirsalih for doing the things for our parents that we are unable to do because of our inability to be there. I am thankful to my sisters-in-law Guli, Akida and Mahinur, and my nephews and nieces—Cameron, Camilla, Aybike, Karen, Eldin, Elanur and Alper. I also wanted to thank my in-laws Cevat and Hulya; elder sister-in-law Mahmure and her husband, Murat, and their son, Eren; and my younger sister-in-law Naime and her husband, Emre, and their daughters, Meyra and Melda, for their love and support.

Writing a book like this is a challenging endeavor that requires quiet time for focus, reflection and research. Noise is inevitable in a house with two small kids, such as my beloved Deniz and Norah. Despite their young age, they seemed to understand they would need to leave me alone evenings and late at night for me to work on this important book project. I am filled with gratitude that my children will not have the same kind of unusual life experience that their father has had. I hope this book will help them understand when they grow up why their father could not spend more time with them and why they cannot meet their grandparents. Finally, I want to express my love and constant gratitude to my wife, confidant and best friend, Nazli. I would not be anywhere near where I am without her love, support and sacrifice. Thank you, Nazli, for being by my side these past twenty years—in both the good and the challenging times. Your decency, dignity, discipline and affection for our children inspire me. You, Deniz and Norah are the light of my life every single day.

Finally, to you, the readers, thank you for engaging with this subject matter. Please lend your voice and support and join me to stop the ongoing genocide and crimes against humanity committed against my people. Finally, after reading this book, I hope you no longer feel distant or even indifferent and realize that this is about us all—civilization, humanity, freedom and pushing back against autocracy in defense of democratic freedom. Together we must prevent the next bad actors from committing genocide against other vulnerable ethnic and religious groups. We cannot let "Never Again" become an empty promise.

INTRODUCTION

THE MAN IN THE TIGER CHAIR

In June of 2017, a Uyghur man in his late thirties sat in a Chinese police station, strapped into a "tiger chair." He was attached to the metal chair by straps that went around his throat, wrists and ankles, so he couldn't move an inch. To even turn his head made it hard to breathe. He had been sitting there for three days, released only for brief, closely supervised bathroom breaks.

The man knew he hadn't done anything wrong. The police also knew that no crime had been committed. His "crime" was that he had a foreign passport, even though he had been born in Xinjiang,[1] the vast, mineral-rich region in the far west of China, where the steppes of Central Asia roll out all the way to the steppes of Russia, which eventually merge with the plains of Eastern Europe. When the man had come home to visit his

---

1 Although Uyghurs refer to our homeland as East Turkistan, for the sake of consistency and ease of recognition I will use the official Chinese name of Xinjiang throughout.

ailing parents, he had been automatically flagged as suspicious by the Chinese security forces.

The police asked him a lot of questions, but they already knew all the answers. Where had he lived? Who had he met? Did he have any illicit contacts abroad? He answered honestly, knowing he had nothing to hide. He had broken no laws.

Suddenly, a printer on a nearby table sputtered to life and started spewing out reams of paper. The men ignored the mechanical whir at first, but the printing didn't stop: the machine seemed to have gone crazy. Long minutes passed as the prisoner in the tiger chair and his interrogators eyed the tsunami of paper tumbling out of the device.

Eventually, one of the policemen went over and started examining the lengthy message. He swore.

"Shit," he said. "How the hell are we going to find all of these people?"

We now know, through leaked official Chinese documents, that there were twenty thousand names on the list. That summer in 2017, Chinese police officers managed to track down and arrest almost seventeen thousand of the people in the course of just ten days. The detainees—among them university professors, doctors, musicians, athletes and writers—had no idea why they were being rounded up.

Perhaps more shockingly, the police officers themselves didn't know why they were arresting so many thousands of people. They were simply following orders that had been pre-programmed by an artificial intelligence algorithm.

The offenses that were listed sound almost cartoonish to the Western ear. They ranged from "having a long beard" to "having WhatsApp on their phone," or "using the front door more often than the back door" or "reciting the Koran during a funeral."

But there was nothing cartoonish about what happened to

those people once they had been arrested by the Chinese authorities.

That vast roundup was the first known instance of a computer-generated mass incarceration, and its victims were almost all Uyghurs, the Turkic Muslim population whose Central Asian homeland, Xinjiang—or as we call it, East Turkistan—was handed over to Mao Zedong by Stalin in 1949, after a very brief period of independence.

Labeling almost all Uyghurs as potential religious extremists and a threat to the Communist Party's authority, the People's Republic of China has rounded up as many as three million of them, as well as other Muslim ethnic groups, into what it euphemistically calls "reeducation camps."

These arrests are extrajudicial, based on an individual's race, ethnicity and religion, the same criteria used by Nazi Germany to round up Jews and Roma. On paper, the reason given for the arrests was "de-extremification." Since 9/11, China has used the Uyghurs' Muslim faith as an excuse to portray the population of eleven million as potential Al Qaeda terrorists—all of them, men, women and children.

But the real reason is this: Beijing does not consider the Uyghurs to be "Chinese" enough. The authorities perceive their centuries-old ethnonational identity, religion and cultural heritage as disloyalty to the party and a source of future political threat to the state. Uyghurs have their own language, literature and history, formed over thousands of years at the point where Buddhist, Manichaeism and Muslim identities have historically overlapped. The Communist party, under General Secretary Xi Jinping, has tried to label anyone who tries to oppose China's crackdown as "separatists" or "terrorists," designations punishable by life imprisonment or the death penalty, just as they did with pro-democracy protesters in Hong Kong and peaceful Buddhist monks in Tibet.

China's main interest in Xinjiang is, however, the land. Lo-

cated on the fringes of Central Asia's vast steppes, the region—
the largest in China, roughly the size of Alaska—contains huge
tracts of natural resources and minerals (petroleum, natural gas,
coal, gold, copper, lead, zinc) and long stretches of fertile agricultural land. In fact, Xinjiang produces about 20 percent of the
world's cotton supplies. To keep this supply chain going, China
has assigned "work placements"—essentially forced labor—for
Uyghurs to toil in these cotton fields, as well as in local factories that get contracts to manufacture goods in the West. Top
brands such as Adidas, H&M and Uniqlo have been identified as
having used cotton from Xinjiang, and the US has recently announced human rights–linked sanctions against eleven Chinese
companies that have supplied material or parts to Apple, Ralph
Lauren, Google, HP, Tommy Hilfiger, Hugo Boss and Muji.

For the first time since the heyday of the antebellum South,
cotton slavery is once again polluting the global economy on
an industrial scale.

Here we are in the third decade of the twentieth century,
witnessing a population's genocide on a massive scale. The tactics used to implement this genocide are reminiscent of Chairman Mao's Cultural Revolution, but on digital steroids. Since
Mao's day, Beijing has updated its technique with an arsenal of
the latest technology, much of it stolen from Silicon Valley and
adapted to its own malignant purposes. The decades-long struggle over its occupation of Tibet—a cause that is largely lost in the
eyes of human rights groups—helped the Chinese refine their
tactics for suppressing an entire people. It became efficient at
eradicating culture and independence while evoking very little
protest from the world.

There is every sign that China is doing all this not just to
brush aside the Uyghurs, Tibetans and Hong Kongers, but to
perfect the art of *digital dictatorship*, a new kind of AI totalitarian state. Already, many of the spying practices used en masse
against the Uyghurs are commonplace in spying on the 1.4 bil-

lion citizens of China. Their social credit system monitors ordinary people's behavior using digital technology. Closed-circuit cameras, spying on phone apps and logging credit card information are used to determine what is known as a person's "social credit score," a *Black Mirror*–style grading of how worthy a citizen is. Littering, buying too much alcohol—or too little, if you are a "suspicious" Uyghur, Kazakh or other Turkic Muslim in Xinjiang—can lead to a Chinese resident being denied the right to buy a plane ticket or even to board a train. If you flee abroad and speak up, the People's Republic will track you down, spy on you, harass you and vanish your family into its prison camp system, or lean on your host country to send you back.

China's ability to combine this dystopian level of AI spying with Chairman Mao–style totalitarianism is a terrifying threat. What is even more bizarre and unprecedented is the hundreds of thousands of Chinese spies sent to live with Uyghur families— often sleeping next to the family members in their cramped bedrooms. They call themselves the "Becoming Family" program, and the spies live in homes to report on suspicious Muslim-related activities. Imagine if the East German Stasi were not just spying on you, but had their spies living inside your flat, pretending to be your family and using your own children to spy on you. That's where we are in this region. Spies' reports are fed into computers and as a result, parents are sometimes carted off in the middle of the night to the camps, their children treated as orphans and sent off to their own Chinese "schools" where they are indoctrinated in Mandarin Chinese against their culture and their own missing parents.

As a lawyer helping Uyghurs to find refuge from this horror, and now as a commissioner on the United States Commission on International Religious Freedom, I often meet with Uyghur parents who have been forced to flee their homes without being able to take their kids with them. Together, we lobby to get their children out. I sit in on the most chilling video calls: desperate mothers and fathers calling home to speak to their kids, only to see a video image of their child sitting on the knee of a Chinese cop. Quite often the children, who have been brainwashed by these officers, will act coolly toward their own parents. It's hard to describe how heartbreaking it is to see parents, afraid they may never see their kids in person again, unable to connect emotionally with their own children.

Given the vast scale of China's persecution, why are we not hearing more about this genocide unfolding before our very eyes? Well, for a start, the world didn't know the full extent of the Nazi Holocaust until US and other Allied troops marched into Dachau and Bergen-Belsen in 1945. And certainly, China has banned journalists and independent observers from being allowed within miles of the camps (although it did allow Disney to shoot the movie *Mulan* almost within sight of a number of concentration camps).

The towns and cities of Xinjiang have been turned into high-tech military camps, with surveillance cameras and checkpoints everywhere. Trucks fitted with highly sensitive listening devices snoop on casual conversations in people's homes, trying to pick up in private conversations what the "Becoming Family" live-in Chinese spies may have missed. China has created, in the words of one Uyghur who fled to the United States after his father vanished into the camps, "a police surveillance state unlike any the world has ever known."

It's extremely difficult to get accurate information out of Xinjiang. Some dedicated journalists have managed to capture glimpses of life in my oppressed homeland. And only through my own extensive links to my community and my work as a human rights lawyer have I managed to establish the contacts and the trust to lay bare what is really going on.

Some of our knowledge comes from satellite images of the sprawling camps, but a surprising amount of photographic and video evidence comes from the Chinese government itself. Having initially tried to deny the existence of the camps, it changed course when incontrovertible evidence started to seep out: Beijing released the images to try to sanitize what they were doing. It publishes carefully curated pictures of the imposing buildings, of Uyghur men in blue coveralls sitting in yards behind razor wire and with armed guards behind them. Then it says to the world, "Look, these are just normal work training facilities." It puts out pictures of little Uyghur kids, separated from their parents in special schools where they are dressed in traditional colorful Chinese robes—red and yellow, with old-fashioned hats on—something not even modern Chinese kids wear to school.

Then there are the testimonials of those who have lived through the camps. These are Uyghurs who have witnessed torture, waterboarding, rape and beatings. We know about dozens of women who have testified to undergoing forced sterilization in a camp before being released—what we now see is a brutal but effective effort to slash the Uyghur population. Having more than the allotted number of two children is a common cause for arrest among Uyghur women. There are only a handful of individuals who've managed to escape from China, and those largely because they were married to foreign nationals whose governments offered them some support. But even that support was often limited, because most governments are too afraid to offend Beijing. Some, such as Egypt's, have even begun deporting Uyghurs at China's request, despite their longstanding claims of "Muslim solidarity" when it came to the occupied Palestinian territories.

Despite the mounting evidence of the horror unfolding, the world continues to allow this to happen. Political and business leaders are afraid of China's economic clout, its military strength and its growing diplomatic muscle. Even as China frantically worked to cover up the full extent of the deadly COVID-19 outbreak in Wuhan—the final death toll will probably never be known—it used its diplomatic influence to get the World Health

Organization to praise its response as the "the most ambitious, agile and aggressive disease containment effort in history," while at the same time parroting official government figures that independent reporting has shown to be highly dubious. A couple of years ago, China even managed to arrest the head of Interpol, a Chinese citizen, and sentence him to thirteen years in jail. The world just accepted it.

Now it is herding millions of its own citizens into camps, using slave labor to bolster its economic strength, bulldozing mosques and Muslim cemeteries in Xinjiang, and building parking lots and theme parks where ancient cultural monuments once stood. Leaked documents quote Chairman Xi—who was allegedly praised by former President Donald Trump, even as the US and China were locked into a trade war over China's theft of intellectual property, and now over the abuse of the Uyghur people—secretly calling on his minions to use the "organs of dictatorship" and show "absolutely no mercy." Any Chinese official who fails to show sufficient ruthlessness in obeying orders risks ending up in jail themselves. As the *Washington Post* noted, "In China, every day is Kristallnacht."

One truly frightening aspect of countries not denouncing China's action is this: they might actually want to copy the lessons learned there. China's burgeoning model of capitalism without democracy will appeal to many authoritarian rulers and will come to shape the ideological struggle of the coming century.

Already, India is building camps that can house up to two million Muslims in the state of Assam, people whom it has deemed to be noncitizens even though many were born in India or lived there for decades. It intends to hold them there until they can be deported to countries like Bangladesh, where India's nationalist government claims they belong. Worryingly, the government intends to expand the program of mass camps to the rest of the country.

"'Never again?' It's already happening," Anne Applebaum

wrote in the *Washington Post*. She is right: What was supposed
to happen "never again" is now being carried out in China, and
on an industrial scale.

The names in this book may sound strange to Western readers; the places might seem remote and hard to picture. But the
people you will meet on these pages are real. They are normal,
everyday people like you and I, unwillingly dragged into the
horrors of China's newest crime against humanity.

Terror and persecution wear people down, hollow them out.
My friends say I too have aged. I can't remember the last time
I had a full night's sleep, because the fear and anxiety gnaw at
me in the darkness. Will I ever see my parents again? Who will
carry my parents' casket if they die? Will we ever meet again,
as I promised them years ago? What further horrors await my
people? And this time, will the world act fast enough to stop a
genocide before it reaches its terrible conclusion?

PART 1

THE STUDENT

1

I've always been my mother's favorite. Our family used to joke that I was an only child, as if I didn't have three younger brothers. It's me that Mom turns to when she gets sad or stressed and needs to talk. She always used to say, as she got older and her health became more fragile, that her one dream was to live long enough to see me marry. I guess that's the bond you forge when you were born in a Communist reeducation camp during China's Cultural Revolution.

And that is why China still uses my mother to torture me, even though I have lived in Washington, DC, as a free Uyghur for more than twenty years. I have not seen her since 2004. I have been able to spend only eleven months—six months in California and five in Washington, DC—with my parents since I left China twenty-seven years ago.

Mom was first arrested when she was about five months pregnant. She was just nineteen years old at the time. Her crime: she had opened the door to some of her father's guests when they used to visit our home in the late 1960s. While the '60s were a decade of cultural upheaval in the West, in China they were an era of extreme repression, when Chairman Mao and his Red Guards were attempting what his late Russian counterpart Joseph Stalin had once described as the "engineering of human souls."

My mom's name is Ayshe. She came from an influential family. Her father had once been a fairly important official in the ministry of culture in the Second East Turkistan Republic, a short-lived and now mostly forgotten country that flourished briefly in the 1940s. It had been backed by the Soviet Union but then ceded by Stalin in post-war horse-trading to China's newly victorious Communists in 1949. The Chinese reverted its name back to Xinjiang in 1954, which in Chinese means "New Frontier," a colonial name that dates back to the mid-eighteenth century, when generals of the Chinese Qing dynasty conquered the region to their far west, a vast area of desert oases, mountains and glacier-fed lakes. It is a beautiful, haunting landscape: in places, it looks like the mountainous forests of California or the sculpted deserts of Arizona. In its farthest western reaches, the grasslands of Central Asia spread out as far as the eye can see, still peopled by Tajik and Kazakh herders in yurts, living the same lifestyle that Turkic tribesmen lived since before the days when the Ottoman and Seljuk Turks moved out to conquer the Middle East. Its ancient cities had been key bazaars lining the Silk Road, a crosscurrent of Middle Eastern, Central Asia and Chinese cultures, where Buddhist fiefdoms slowly ceded to the eastward advance of Islam a thousand years ago. But its capital, Ürümchi, is one of the largest and most modern cities in Central Asia.

My grandfather, a jeweler by trade, used to keep up with his old contacts from those heady days of independence, and they would pay social visits to his house. This obviously marked him in the Communist Party's eyes as a highly suspect person. So he was carted off to a camp and his daughter was sent for "reeducation," accused of being "intoxicated with separatist ideology." Guilty by association.

While my mother, with me in her belly, was being "educated" into the joys of Mao's workers' paradise of collectivization and labor camps that cost the lives of millions, my father, Ablikim—who had been raised in the north of what we Uyghurs still call East Turkistan—had been sent to an agricultural labor camp. A math teacher, he knew little about working in the fields from dawn till dusk. But he had cousins who, during the Chinese reannexation of our land, had ended up on the other side of the border, in the Soviet Union. By the late 1960s, China and the USSR were no longer friends. My father's crime was listed as "intoxication with Soviet ideology" and having relatives in a hostile country. And so it was, just about a year after they were married, that both my parents entered the vast Communist penal system.

The reeducation camp wasn't hidden out of sight, like Stalin's gulags that had once sprawled just across the border in Siberia. In fact, this one was in downtown Kashgar, in an old Soviet-era government building, a brutalist slab of early-twentieth-century concrete whose windows were boarded up to prevent inmates from seeing more than thin cracks of sunlight.

In these gloomy confines, I came into the world in 1970. Food was scarce and my mother suffered terribly, both physically—there was little nutrition for anyone, let alone the mother of a newborn baby—and mentally due to her worry over me. She wasn't quite sure what she had done to offend the rulers in Beijing, but she could see quite clearly the effects of her incarceration on her baby. I was badly malnourished because she was malnourished. When she tried to breastfeed me, almost no milk came out and she would cry in pain. I was a scrawny infant, lacking calcium and vitamin D because so little sunlight came into the prison. The only times she was allowed outside were for the raising of the red flag at dawn and the singing of songs about the glory of Chairman Mao at sunset, after eating the scraps that passed for dinner.

Between those tiny cracks in the boarded-up window, she could just steal glimpses of Kashgar, a city that was already a trading post on the Silk Road two thousand years ago. The onetime desert oasis now blended timeless markets and twisting alleyways with modernist monstrosities like the one she was trapped inside. If you have ever seen the movie *The Kite Runner*, then you have seen old Kashgar, before the authorities knocked it down and built a new Disneyland-like heritage site to attract tourists and spy on the residents: Kabul was considered too dangerous to shoot the movie in, so Kashgar became the Afghan capital's stunt double. Every day, her mother would stand in the street outside the prison, hoping to catch a glimpse of her and the new grandchild she had never laid eyes on, and praying for some sign they were both still alive. And somewhere out there, beyond the city limits, was her husband, a man twelve years older than her whom she had met at a university dance just a year or so before.

My father came from the town of Ghulja in the north, near the border with Kazakhstan, a more European part of the country where the Soviet influence had taken greater hold than in the more conservative and religious south, where my mother hailed from. My father was the son of a famous Uyghur dancer who was known across the country, the way a celebrated tango dancer might be known in Argentina at the time. Dad was a good dancer and had been brought by authorities to Kashgar as part of a move to integrate Uyghur intellectuals from the north into the ancient city of Kashgar, once a hub for scholars, merchants and artists but now a conservative, traditional town.

As a young high school teacher, he was showing off his ballroom dancing skills at an event when my mother, then only 18, caught his eye. She had fair skin and light brown eyes, and Dad was immediately smitten. He asked her to dance, but she was too intimidated by his fancy footwork, his suit and his tie. So instead, she offered to hold his coat while he danced with another young lady. But my father has always been a persuasive man and was determined to dance with her. Eventually, she relented, and a romance quickly blossomed. Even though they were from different parts of the country, their parents shared a connection: his mother and her father, who was also a musician, worked in cultural affairs such as performing Uyghur music and dance to various audiences including the soldiers in the East Turkistan Republic Army. Despite the age difference, her parents were happy with the match, and in 1969—three years after Mao declared his Cultural Revolution—they were married. By September 1970, when I was born, they were both behind bars. Sadly, thousands of Uyghur children, if not millions, are in a similar situation today as I was fifty years ago.

Weakened by hunger and nursing a scrawny newborn, my mother—still only 19 at the time—had a hard time surviving in what was, despite its euphemistic title of "reeducation center," a prison camp. One of the guards was a Uyghur woman, a party loyalist who had taken a particular dislike to the pregnant young inmate. She used to beat her frequently, even hitting her across her swollen belly. This woman would kick her and call her a whore for marrying an older man, and repeating the absurd, trumped-up accusations against my father. Mom was terrified she would miscarry and lose her first child. But she was young and strong and that's what saw her through. Then one day, just weeks before she was due to give birth, she fell down a flight of steps, weak and dizzy from hunger. Her ankle and hip bone were fractured. When she finally gave birth to me, her hip bone was still broken, her body in a cast from the waist down.

When I was about five months old, we were released from prison. We had both survived, but my mother never made a full physical recovery. When I was growing up, on cold winter days she'd struggle to find a comfortable position to sit in the evenings as we gathered around the coal stove in our living room. When we went out walking in Kashgar, I would notice her limp as we walked downtown. We would often pass the building where I'd been born. She'd point up at a second-floor window and say, "That's the one, that's where we were locked up."

It was hard to miss the building: it loomed over the entrance of the old bazaar where two of my uncles had shops selling Chinese products to tourists from Central Asia. At weekends I would help them out in their stores and would pass the place where I was born. As I got closer to my teen years, my mother would tell me about how I was barely able to open my eyes when she was allowed to take me outside, because I was so accustomed to living in the gloom of the prison.

I was a studious kid. I read a lot—in part because we had no video games or cable TV—and in my spare time I'd play soccer or run, or join a school friend to play keyboard and guitar. While some of my friends would mix in Chinese expressions when speaking Uyghur, I was always careful to keep the two languages separate. Even at that young age, I had started sensing that one would inevitably dilute the other.

Not surprisingly, I never aspired to join the Chinese elite. I knew what the Communist leadership had done to my family and to my people. I also saw the discrimination against my own people—the "Uyghurs need not apply" at the bottom of the job advertisements, and the fact that the Communist Party always loomed large in every aspect of daily life.

So instead of Beijing, my eyes turned to the West and the allure of freedom. I wanted to be free and live with respect and dignity.

I was one of those "lucky" students selected by the regional government to attend college in China proper after I graduated from the Kashgar Uyghur High School, one of the top schools in the region. The authorities had renamed my school from No. 6 High School to Uyghur High School in the '80s, along with establishing the first and only Uyghur publishing house in Kashgar. I was always a good student and a short-distance runner in high school. Every student who was not a native Chinese speaker was required to attend a two-year language course before going to universities in China proper—it was a soft-power method of trying to Sinicize the Uyghurs. I went to study the language in Ürümchi, the largest metropolis in Central Asia. Some American travelers liken the city to a combination of Houston and Los Angeles. It lies in the northeast of Xinjiang, the most cosmopolitan part of the region, where my paternal grandmother, aunts and other close relatives lived.

Even though it was the capital of the Uyghur region, more than 80 percent of the population of Ürümchi was already ethnic Chinese by the time I arrived. After completing my Chinese language training, I was sent at the age of 20 to the Northwest A&F University in the Yangling District of Xiangyang, a city of some seven million people in Shaanxi province.

While I was studying there, the world started to change in dramatic ways.

2

The 1980s had seen something of a cultural renaissance for the Uyghurs. After the genocidal excesses of Chairman Mao, whose efforts to completely reshape China in the "Great Leap Forward" and then the "Cultural Revolution" cost the lives of tens of millions of people, came a more reformist leadership under Deng Xiaoping, who introduced some free market elements to revive the devastated central-command economy. Deng's right-hand man, Hu Yaobang, who was the first top Chinese leader to dispense with the Chairman Mao uniform and wear Western business suits, allowed the Uyghurs more breathing space in their cultural life and education, triggering a flourishing of the Uyghur region while I was at high school.

Those were hopeful days in Xinjiang. My father had been released from the labor camp after three years but had been barred from working until the late 1970s, and even then, was only allowed to take a menial job organizing a high school library and distributing newspapers to various offices. My mother had been obliged to take a job in a grocery store just so we could get by. Now he was allowed to return to his lectern and once again teach math.

The new attitude also opened up potentially lucrative investment and cashed in on tourists curious to see this remote and strangely exotic corner of the world.

The Soviet-era monstrosity where I had been born was knocked down and replaced by a shopping center, designed in a traditional Uyghur architectural style, with an ornate spiral staircase. Much of ancient Kashgar was redeveloped, its ancient bazaars revamped, and the old livestock market moved outside the city. I used to go to see movies in the theater, an odd experience given my history with the place, but there was nowhere else to see the latest releases in Kashgar. Right around the corner was a famous Uyghur restaurant that made the best "polo," or pilau rice, a famous Uyghur dish. Two of my maternal uncles had shops nearby, on the most scenic old street in the city, covered like a European arcade and full of shops selling traditional trinkets and clothing to the new visitors arriving from overseas.

They even went as far as restoring the crumbling mausoleums of medieval Uyghur leaders and scholars, including that of Mahmoud Kashgari, who compiled the first Turkic dictionary in the eleventh century for the Arab caliphs in Baghdad, to help them communicate with their new Turkic allies in Central Asia—the same ones who would soon eclipse the Arabs' power. Another of them, the tomb of Yusuf Has Hajip—a poet, scholar and royal adviser—happened to be right inside a Chinese elementary school, and the authorities actually carved out a piece of land within the school to restore his mausoleum. That is an unthinkable act these days when Uyghur mosques and cemeteries are being bulldozed by the dozen to build parking lots, and to erase our historic ties to the land.

We may not have had our own country, but we had an "autonomous region," at least on paper, that allowed us to practice certain aspects of our culture. But real governing power was still in the hands of the Chinese Han elites. Nevertheless, it was an interlude between the horrors of Mao and the terror lurking, unbeknownst to us then, just around the corner. We could celebrate Kurban, the feast that ends the fasting month of Ramadan, and I was able to take all my classes in my mother tongue, learning to write poetry in the sentimental style of the Uyghur language. One of my compositions that my father helped me write was read out on a Uyghur radio station. He may be a mathematician by profession, but he has always been an avid reader and is a gifted writer.

Then in 1989, the Berlin Wall came down. The failure of the Soviet system became clear to the whole world. Across Central Asia, the Turkic republics that had once been part of the Soviet empire declared their independence: Kazakhstan, Kyrgyzstan, Turkmenistan, Tajikistan, Uzbekistan. New countries sprang up across the region. Long-suppressed nationalist sentiments started to rise again, and we saw the dark side of that seismic shift when Yugoslavia slipped into a brutal civil war. Where the rotted old Communist structure collapsed, old dreams of liberty arose, but alongside long-buried resentments.

In April of that same year, Hu Yaobang died. The reformist had been forced out as secretary-general of the Chinese Communist Party a couple of years earlier by party hardliners who blamed him for anti-Communist student protests. The hardliners wanted to shut down the reforms he had led, so they gave him a very low-key funeral. Thousands of pro-reform students in Beijing took to the streets demanding a state funeral, centering their protest on the Monument to the People's Heroes, on the capital's Tiananmen Square.

Already alarmed by the breakup of the Soviet Union, the Chinese regime cracked down hard on the Tiananmen Square protesters, killing hundreds if not thousands. The subsequent bloodshed in Yugoslavia in the early 1990s, turbocharged by long-suppressed ethnic rivalries and resentments, further spooked the Communist leadership. The Uyghur renaissance came to an abrupt halt.

As I finished school, in my early twenties, I could see no future for myself in China. I started to lose interest in staying there, and devoured the news from overseas. At the time, the US had just invaded Iraq to free Kuwait from its occupation. It inspired me and gave me hope that another country would go to war against occupation and oppression. I was also envious of the Turkic republics that had gained their freedom, and I was young and naive enough to hope that the end of the Soviet Union might presage the end of China's Communist Party. Tiananmen Square cured me of that. Now it seemed to me—as it had to so many before me—that America was the only safe place for me to go.

3

As a young man stuck in China and desperately trying to find a way to get to the US, I'd spend several hours a day studying English. I knew it could be my ticket out of a world where, as a Uyghur, I would be constantly treated as a second-class citizen, maybe landing a government job where the keys to promotion were either being Han Chinese or a member of the Communist Party. Eventually, I passed the TOEFL exam, which was required for nonnative speakers who wanted to apply for college or graduate schools in the United States. Back then, it was still quite unusual for students from China to go to the US: China was still quite a poor country at the time. It was even rarer for Uyghurs. So I was even more ecstatic when I received an admission letter from the University of Idaho. How did I end up applying to the University of Idaho? I briefly dated an American woman from Seattle who was born in the university's town of Moscow, Idaho. Her parents came to visit her in Xi'an, and her father encouraged me to apply.

There was only one more problem: getting a visa to the US was next to impossible. You needed a full scholarship or a stipend, neither of which I had. We had only my father's meager salary as a math professor in Xinjiang and some of my mother's savings from her retail business. The US diplomat who interviewed me at the consulate rejected my visa application because I displayed "immigration tendencies," a euphemism in the State Department for a person who might come into the country and never leave. How right he was!

When I got the rejection, I felt like I had been hit in the head with a hammer. I was devastated, completely lost. Job opportunities in Xinjiang did not look promising. If I returned home, I'd get sucked into the state employment system with no hope of freedom or upward mobility. But then my luck turned around. Thanks to all my hard work learning English, I found a job with an American consulting company in Beijing as a project manager for foreign banks that were financing infrastructure projects in China, including in Xinjiang. It was a most fortuitous moment. Overnight, I was making three times what my father earned as a university lecturer.

One night when I was out with some engineers and business partners from Finland at an upscale hotel restaurant in Beijing, I bumped into the American foreign service officer who had interviewed me for my visa. He was a nice guy and remembered me from my visa interview. We exchanged business cards and would meet regularly for beers or lunch. Then, one evening in the spring of 1995, I went back to my hotel room and saw that someone had been rifling through my things. My business cards with all my foreign contacts were gone. It was deeply worrying, and I voiced my fears to my American diplomat friend. On his advice, I renewed my admission letter from the University of Idaho and reapplied for a new visa. A couple of months later, I met him again at a Pizza Hut near the US embassy in Beijing. (Pizza Huts in China are more upscale than the ones in the US—and the eight-inch pizzas are much smaller in portion size, too!) He had a somber look on his face.

"I'm sorry, Nury," my friend told me. "No visa."

For the second time, I was crushed. I felt like the wind had been knocked out of me. But then he pushed a yellow envelope across the table and smiled. The visa had been approved. I almost knocked him out for playing tricks on me, but I was too elated to stay mad. I have stayed in contact with this official over the years, and he is now a senior diplomat representing the United States. I bumped into him on a metro in Washington about three years ago. He spoke encouragement and complimented me on my Uyghur advocacy work.

Once I had the visa secured, there was one last issue. In the weeks leading up to my flight, I began to worry about the possibility of being detained or denied travel. It was easy for Chinese officials to pick on a poor Uyghur student: some self-important policeman could block my exit just because he thought a Uyghur going to the US looked suspect. Would the Chinese actually let me fly out?

To make the matter worse, I left my seriously injured mother in a hospital bed in the care of my father and a dental student friend. My mother came to stay with me to cope with the loss of her youngest sister, who died earlier in the year. Unfortunately, about a week before our departure home, she got hit by a reckless driver while passing a pedestrian crossing. The local police took the driver's side and were unwilling to order him to pay for the medical bills. I felt irresponsible to leave my parents in such a complex and uncertain situation. But my mother did not want to lose this once-in-a-lifetime opportunity and told me to go. The sad look on my mother's face, trying to hide her tears while lying in a hospital bed while I was leaving the room, still haunts me. Her pelvis was fractured just like the injuries in the reeducation camp in 1970. She had a metal implant in her right thigh. It was a strange turn of events and a repeat of similar injuries twenty-five years before.

When the Chinese passport official examined my US visa and waved me through airport security, I could have cried. It was August 1995 and at the age of 25 I was taking my first-ever international flight. First to Tokyo, then LA, then Spokane, and from there a bus to Idaho. It never occurred to me that this would be my goodbye to China, a place filled with so many bittersweet memories.

My friend's family had arranged for a host family to let me stay with them for the first few weeks while I got settled into my schooling. The US was such a refreshing change from China, though it did have its share of cultural and social norms that took some getting used to. For one, I was so impressed that individual freedom was respected. My hosts were wonderful. They would ask me what I wanted for dinner. They would drive me around to run errands. They invited me to their family dinners on weekends. One of the biggest shocks was the free and open discussion at the dinner table. In Xinjiang, if you had a difference of opinion, you could end up in jail if you had someone there monitoring your conversation. I remember having Thanksgiving dinner with my host family and marveling at the political discussion that was taking place. People at the table disagreed with each other, and then just moved on.

Another related cultural shock was the freedom I had in class. In the Chinese education system, you're not supposed to speak. If you speak up, you're disliked. It was so awkward for me at first. I had been trained not to speak in front of other people. One time while studying in China, I was scolded for correcting my calculus teacher for teaching something incorrect (remember that my father was a math teacher and I was pretty good at math).

In my spare time, I fell in love with the Discovery Channel and the History Channel and watched every show on American history, and in particular on the revolution against Britain.

I also shared the American obsession with true crime shows, of which there were plenty on cable television.

Because I was in the country on a student visa, I was only allowed to work twenty hours a week on campus. I got a job at the student center Taco Bell, and became fond of their hard tacos. There were two novel things that struck me about my work at the Bell. I was dumbfounded that you could call in sick or stay at home to study for an exam—something that was unthinkable where I grew up. Then there was the freshness date on food. As much as you might joke about Taco Bell having fresh food, they did have dates by which prepared food should be served. In China, if it smells okay, you keep on selling it.

I made a lot of friends at my job, but also had to answer to a lot of strangers who'd ask me the same question, "Where are you from?" in a tone that could range from pleasantly curious to xenophobically hostile. The two most common responses after I answered them were, "Quaker?" and "Where the hell is that?" One final observation from my early months there: I was shocked that there were some people who came from very well-off families who still worked for money. There was a sense of equality and meritocracy that I'd never experienced before.

Among the harder-to-adjust-to differences in American life was the openness of people's sexuality and affection. I saw boys and girls kissing in public, even one time in front of their parents. Uyghurs might hold hands or kiss each other on the cheek, but never on the lips and certainly not open-mouthed for all to see. Then there was the one time I went to a bar and saw a very handsome white man dressed in women's clothes wearing heavy makeup. It was definitely not something that I would have experienced in China. Later that night, when I was leaving, I saw the same man smoking a cigarette and realized he was one of my professors! It made for an awkward Monday in class for me.

4

I had initially planned to finish my studies in the States and return home to find a job that might be useful to my people and my homeland. But in February 1997, trouble broke out in my father's hometown of Ghulja, in the north of Xinjiang. A peaceful demonstration was held in the town by thousands of Uyghurs to protest against the execution of thirty Uyghur independence activists, as well as against China's crackdown on attempts to revive traditional tribal gatherings known as "Meshrep" and other aspects of our culture. Thousands of community and cultural leaders had been arrested, some of whom died after being tortured in jail.

Uyghurs have long been disturbed by, and quietly resentful of, Beijing's decades-long push to fill our sparsely populated homeland with Han Chinese. In 1944, Uyghurs made up three-quarters of the region's population of less than four million people, and the Han—that is, the ethnic Chinese—were less than two hundred thousand. But after Stalin delivered the

Uyghur homeland to Mao on a silver platter in 1949, there was a concerted, state-controlled push to "settle" the region with Chinese people. By 1975, there were almost five million Han in Xinjiang. Today, there are around eleven million Uyghurs and 8.2 million Han Chinese living there. And resentment has been stoked by the fact that almost all the best jobs go to the Han, even if the position of regional governor is held by a Uyghur loyalist handpicked by Beijing. These same tactics were laid out in Tibet. (Why do you think there's a high-speed train to Llasa? It's not so that the Dalai Lama can make the 32-hour trip from Beijing to his forbidden homeland. It's to dilute the cultural identity of Tibetans to create a more homogenous China.)

Despite those bubbling tensions, the demonstrations were peaceful. The authorities' response was not. The police used billy clubs, water cannons and eventually live fire to break up the crowds—the official death toll was nine. Unofficially, it may have been as high as 167, but given China's opacity, we may never know for sure. It was a worrying augur, though even then nobody could quite guess the scale of the horror that was awaiting us.

That brutal response forced me to rethink my plans to return home after college. Yet once again, my options were limited: the money I'd earned working in China might have been a lot compared to what my father made in Kashgar, but it wasn't much to live on in the States. It had just about run out by the end of my stay in Idaho, and as an international student, I wasn't legally permitted to work outside the campus. I couldn't bring myself to continue to put a financial strain on my parents.

I contacted a Uyghur friend of mine, Örkesh Dölet, who was living in San Francisco and who had been one of the student leaders at Tiananmen Square in 1989. Ironically, he is better known around the world by the Chinese version of his name, Wu'er Kaixi, the student leader who interrupted Chinese Premier Li Peng on national television when he met with the representatives of the Tiananmen protests, before ordering their bloody repression. Örkesh was listed as the second most wanted man in China before he managed to flee the country (the most wanted person was another Tianenmen student leader, Wang Dan).

Örkesh introduced me to an immigration lawyer he knew named Steve Baughman. A fluent Chinese speaker, Steve is a China expert and represented a number of scholars and students who escaped from the Communist People's Republic. He told me I was eligible to apply for asylum in the States, and helped me get the necessary papers ready, including a support letter from Harry Wu, a Chinese human rights activist who spent two decades in labor camps before escaping to the US. Harry had returned to China in 1995 as a US citizen, but that status was not enough to protect him from being arrested and sentenced to sixteen years in jail. The asylum officer who interviewed me was a middle-aged woman who was, thankfully, fully aware of China's appalling human rights record and had even heard of the Uyghur struggle—a rarity back in the '90s. At the outset, she asked me one of the commonly asked questions in any asylum interview: "Have you ever been subjected to harm?"

I knew I had to answer honestly, yet simply. "I was born in a Communist reeducation camp." I told her what had been done to my family and why I had left China. The interview did not last long after that. She turned to my lawyer and said, "Mr. Baughman, I have no reason to deny your client's request for asylum." She then advised that I would receive the approval notice in the mail.

I felt like I was floating on air when I walked into the bright San Francisco morning. I was so elated that I asked Steve if I could officially change my birthday to that day. He said with a smile, "Nury, it doesn't work like that."

"Yours is an honorable profession, Steve," I told him. "I wish I could become a lawyer, too. But my English isn't good enough."

And that was when Steve told me that I could become a lawyer if I really wanted to. One of the partners in his law firm was a nonnative who had become a successful lawyer. That was it. I decided then and there I was going to become a lawyer, to fight for human rights and help my people.

5

I stayed on in San Francisco, working a variety of jobs for several years to save up enough money to go to law school. Ironically, one of these gigs was working in Chinese restaurants. I wasn't too keen on being a busboy, but working in a Chinese restaurant was the only suitable option at the time. I encountered a lot of the casual anti-Uyghur sentiment I'd experienced back in China—it is rather like the old attitudes to the Irish or Italians in America in the early twentieth century. Uyghurs are seen as hayseeds, a bit dim, and our women are viewed as being easy. I worked hard though and soon became a popular waiter at Chinese restaurants, then took a job as a tour guide at a Taiwanese tour company. I didn't experience the same attitudes there, fortunately—it is only in mainland China that such friction exists between the Han majority and the Uyghur minority.

Soon after my arrival in San Francisco in 1996, I decided to take advantage of my newfound political freedoms, which I had never enjoyed in my old country: speaking up there on any issue could easily land you in jail. One of my most exhilarating early memories of life here was the first demonstration I attended outside China's embassy. It cost me a month's salary for a flight to DC, but it was worth it: I stood with a small crowd of people protesting the treatment of political prisoners, religious minorities and ethnic groups by the Communist Party.

At one point I saw a telephoto camera lens at one of the upper-floor windows, recording the scene and sending back pictures of the "troublemakers" to Beijing. It was a Rubicon moment: thrilling to be able to express myself politically and publicly without fear of arrest, but aware that I still had family back home who would be vulnerable to the Communist Party's retribution.

I also met a girl in San Francisco, at a Turkish event hosted by some friends. When she heard I was Uyghur she said, "Oh, you're an ancient Turk!"

Nazli had grown up in Turkey before coming to the US at the age of nineteen. When she was little, she had been taught in school that Uyghurs were a Turkish sect that had disappeared long ago. She didn't know there were any Uyghurs left.

Contrary to what many people may think, the Turkic peoples didn't originally come from Turkey. They originated in the vast grasslands of Central Asia, as herders and nomadic horsemen whose rugged lifestyle and hunting skills made them fearsome warriors. Throughout history, they have burst out of their homelands to shake empires and shape history: the Huns, descended from the Xiongnu tribes—whose territory included regions of the Uyghur homeland—terrorized the Roman Empire and even invaded Italy under the leadership of their most infamous leader, Attila. (When I managed to get my three brothers out of China, one by one, Mamutjan started out on a scholarship in Budapest, Hungary, which was offered to the descendants of the Huns.) Their expansion also forced the Gothic tribes of Eastern Europe to migrate westward and into conflict with Rome, eventually leading to the collapse of the imperial city.

A thousand years ago, the Seljuk Turks conquered Baghdad and took over the Middle Eastern empire of the Arab Muslims, while in 1453 the Ottoman Turks eventually took the last redoubt of the eastern Roman Empire in Constantinople, before pressing on into southeast Europe as far as the gates of Vienna. The Ottoman Empire was only dismantled at the end of World War I, giving way to the modern secular state of Turkey, where many Uyghurs now seek refuge from Chinese oppression.

These restless sweeps of Turkish history have left a variety of modern Turkic states in their wake—Kazakhstan, Azerbaijan, Uzbekistan, Kyrgyzstan and Turkmenistan, to name but a few. But there are also smaller Turkic peoples, such as the Crimean Tatars, the Bashkirs, the Qashqai and the Kumyks scattered across tracts of Russia, Iran and other Central Asia countries.

In this vast kaleidoscope of Turkic peoples, the Uyghurs have often been overlooked or forgotten. Until now.

Nazli was younger than I was, but she had a maturity and a respect for manners that Uyghurs value. I had no social status, or big bank accounts, but she saw the good in me and we started to date long-distance, after I moved to DC for law school sometime after we met. In 2003, she transferred to George Washington University in Washington, and on October 31, 2007 (yes, Halloween), we were married in the gorgeous coastal city of Bodrum, Turkey, where her family hailed from.

My time in San Francisco was an exciting period to be in the city: it has always been a lively, fascinating place, but for someone from China whose previous experience of the US was limited to Idaho, it seemed impossibly exotic. A lot of the parties I went to at that time were full of young tech nerds excited by the explosive growth in Silicon Valley. It wasn't really my thing, but many of the new technologies being discussed by these fresh-faced entrepreneurs—who dreamed of the internet as a new tool of an open, democratic and global society—were soon to be hijacked by China to launch its own high-tech industry, which was to be bent to far darker ends.

In August 2001, I moved to Washington, DC, to finally study law. However, my course had only just begun when the United States was attacked by Al Qaeda terrorists, including a hijacked plane that smashed into the Pentagon just a few miles from where I was sitting in a rather dry contracts class at American University, studying the foundations of English common law.

The shock among my fellow students was palpable. The whole world was stunned by the sheer scale of the unprovoked terrorist attack. But as it quickly became clear that Islamist extremists—most of them Saudis—were behind the worst attack on US territory since Pearl Harbor, my initial reaction was: China will find a way to use this against the Uyghurs, just as Muslims around the world felt the fear of being branded potential terrorists.

Unfortunately, I was more correct than even I could have guessed. On October 7, 2001, the US launched Operation Enduring Freedom, the invasion of Afghanistan to overthrow the Taliban who had been sheltering Osama bin Laden and his Al Qaeda group. Kabul fell by the middle of November, and US forces began hunting down bin Laden and his foreign fighters in Tora Bora—in remote villages and training camps, they captured Saudis, Yemenis, Pakistanis and Algerians. In all, there were nationals from some fifty countries who were captured and shipped to the US military base at Guantanamo Bay in Cuba. There, they were interned in a hastily built, extrajudicial prison camp for what were loosely termed "unlawful combatants" and "battlefield detainees." Their legal status was kept deliberately vague, meaning they could be held in judicial limbo indefinitely, because even terrorists get their day in court.

There was one group of people detained who were almost entirely overlooked at the time in the media: twenty-two Uyghurs. A few of them had been arrested in Afghanistan, but most were detained in Pakistan. Some had originally fled China after the

Ghulja massacre in 1997, a few years earlier, and had wound up in Afghanistan, which is not far from Xinjiang and was open to stateless Muslims fleeing repression at home.

At that time, President George W. Bush was already preparing to invade Iraq and was scrambling to build international backing for his "global war on terror." There was growing skepticism about the US plans, however, which were based on clearly unreliable intelligence.

For Beijing, which had far friendlier ties to Washington at the time, this represented a golden opportunity to crush any separatist leanings that decades of heavy-handed colonialism in Xinjiang had inspired. The Communist leadership quickly grasped that a handful of Uyghurs swept up in the US dragnet for Al Qaeda operatives might allow them to rebrand Uyghurs as dangerous Islamic extremists.

The Chinese authorities started insisting that any act of violence in Xinjiang was motivated by Al Qaeda sympathies. They also offered up a murky group called the East Turkistan Islamic Movement as the culprits behind such attacks, and offered to join Washington's crusade against Islamist terrorism. Years later, Richard Boucher, who was a top State Department spokesman under the Bush administration, said that China had been asking Washington for years to designate the ETIM a terrorist organization. "We'd say, 'Who are these guys? We don't see an organization, don't see the activity...' It was done to help gain China's support for invading Iraq."

And there were some acts of horrific violence in Xinjiang in the decade that followed, which China always blamed on Uyghurs, who were either sentenced to death or sent to prison for life in brief show trials that often lasted as little as a day. In March 2014, a group of knife-wielding attackers allegedly stabbed passengers at the Kunming railway station, killing thirty-one people and wounding one hundred and forty more. The police said they had found a hand-stitched Uyghur flag on one of the kill-ers, "proving" they were separatists. Radio Free Asia, the US government–funded news service, said the attackers—six men and two women—appeared to be Uyghurs from Hotan prefecture in Xinjiang, where police had killed fifteen people and wounded fifty when they suppressed a demonstration against a mosque being forcibly closed. International human rights groups criticized the lack of transparency surrounding the investigation and the trial.

In the aftermath of the invasion of Afghanistan, Washington was initially dubious about such claims of Uyghur terrorism: in March 2002, Assistant Secretary of State Lorne Craner reported that the Chinese Communist Party had "chosen to label all of those who advocate greater freedom in [Xinjiang], near as I can tell, as terrorists. And we don't think that's correct."

But as the war on terror got messier, and allies began to peel away when the justifications for invading Iraq frayed, the Bush administration forged closer ties to China. As Washington geared up for its disastrous invasion, having a powerful ally with a permanent seat on the UN Security Council became of vital importance. Even though the interrogators at Guantanamo were reporting that many of the detainees in their charge had just been "Mickey Mouse" bystanders randomly swept up in the US Army's roundups, the government insisted they were all dangerous terrorists and could not be released.

In reality, there were few places that would actually take them either. So the Uyghurs languished in Camp Iguana for years. In a sop to China, the US State Department added the East Turkistan Islamic Movement to its terrorist blacklist later in 2002. That would light the fuse for the disaster unfolding today for the Uyghurs.

China had played its hand very well.

By this time, my growing activism had led me to join the Uyghur American Association. Though still only a law student, I was tasked with leading the group's response to the Uyghur detainees in Guantanamo. I wrote to Colin Powell, who was the secretary of state at the time, and pleaded with him not to repatriate the men to China, where they would likely face execution, and would play deeper into Beijing's efforts to brand Uyghurs as extremists. In August 2004, Secretary Powell said in an interview with Radio Free Asia that the Uyghurs are a difficult problem, but they aren't going back to China, and finding a place for resettlement has been difficult. In fact, they never went back to China. And in 2005, I actually got to visit them in prison at Gitmo.

My concern over the fate of these men, and of my people in general, led me to attend an interfaith and interethnic conference in 2003 that was funded by the National Endowment for Democracy in Boston. Massachusetts Congressman Barney Frank was one of the speakers at the event. Frank was highly critical of the Bush administration's support for the Chinese crackdown in Xinjiang and was deeply skeptical that it was designed to crush would-be Islamic extremists. Afterward, I managed to get a meeting with him and some of the NED leaders and explained to them my position. They suggested I set up a human rights research group, much like a think tank, to promote the Uyghur struggle.

I'd never done anything like that before, but the idea caught my imagination and I already had lots of contacts in DC. And that was how I came to co-found the Uyghur Human Rights Project, on a seventy-five-thousand-dollar grant from the NED. I used the money to rent a tiny office at 1700 Pennsylvania Avenue, knowing the significance of the address would not be lost on Beijing. Even though we had only one phone and two computers, we were right next door to the White House, prompting China to instantly label us a "soft power CIA" group and to dismiss me as "just a Uyghur."

In 2003, I testified in front of Congress about the Chinese government's oppression of the Uyghurs. At the time, I was focusing on China's imprisonment of Rebiya Kadeer, probably the most famous Uyghur dissident in the world. She and I had met—she was a friend of my late aunt Tangnur, who was herself a poet and is the widow of the best known Uyghur playwright of his generation, Mamtili Zunun Teshnahi. Ms. Kadeer and my aunt were old friends from Ürümchi and had set up a nonprofit to help empower Uyghur women in the workplace.

Born into poverty in 1946, Ms. Kadeer had started out making and selling clothes, then, when Chairman Mao's Cultural Revolution wiped that business out, she started her own laundry to feed her eleven children. She later opened a store selling Uyghur ethnic clothing, and as that business flourished she moved into real estate. She eventually became a multimillionaire, owning a number of commercial properties in Ürümchi during the brief Uyghur renaissance of the 1980s and early 1990s. That was when she and my aunt Tangnur started their 1,000 Mothers Movement to help Uyghur women start up their own business ventures. Ms. Kadeer eventually got involved in politics and for a while sat on the National People's Congress, nominally the country's parliament but in reality, a somewhat toothless body stacked with Communist Party loyalists, alongside a small number of ethnic minorities for appearances' sake.

But her husband, Sidik Haji Rouzi, was a believer in independence for East Turkistan. He was exiled to the United States mainly because he accused the well-known Chinese composer Wang Luobin of stealing Uyghur music. Rouzi later worked for Radio Free Asia as a commentator. Ms. Kadeer refused to publicly denounce him, and so China accused her of passing along internal reports on separatism that she as a politician had access to.

Then, in February 1997, the Ghulja massacre occurred. When a US congressional delegation visited China, Ms. Kadeer tried to contact them to tell them about the widespread human rights abuses. She was arrested, stripped of her assets, and in 2000 was jailed for six years—the first two years in solitary confinement, which took a terrible toll on her health.

Before her arrest, when I was still living in San Francisco, she had made a visit to DC and had sent me a plane ticket to come meet her in 1997. She was always on the lookout for potential future leaders in the Uyghur community. We met on the steps of the Lincoln Memorial, since she was probably being followed by Chinese spies even in DC, and later we spent a few days with other activists at a hotel in upstate New York, discussing the plight of our people. I became intensely motivated by the injustice being visited upon a leading Uyghur rights activist.

Living in DC as a student and being politically active, I was building up a network of contacts to help me in my campaigning. Young congressional aides on the Hill were regularly calling me up, telling me I had to meet some expert on China or inviting me to cafés to brief them on the finer points of life in China for the Uyghurs.

Obviously, this was not the life of your average student. While my classmates from American University were out living it up in the watering holes of Adams Morgan, I was writing briefings in my room or cramming to catch up on my studies, in which I was already at a disadvantage, not being a native English speaker. And to boot, I was having to rack up huge debts to pay for the course, so I was also working in the law school computer lab to cover some of my expenses.

Then one day, after I had received poor grades in one of my first-year required courses, John Corr, my professor of civil procedures, took me to the cafeteria and sat me down. "Nury," he said, "I think you need to focus more on your legal scholarship than your activism. If you're not a good lawyer, how can you help your people?"

He was sympathetic, but the message was clear, and it hit me like an electric shock. I was at risk of flunking out. But there was simply too much to do on the human rights side of my work. I couldn't give it up. I just had to work harder, and longer. It was a tough time, but in the end, I managed to graduate with good grades in May 2004, and with a burgeoning network of contacts in the most powerful city in the world.

PART 2

THE LAWYER

6

It was one of my contacts who launched me into the next stage of my career in 2005. The extrajudicial incarceration of the prisoners at Guantanamo had caused outrage among lawyers across America. The Center for Constitutional Rights (CCR) based in New York organized a team of high-powered pro bono lawyers from America's white-shoe law firms to fight back. They had obtained the names of the detainees being held at the military base in Cuba, which included the names of Uyghur prisoners. Quickly, defense teams formed, and they started to learn more about the Uyghurs and their plight. One of my former professors, Rick Wilson, was representing Omar Khadr, a Canadian national who had been detained in Afghanistan just before his sixteenth birthday and was now being held at the camp. When Professor Wilson heard about the Uyghur detainees, he immediately suggested his students at the human rights clinic at my law school reach out to me asking if I would be interested in connecting with the pro bono team representing Uyghurs, as a translator, legal counsel and expert on their situation as they worked on the habeas corpus petition to either have the men brought before the judge or be released if no lawful grounds could be shown for their detention.

The legal team was led by Sabin Willett, a well-known bankruptcy litigator who also happened to be a successful novelist. The Justice Department didn't want to allow me to visit Guantanamo because I didn't have the necessary security clearance: in a federal court in DC, Sabin Willett used all his eloquence to argue for my inclusion.

"Frankly, your honor, I would like to be able to speak to my clients, and they don't speak English and I don't speak Uyghur or Chinese."

The DOJ still tried to throw up any hurdle it could, arguing that I didn't have the necessary security clearance. I ended up bypassing this hurdle by being assigned my own Pentagon minder, a gruff, chain-smoking middle-aged man who was my escort monitoring me and the Uyghur detainees we would be visiting.

We flew first to Fort Lauderdale, Florida, where we changed planes to a noisy nine-seater puddle jumper for the three-hour flight over to Cuba. The Guantanamo base is completely split by the eponymous bay: visitors arrive on the leeward, or western, side of the base, while the prisons are located on the eastern shore of the bay. There is no road connection between the two, given the relatively small size of the base and the length of the bay.

Guantanamo naval base is both beautiful and unnerving, especially for someone born in a prison camp. On the one hand, you have the breeze from the sparkling Caribbean Sea. On the other, you are surrounded by razor wire and stern-looking, heavily armed men in uniform, who are based on a tiny sliver of land in what is essentially a hostile Communist state. Add to that the fact that there were some undeniably frightening characters in the cells just across the water, including eventually Khalid Sheikh Mohammed, the man who masterminded the 9/11 attacks that killed almost three thousand people.

When we landed, half deafened by the noise of the twin-prop, we were picked up in a small bus and driven to the "hotel," a no-frills guesthouse where we could sleep and which had a common room for visitors to grab a coffee or a meal at a cafeteria nearby.

There were plenty of lawyers there in the evenings, discussing their client meetings and court battles. That first night, I was impressed to hear from one of the female lawyers that she wore a headscarf when she met with her client. I did not expect this level of respect toward those detained in Guantanamo after 3,000 Americans were killed as a result of terrorist acts by Muslim individuals.

The next morning, we were bussed to the ferry crossing and shipped across to Fisherman's Point, where Christopher Columbus had briefly landed on his second expedition to the New World in 1494. After a quick coffee stop at the McDonald's—no better way to remind ourselves that we were still on US territory—we were taken to Camp Iguana to meet our clients.

The meeting was in a rec room adorned with a TV that only played cartoons, a couple of couches and some chairs. When the Uyghurs were brought in, they greeted Sabin and me in the traditional Uyghur manner—with a bear hug. My Pentagon escort looked stunned when they did the same to him—he stood there, arms awkwardly dangling by his side as he was enfolded in the arms of a man in a prison uniform.

I tried not to laugh at his visible discomfort with these friendly hugs by individuals detained by his own Defense Department.

The two men we met first that day were called Abu Bakr Qassim and Adel Abdul Hakim. They had been captured by Pakistani bounty hunters in the winter of 2001 as they fled on foot across the Afghan border from the US bombing raids that had killed dozens of other people in the village they had been living in. As well as dropping bombs, leaflets advertising the reward were flying off the US military airplanes with promises such as "You can receive millions of dollars for helping the Anti-Taliban Force catch Al Qaeda and Taliban murderers. This is enough money to take care of your family, your village, your tribe for the rest of your life. Pay for livestock and doctors and schoolbooks and housing for all your people."

They initially did not tell their captors they were Uyghurs, terrified that they might be sent back to China. They had fled several years before, after taking part in the Ghulja protests on February 5, 1997. From there they had been forced from country to country across Central Asia—each place they sought refuge eventually bowed to Chinese pressure and the men had to flee, in fear of arrest and deportation. Eventually, they found their way to Afghanistan, which they described as "the end of civilization." There was a remote village where they heard they would be accepted, no questions asked.

Despite strong anti-American sentiment shared by others in Afghanistan at that time, the Uyghurs perceived the US as a natural ally in the decades-old struggle against the Communist Chinese regime. Qassim later told the *Wall Street Journal*, after his release, that he had told the Pentagon tribunal examining his case that he believed the US should have helped the Uyghur people, "and now they are saying we are the enemy... We Uyghurs have more than one billion enemies and that is enough for us."

The first US bombing raid wiped out around two-thirds of the village—the US military would later describe it as a training camp, but the Uyghurs said it was more of a run-down village. As Sabin argued in court, the presence of a gun range transforming a "village" into a "military training camp" would mean half of Northern Virginia could be defined as a camp.

Fleeing across the border into Pakistan, they were caught by the bounty hunters who sold them to US forces for five thousand dollars a head—the promised "millions" would have only applied for the capture of Osama bin Laden or one of the other high-value targets. But the Uyghur men were happy to see the American patches on the soldiers' uniforms: they thought they would be safe now. Instead, they were accused of being Al Qaeda terrorists and taken to a US military base in Kandahar where they were reportedly tortured and then shipped off to Gitmo.

On one of the first nights I spent in the hotel at Guantanamo, I struck up a conversation with a military official who was also visiting. He told me that it was a mistake to bring the Uyghurs to Guantanamo, and what the US should have done was train the Uyghurs up, put them in uniform and send them back to Afghanistan to work alongside the US troops deployed there to help restore order after the fall of the Taliban. Even then, US officials recognized that these men appeared to be more potential allies than terrorists or security threats to the United States.

The most powerful thing I took away from that visit was that the men I met never once complained at all about their conditions and the restrictions that they were subjected to. Instead, they seemed to be concerned about the impact that their imprisonment in Guantanamo might have on the greater Uyghur struggle for freedom.

I left Guantanamo with a heavy heart and further appreciation for my free life in America. Even more so when it emerged that the US had, in the early days of Guantanamo, not only allowed Chinese interrogators in to "question" the detainees (by "question," they meant threaten them with repercussions for their families if they did not admit to being terrorists) but had even agreed to a Chinese request to "soften up" the detainees prior to the interrogations, by depriving them of sleep, slashing their rations and turning the temperatures of their rooms down extremely low.

In the end, we managed to get the military to acknowledge the men posed no security threat (since they were classified as "No Longer Enemy Combatants") and agree to release them, as they eventually did, along with hundreds of other men who had been locked up for years. It wasn't easy, as few countries wanted them. One group, including Abdul Hakim and Abu Bakr Qassim, was sent to Albania. I went to Albania shortly after their arrival to assist with the resettlement and rehabilitation. We dined in at a Turkish restaurant and strolled on the streets of Tirana while listening to their reflections, regrets and concerns. It was fascinating to observe them watching Western movies in my room in the Sheraton Hotel: they had not seen any movies during their years in the mountainous regions of Afghanistan-Pakistan and then Guantanamo, and now at a UN refugee camp.

The problem was that Albania wouldn't allow the former detainees' families to join them. That was less hard for the unmarried men—Abu Bakr eventually found a job in a pizzeria and then found a Uyghur wife on an online dating site—but for Adel, it was hard. When he was invited to give a talk on human rights in Stockholm—where his sister lived, also in exile—he applied for political asylum, which was eventually granted.

I was able to reconnect with Adel in Stockholm in October 2017 when I was there to help train a new generation of Uyghur civic leaders. He was as calm and thoughtful as he had been in Guantanamo. No complaint about his capture or years in jail. Instead, he praised the United States for championing Uyghur human rights. He was extremely concerned about the deteriorating situation in the homeland.

While living in Sweden, China sent a Uyghur man to spy on him, pretending to be a disillusioned former party official but in fact tasked with sidling up close to the exiled Uyghur leadership and spying on their movements and actions. I actually saw this same man in the south side of the US Capitol one time, casually standing next to the spokesman of the World Uyghur Congress at one of their annual meetings. We had no idea who he was until the Swedish secret service picked him up and charged him with spying on the refugee community there.

As well as securing the liberation of the Uyghurs from Guan-

tanamo, we also managed to finally get Rebiya Kadeer freed
from a Chinese jail. I had been lobbying the issue with Frank
Wolf, a Virginia Republican congressman who was an outspoken critic of China's human rights record. Frank urged Secretary
of State Condoleezza Rice not to visit China during a diplomatic tour of Asia in 2005 unless Ms. Kadeer was freed. There
were worrying reports circulating that Beijing was offering to
release her only if Washington would agree to deport some of
the Guantanamo Uyghurs to China. I heard that some people
inside the administration were open to the offer, so I quickly
contacted Ms. Kadeer's husband and told him about it. He burst
into tears and said his wife would rather spend the rest of her life
in jail than submit to such brutal blackmail, so we managed to
scotch that effort. In the end, Secretary Rice went to Japan and
it looked like she was about to snub Beijing when Ms. Kadeer
was suddenly released. She moved to the United States, where
she became the head of the Uyghur American Association and
Germany-based World Uyghur Congress.

By chance, one of my brother Mamutjan's best friends was
dating Ms. Kadeer's adopted daughter at the time, and he arranged a date between him and Ms. Kadeer's daughter Akida.
After dating for a year, they got married in July of 2007.

My brother's marriage to the daughter of such an outspoken
human rights critic as Ms. Kadeer only added to the pressure
on my family. After their engagement was announced, Chinese
security pressured my parents to stop my brother's marriage
to Ms. Kadeer's daughter. It was a beautiful spring morning in
DC and I was enjoying my coffee while checking emails. Mom
called and said there was someone there who wanted to have a
word with me. Of course, it was some goon from the security
services, waiting at my parents' home for me to call. He told me
to tell my brother not to marry the daughter of someone who
had "harmed" China. I was coolly polite, for my parents' sake,
and told him I was not in the habit of dishing out advice to other

people on whom they should fall in love with. The man quickly started shouting and threatening, so I hung up.

I had been out of law school for only a couple of years at that point, but I had already made a name for myself as an advocate for the Uyghur cause. And that meant, inevitably, that I started to pop up on China's radar.

Mamutjan and his wife married in July 2007 in the Washington Hilton with the attendance of hundreds of Uyghurs from all over the world. My parents had of course planned to come to the wedding. But China wanted to punish us, so they took their passports away.

In spring 2007, Chinese security called and pressured me to stop the marriage. Otherwise, there would be consequences for giving moral support to the "state-enemy" Rebiya Kadeer. It is typical that the Chinese authorities believed I could and should interfere in other adults' love affairs because of Beijing's disapproval. I refused to comply with their intrusive and absurd request.

For obvious reasons, I could not travel safely to China. The last time I saw my mother was when she and my father managed to get to the United States for a visit in 2004, close to twenty years now. Since that time, we have only been able to speak by phone, with Chinese police listening in on our conversations. Sometimes they are waiting at my parents' home when I call, wanting to take the phone and taunt me or try to order me to relay threatening messages to other Uyghurs living in exile. My mother had always told me, since I was a little boy, that her greatest dream was to see me married and to come to my wedding. When that eventful day arrived in October of 2007, however, she and my father were unable to fly to Turkey to attend—their passports were still being held by the authorities. But that wasn't enough: on the night of my wedding party in Bodrum, on Turkey's beautiful Mediterranean coast, my father was hauled before the head of the university where he once taught and was shouted at for hours, accused of disloyalty and threatened with repercussions for his sons' decisions.

By a strange twist of fate, the Uyghur official who gave my father that dressing-down happened to be the son of the woman prison guard who once beat my pregnant mother in a re-education camp. And despite his brutal party loyalty, I later discovered that he too has been sent to the camps. Being a Uyghur trumps being a loyal member of the Communist Party.

My brother Mamutjan later developed heart disease. I have often wondered if this is partly due to the stress and guilt of knowing that because of who he fell in love with, my parents may never escape China and could one day die in a concentration camp. And of course, the day Mamutjan was taken into hospital for surgery, the Chinese authorities decided to detain my mother and harangue her, yet another way of adding to our distress. While all this was happening, I was at George Washington Hospital attending my wife who had given birth to our first child.

Despite this constant persecution, my mom has always supported me. But the relentless torment is hard, especially now that it has morphed into what appears to be a campaign to eradicate an entire people. Recently she has started showing signs of cracking under the strain. She was arrested when she was taking my father to a hospital in Ürümchi to treat his diabetes and heart condition in the summer of 2016. She was held for less than a day, but it was clear that this tough, kind lady was reaching her breaking point. When I managed to finally reach her on video chat, she was sobbing.

"I wish we'd died five years ago, before all this happened."

I felt my heart clench up. What can you say to that?

I tried to reassure her, of course, to tell her it would all be okay. But we both knew that wasn't true. Police had put her on a watch list that alerted the authorities when she checked into a hotel in Ürümchi.

7

You might think that crimes against humanity are uncovered by newspaper reporters, diplomats, human rights organizations or spies. Sometimes they are, for sure, but when the powerful governments behind an atrocity can block all access to the afflicted region, the work of unearthing the crimes can fall to a few individuals. In 1899, a young Polish seaman with ambitions to be a writer published a novella about the genocide that Belgium's King Leopold was perpetrating in the Congo, where some eight million people were worked to death collecting rubber. Joseph Conrad's *Heart of Darkness* was listed as fiction, but it was in fact the first written testimony of the horror in Africa that was subsequently investigated and exposed thanks to his work.

A few decades later in 1933, a lone Welsh freelance journalist called Gareth Jones gave Stalin's secret police monitors the slip and managed to covertly enter Ukraine, where he became the first person to report on the Holodomor, the starvation and economic collapse that killed some six million people when

Stalin collectivized peasant farms in the Soviet Union's bread-basket. The rest of the press corps had stayed in Moscow, either too afraid of arrest and deportation, or deliberately trying to uphold Russia's image as a workers' paradise. Even the *New York Times* was denying the rumors of the mass die-off for fear of being thrown out of the country. After Jones's story came out, with descriptions of villages full of dead and dying people, the *Times*'s Moscow correspondent, Walter Duranty, even published a rebuttal of his reporting, calling it a "big scare story."

Less than ten years later, the horror of the Nazi death camps was first brought to light when a Polish cavalry officer, Witold Pilecki, volunteered to be captured and taken to the most deadly of the camps, Auschwitz, from where he smuggled out reports on the horrors for years. The Allies failed to act on his intelligence reports, carried by a handful of prisoners who actually managed to escape. More than a million people died in the sprawling complex of Auschwitz-Birkenau, although Pilecki himself miraculously survived the war.

In Xinjiang, the first people to bear witness to the destruction of my people included an American-Russian student who was working on a review of Uyghur cuisine in 2016, a born-again German data researcher, and a Chinese student living thousands of miles away in Canada who had fallen foul of the authorities back home with a facetious tweet.

Of course, many of us linked to Xinjiang had already spotted that something new and sinister was unfolding. We just didn't know at first what to make of these worrying portents.

In my own case, the first sign came in 2015, when my parents received one of their regular visits from the security forces. I hesitate to say they were used to such frequent harassment visits, because you never get used to systematic abuse. But it had become somehow standard after so many years.

This time, however, there was something markedly different. The police weren't arresting or browbeating them. Instead, they insisted on cutting a snippet of hair from each of their heads.

The local authorities had been pestering Mom and Dad for a while, saying they needed to go to a state clinic for a health checkup, including blood tests. My mom refused, telling them that my father's university pension plan already provided health coverage. This had gone on for a while, but then the police suddenly showed up at their house demanding that my mom and dad allow them to cut samples of their hair. This was clearly not a medical checkup.

Mom still refused. My elderly father held up his hands in a gesture mimicking being handcuffed. "Why don't you just arrest me again, instead of this constant humiliation?" he asked.

One of the policemen stared at my mother. "If you don't give us a sample right now, we'll go to a local barbershop and just take some hair from there and say it's yours."

My mom is a shrewd woman, and this worried her. Were they looking for forensic material to try to frame them for something? When the Chinese authorities had denied them passports to come to my brother's wedding back in 2007 and afterwards, they had tried to justify their decision by saying they had criminal records—an absurdity, given that my father is a law-abiding elderly math professor. Mom feared this might have something to do with that. To avoid being framed for whatever fake crime they might be cooking up, they submitted. The police cut a lock from each of their heads and left. It would be years before we found out what the samples were really for.

Around that same time, aside from the regular harassment of my family, I started to hear stories from other Uyghurs that something was afoot. A Uyghur friend of mine, a successful businessman who lives in one of the southern states, went home to visit his family in Ürümchi. When he went to the apartment block where his sister lived, he was surprised to find a locked gate and a guard. There was a facial recognition camera on the gate that refused him entry, but the guard took pity on this visitor with a US passport and phoned up to his sister's apartment. My friend was shocked when she refused to come down, or even acknowledge the existence of an American relative. He left, confused and saddened.

A steady stream of these stories started to leak out of Xinjiang: people being arrested for no apparent reason, more and more security cameras and checkpoints appearing in the streets, mosques being demolished and strange directives issued by the authorities over what people could say to each other, where they could go or even where they could live. People were reluctant to talk on the phone or social media about what was going on inside Xinjiang, especially with relatives living outside the country. A few reports trickled out of new prison camps being built, but Beijing denied anything had changed. Journalists and other foreign visitors suddenly had very limited access to the region: they were turned back at checkpoints, or had minders following the few who managed to get there. It was starting to feel more like North Korea than China.

There were very few Westerners living in Xinjiang at the time. One of them was Gene Bunin, a Russian-born American who had been doing a PhD in mathematics in Switzerland. In 2007, Gene had upped sticks and traveled to China and lived in a small town not far from Shanghai, where he worked as an English teacher and learned Mandarin. During his stay in China, he traveled to Xinjiang as part of a tour of the country. At the time, he had no idea who the Uyghurs were—he even tried speaking Russian to them (Russian is spoken in neighboring Kazakhstan), but was met with blank stares. When his teaching contract in eastern China expired the following year, he made a spontaneous decision not to go home, but to move to the exotic Central Asian region that had grabbed his attention. He resolved to learn Uyghur, but found the language much harder than he had expected, in part because he already spoke Mandarin, so people would naturally default to that. Eventually, he returned home to resume his mathematics studies.

But he was drawn back to Xinjiang in 2009, when the bloody riots broke out in the summer in Ürümchi. These protests have become so well-known in the story of my homeland that people simply refer to them as "July 5," the way Americans talk about 9/11. They were sparked by an incident in southeastern China, where Han workers in a toy factory had set upon hundreds of Uyghurs who had been sent to work there.

The attacks started out after false rumors circulated of Uyghur men sexually harassing a Han woman—the classic trigger for lynch mobs in racially segregated societies, such as the old American South. Chinese police later charged a disgruntled Han former worker with spreading fake allegations and inciting the fight, in which a mob of Chinese men attacked the dormitory where the Uyghur men were sleeping at night and killed two of them. The massive brawl—which came on the back of years of open discrimination against Uyghurs in the workplace— brought thousands of people onto the streets of Ürümchi, demanding a full investigation.

The authorities in Ürümchi responded instead with heavily armed riot police, equipped with live ammunition, billy clubs, tear gas and Tasers. The peaceful protest degenerated into violence: the Chinese authorities not only blamed the Uyghurs but said the violence had been planned by Uyghur exile groups. In the US, Rebiya Kadeer accused the authorities of planting agents provocateurs in the crowd: when protesters starting throwing rocks at the police, they responded with deadly force.

By nightfall, there was a fully-fledged race riot in the city, with cars being torched and bystanders attacked. It took almost two days for order to be restored, by which time a significant number of people were dead and hundreds more injured. There were reports of police gunning down groups of rioters in the streets. It was a dark day, and in the aftermath, thousands of Uyghurs were arrested, the internet and phone lines were cut, mosques were shut down and dozens of people were ultimately sentenced to be executed.

When he heard what had happened, Gene wanted to help the Uyghurs. Even living in Switzerland, doing his mathematics PhD, he had kept up with his Uyghur language learning. Each weekend, he took a train right across the country to take lessons from a Uyghur exile he had found living there. The best way to help now, the young academic decided, was to compile a book about the Uyghur language, since almost none existed in the West at the time. So began a decade-long project that took him back to live in Xinjiang in 2014, where he freelanced as a translator to fund his studies.

As a side project, he decided to write about Uyghur cuisine. He started traveling around Chinese cities, interviewing Uyghur restaurant owners and picking up tips about the preparation of laghman noodles and pilau rice. The owners and chefs were always glad to see him and to share some tea and a meal and talk about life, and the discrimination they faced among the Han Chinese. One restaurant owner, who looked Middle Eastern in appearance, told him that he would sometimes check in at a hotel and speak English to try to get a room. The receptionist would be glad to accommodate him until he saw the word "Uyghur" on his Chinese identity card, at which point he would abruptly be told there were no vacancies.

But in 2017, the menus started to change. Traditional Uyghur food was vanishing, replaced by generic kebabs and Chinese rice dishes. When Gene asked why, he was told that the Uyghur cooks and staff living in inner China were being ordered back to Xinjiang en masse, a three-to-five-day train journey from which most did not return, most likely disappearing into the camps.

Usually when Gene visited a restaurant, the owner and staff would want to take a photo with this exotic-looking blond foreigner, but as 2017 wore on, the selfies became fewer and fewer as the fear began to seep in. In May that year, he was talking to some Uyghur friends in a city in eastern China and telling them he was planning on going back to live in Kashgar—the men told him it was not a good idea to be in Xinjiang right now.

But he did go back. When his train pulled into the station at

Ürümchi, there was a huge line of people showing their ID papers to police as they *exited* the station, not upon entering. Outside, there seemed to be police and sentry posts every hundred yards or so. Gene traveled on to Kashgar the next day, where he began rooming at a hostel, and found the situation was the same there. Many of the shops on his street had closed: he was told one of his oldest friends there had been arrested. People were reluctant to say exactly where the missing had gone. They started using the word *"yoq"* a lot—it simply meant "away, gone" with the implication that it was not safe to say any more about where the missing person might have gone.

When Gene went to Kashgar's night market, where food stands offered cooked meals just across the street from the main mosque, there was only one chef cooking large vats of pilaf rice (polo in Uyghur), where before there had been at least three or four. A few days later, that last man too disappeared. His wife took his place for a week, before she vanished as well. His favorite pilau restaurant was suddenly staffed entirely by women—all the men had disappeared.

Another friend of Gene's happened to be a bookseller—his shop was now closed. It opened again briefly in November, but was now run by his daughter-in-law. She told him the bookseller had been jailed for seven years in Aksu, another prefecture in Xinjiang. Then her husband was taken off to a camp, too. Eventually, she had to shut the bookshop down—too much of the old Uyghur literature she was selling was now deemed "unsuitable" by the authorities, and they could only sell the state-approved books that nobody wanted.

Gene noticed that a training center near his hostel had been abruptly transformed into a prison camp: the fence became a high wall topped with razor wire, the gate was permanently shut and a police checkpoint was set up outside. It was unnerving, especially as he could not speak to anyone about it. His conversations had been pared down to "Hi, how are you?" when he met Uyghurs in the street—people were afraid that interaction with a foreigner would land them in jail.

In February of 2018, when he was traveling back to inner China to try to continue his guide to Uyghur food and restaurants, he was picked up by the police in a textile factory town where he was spending the night.

Like most Americans, Gene had never been interrogated before. The plainclothes police came to his hotel room, gave him a few minutes to get dressed and then go with them. They were suspicious of a Westerner going around Uyghur restaurants, speaking to people—they thought he might be a journalist working undercover. They also asked him what he thought about Chinese politics: he said he wasn't interested in Chinese politics.

"Oh, we think you are *very* interested in Chinese politics," one of the cops said slyly. He then produced a cell phone and scrolled through to a sarcastic comment Gene had posted on his Facebook page about Xi Jinping abolishing term limits on the presidency, opening the door for him to stay in power indefinitely.

Gene had been suffering from panic attacks for several months by that point—the disappearances, the paranoia, the fear that someone could be jailed and tortured just because of a careless move on his behalf—but now, for the first time, he felt himself to be directly under threat. He was released without charge after several hours of questioning, but the message was clear. He had to get out of China.

He spent a month back home in Boston, but felt bad about not being in Xinjiang. He felt he should be there, bearing witness. So he flew back to Kazakhstan and entered the country overland. This time, he was detained for six hours; the police asked who his Uyghur friends were and what their phone numbers were. He played dumb, said he didn't really know that many people, and explained he was just researching Uyghur food. At ten that night, he was released again after the police confirmed he was not a spy or a journalist. Behind him was a man who

NO ESCAPE

had been sitting in handcuffs the whole time Gene was being interrogated. As Gene was led out, he heard the cops turn to the man and say, "Right, now finally it's your turn."

When he went back to the hostel in Kashgar he had always stayed in, however, he was told the entire establishment was shut down for "fire safety" reasons. He tried to check in to other places, but was denied accommodation everywhere. He had been blacklisted. He left Xinjiang for eastern China, but even there he was hassled by police who warned him about getting mixed up with "bad Xinjiang people." He decided he could no longer stay in China and headed for Hong Kong. As he was leaving the mainland, he heard that his restaurant owner friend—the one who had sometimes posed as a Middle Easterner to get a hotel room—had died in prison.

Depressed and suffering from ever more frequent panic attacks, Gene left for Kazakhstan.

By the time he got there in 2018, the first media reports were coming out about the security crackdown in Xinjiang, though none quite captured the fear on the scale that Gene had just witnessed. Some Kazakh activists were mobilizing to rescue relatives on the other side of the border who had disappeared into the camps and prisons. Gene hooked up with a group called Atajurt, which had started tracking down Kazakh citizens whose relatives across the Chinese border had been detained, and getting them to make video testimonies that they then released online in order to pressure China into releasing them. They had thousands of people, many of them poor farmers, sit down with pictures of their relatives, and talk about where and when they had been arrested. Eventually, their efforts put enough pressure on the Kazakh government—which lived largely in fear of its powerful neighbor—to petition Beijing for their release. Amazingly, hundreds of ethnic Kazakhs were freed from the camps and fled across the border into Kazakhstan.

That summer, one of the Chinese Kazakhs who managed to get out of China was actually put on trial by Kazakhstan for

83

crossing the border illegally. Her name was Sayragul Sauytbay, and she was a forty-one-year-old trained medic and school
principal who had an extraordinary story to tell, and which
she began to share with the local Kazakh media. Sauytbay said
she had been forced to work as a teacher of Chinese in one of
the newly built concentration camps in Xinjiang, so that the
prisoners—all of them ordinary people, all Muslims—could be
better indoctrinated in Communist propaganda.

In the camps, she had witnessed utter horror: mass arrests,
gang rapes, brainwashing, beatings and torture. She recalled an
ethnic Kazakh woman had been executed merely for sending a
short video clip of a Chinese flag-raising ceremony—something
the Uyghurs and other Muslim groups were by then being forced
to attend every week—to a relative in Kazakhstan. Her testimony in court sent shockwaves across Kazakhstan, and finally
caught the attention of the international press. For the first time,
here was eyewitness testimony of what was going on behind the
razor wire in Xinjiang's camps.

Sauytbay's lawyers argued for her to be granted asylum, arguing that if she were sent back to China she would surely face
execution. In fact, she had only been arrested by Kazakh border
police because China itself had put out a warrant on her. Kazakhstan initially granted her a stay of deportation as her asylum
request was examined. She fell silent again as she awaited a decision, fearing that aggravating the Kazakh government might
get her sent back. When it looked increasingly likely that this
would be the case, she managed to escape to Sweden.

As the scale of what was going on started to become apparent, Gene decided to build an online database to list Xinjiang's
missing—their names, ages, where they vanished, what they
were charged with and where they were thought to be. Most
important, the site had photos of many of the missing, something
that brought the victims to life and humanized them, stopped
them from just becoming another horrific statistic. Over the
summer of 2018, Gene built the Xinjiang Victims Database,

which to date has the details of more than thirteen thousand people—some of them as young as three years old—who have been "vanished" by the authorities, a fraction of the number who have actually disappeared to be sure, but a concrete base from which to gauge the staggering scale of the tragedy unfolding in Xinjiang.

Predictably, China denied there were any camps. It had been denying their existence for months by that time, ever since the first reports leaked out about growing numbers of arrests in early 2018, when Radio Free Asia's Uyghur-language service estimated that one hundred and twenty thousand Uyghurs had been detained in the region of Kashgar for showing signs of "extremism." As a result of those reports, the Chinese had arrested the relatives of the RFA reporters and put *them* in camps.

But a lack of any hard evidence of the camps' existence made it harder for outsiders to argue against Beijing's denials.

It was this persistent stonewalling in the face of mounting testimony that angered Adrian Zenz.

Zenz, a German anthropologist, knew how ruthless China could be, because he had researched that very subject in Tibet. His PhD in social anthropology from Cambridge University in England had focused on how the higher education system in Chinese-occupied Tibet had shaped the ethnic identities and job opportunities of young Tibetans. His 2010 PhD thesis, "Tibetanness Under Threat," was a rather dry and academic report, and had gone largely unnoticed at the time. But now his methodology was to prove to be downright revolutionary.

Zenz, who speaks and reads Chinese, had scoured the internet looking for official job adverts in the Tibetan region. In the run-up to the 2008 Beijing Olympics, Tibet had been rocked by a series of mass street demonstrations and self-immolations by Tibetan Buddhists in protest at Chinese attempts to stamp out their culture and replace it with Chinese Communist Party propaganda. With the eyes of the world watching, China didn't want anything as unsavory as human rights protests or mass suicides of the oppressed diverting attention from the spectacle at its amazing Bird's Nest stadium.

Zenz's search focused on the government recruitment of teachers; instead, what he found online was a massive increase in job ads for police and security services. In 2007, before the protests in the Tibetan capital, Lhasa, that demanded more autonomy, the Chinese authorities had advertised two hundred and sixty police-related positions. Between 2011 and 2016, that number shot up to 12,313.

Intrigued, Zenz started looking at government construction bids and contracts, and managed to unearth a huge construction program for police stations, jails and surveillance operations in Tibet.

Zenz's job at the time was teaching social research methods at a theological school near Stuttgart in Germany. In 2016, he presented his findings at the International Association for Tibetan Studies conference in Norway. An outsider—he is a born-again Christian who co-authored a book about the Rapture with his American father-in-law—Zenz describes himself at that event as "an exotic insect that people could maybe admire from a distance but don't really know what it's supposed to do." Nevertheless, when his presentation was over he was approached by James Leibold, a professor at La Trobe University in Australia, who is an expert on China's ethnic policies. He asked Zenz to apply his painstaking research methods to the situation in Xinjiang.

Zenz once again began scouring the internet, looking for specific construction bids: the telltale elements like high walls, watchtowers, razor wire and surveillance systems to be installed. With his background in scrutinizing Tibet's job opportunities based on educational qualifications, he also spotted what appeared to be suspiciously low educational requirements for staff in camps that purported to be offering "vocational training." That raised the question of what the camps were really for.

He put in hundreds of hours, financing the research himself for a long time, but driven by a passion to unearth the truth and help the ethnic groups living under Chinese oppression. He felt he was doing God's work.

In 2019, he was able to make an estimate based on his meticulous research, and it was stunning. As many as a million people had been detained and sent off to China's concentration camps. His calculation quickly became universally accepted, with the United Nations formally adopting it in March of that year.

While Zenz was trawling official Chinese government online recruitment ads from Germany, in Canada, a Chinese second-year law student was also doing his part to piece together crucial evidence of what was happening in Xinjiang.

While in Canada, Shawn Zhang had already gotten into hot water with the authorities back home by posting social media comments mocking Western corporations that are forced to kowtow to the Chinese Communist Party in order to keep operating in China. What had really yanked their chain was when Shawn posted on social media an image of a "Free Tibet" flag on a page of the Marriott hotel, which had recently been forced to apologize to China for accidentally listing Tibet—invaded by Mao's troops in 1950—as an independent country in its hotel rewards program. China had been furious, and the hotel chain had been forced to issue an abject apology.[2]

Because of that small gesture of defiance, the authorities visited Shawn's parents at their home near Shanghai and told them to make sure their son shut up.

Zhang had already decided however that he would not be returning home when he finished his degree at the University of British Columbia in Vancouver. He found the lack of freedom in China suffocating, and the influence that Beijing is able to exert globally with its growing economic might and military

---

2   In May 2021, Hollywood star John Cena was forced to record an effusive apology in Mandarin when he called Taiwan a country—as opposed to part of China—while promoting his latest movie, *Fast & Furious 9*. China has the largest box office in the world. "I'm very, very sorry about my mistake. I'm sorry. I'm sorry. I sincerely apologize. You must understand that I really love and respect China and the Chinese people. I'm sorry."

muscle disturbed him to the extreme. So in early 2018, when he heard stories circulating online and in the media of mass detentions in the far west of the country, he decided to use his language and computer skills to investigate.

He searched on Baidu, the Chinese equivalent of Google, for terms such as "reeducation center" and came up with pictures of newly built facilities, often featuring a gate or a wall or a sign, together with their GPS coordinates. He then went a step further and plugged these coordinates into Google Earth and found there were actual satellite images that showed the size and layout of the compounds.

When he first started mapping and identifying them, Zhang had been skeptical of reports that so many Uyghurs could have been detained. What he saw now convinced him it was all too feasible. He downloaded and stored the pictures, and in the coming months went back to the same coordinates on Google Earth: that was when he realized the facilities were getting bigger and bigger. He shared the images online, on his blog and Twitter accounts, and soon journalists from major news outlets were knocking on his door for help researching their stories about Xinjiang.

There was one more vital link between what had happened in Tibet almost a decade before and what was happening now in Xinjiang. And that was a man called Chen Quanguo, the Communist Party boss who had masterminded the crackdown in Tibet that Zenz had uncovered. In 2016, Chen had been transferred to Xinjiang, to repeat what he had done in Tibet and to elaborate on it. The stern sixty-one-year-old moved into a government-owned hotel guarded by the People's Liberation Army and installed a high-speed data line run into the region's digital-security infrastructure. Artificial intelligence and high-tech were to be at the core of his crackdown.

Chen came from a poor rural background in Henan province, and served a four-year stint in the artillery before getting a job at a car parts factory. A party zealot, he slowly worked his way up through the Communist Party ranks to become governor of neighboring Hebei province before being sent in 2011 to the Tibet Autonomous Region (Tibet proper was sliced up after Mao invaded in 1950—otherwise it would be the 10th largest country in the world). And that was where he made his mark, rolling out massive recruitment of impoverished local Tibetans into low-level security forces, mimicking what many European colonial powers had done in the nineteenth century by using "native" troops to keep order in their sprawling overseas domains.

With those extra security forces, Chen built up thousands of local "convenience police stations," concrete or prefabricated huts with no more than five hundred meters between them, inside Tibet's towns. This was known by the party as "grid-style social management," segmenting communities into very small sectors overlooked by police, security guards and a dense network of surveillance cameras. In place of naked brutality, Chen planned to crush the Tibetan spirit methodically, almost mechanically.

Soon, Tibet's dissenting voices had been once again stifled, and Chen—the rising star of the party—had been dispatched to Xinjiang to do the same, crushing any group that failed, in the paranoid imagination of the Chinese Communist leadership, to conform to its image of "unity" in the vast nation.

"Round up everyone who needs to be rounded up," he ordered when he arrived in Ürümchi. He was there, he said, to "gnaw bones."

Within the space of that first year, he had recruited more than ninety thousand new security agents—often low-level assistant police officers, more brute muscle than actual law enforcement officers—and deployed them in some seventy-five hundred new convenience police stations. Xinjiang's transformation into an open-air prison camp had begun and Chen—who has been compared to Adolf Eichmann, the man who engineered Nazi

Germany's "Final Solution"—had won himself a coveted place on China's Politburo, one of only twenty-five members at the core of Chinese power.

Faced with such mounting evidence of oppression from Zenz and others, China was forced, in November of 2018, to admit that the camps did actually exist. But now it resorted to the big lie: the camps were only there as "vocational reeducational facilities," to train poor Uyghurs and allow them to escape poverty, or to draw them away from extremist tendencies.

The fact that so many of the detained were successful professionals—doctors, lawyers, entertainers, professors—showed the utter absurdity of the "vocational training" lie. As for the "de-extremification" line, should Britain lock up every Muslim in the United Kingdom because a handful of extremists carried out attacks on London's buses and Underground? Should France herd its large Muslim population into camps because some French citizens fought in Syria? No, clearly not. That is a policing matter, and what was happening in Xinjiang was something far more sinister.

Yet the official lie persisted.

What China had failed to take into account was that some of the people it had sent to the concentration camps might actually have the tenacity—and often just the sheer luck—to escape the country. They would then show extraordinary courage in speaking out about what had happened to them.

And I would get the chance to help them tell their stories to the world.

PART 3

THE WAR ON UYGHUR WOMEN

8

Long before the internet sleuths and nervous dissidents started spotting signs of newly built prisons popping up on satellite images, or in the dry pages of government budget reports, ordinary Uyghurs had already started to feel the walls closing in. Some spotted the signs before others. Rumors first filtered into Xinjiang's cities from the countryside that something was wrong, detailing roundups that almost emptied remote villages. These were relatively easy for residents of Ürümchi and Kashgar to ignore, given China's periodic crackdowns on any organized group that wasn't the Communist Party, such as the Falun Gong spiritual movement, political dissidents or religious organizations. "These things happen sometimes in authoritarian regimes," people thought. "It won't happen here."

Many were simply oblivious. For young Uyghur students living overseas, the first they knew of the dawning era of repression was when they flew home to see their families during summer break of 2017. They were met at the airport not by joyful par-

ents but by state officials, who greeted them with chilling, ro-
botic speeches, like the scripted spiels you get from fundraisers
in the US, only these were informing them that their mother
and father were "in a training school set up by the government."
When these officials were met with confused, stunned faces,
they continued their pre-scripted speeches, laden with menace.
"I'm sure you'll support them because this is for their own good.
And for your own good."

The first hint of this repression that Qelbinur Sidik got was in
2015, shortly after fellow teachers at her high school in Ürümchi returned home to their provincial towns and villages for
the summer break. When they came back to Ürümchi in the
fall, they told disturbing stories of mass arrests in the countryside, of police checkpoints everywhere. These word-of-mouth
reports were unsettling, but easy for her to ignore. Qelbinur,
a small, earnest but kindly lady now in her early fifties, who
looks every inch the veteran high school teacher, ostensibly had
little to worry about: an ethnic Uzbek, she had been a teacher
of the Chinese language to fifth and sixth graders for almost
three decades, and was also a school administrator. In short, a
pillar of the community, and not a Uyghur, though Uzbeks
are also Turkic Muslims. Uzbek and Uyghur people have a lot
in common—they look similar, have similar music, dress and
types of food. Their languages are different, but mutually un-
derstandable. She enjoyed her job. She loved the way the light
streamed in through the large glass windows of her classroom,
and the chance that every day brought to implant new knowledge in the minds of her young Uyghur students.

It is part of human nature to downplay disturbing news over
which one has little control: psychologists call it "normalcy bias."
With hindsight, it's easy to say that people should have seen a
disaster coming. So Qelbinur brushed off what she heard from
other teachers and got on with her life with her husband in their
middle-class neighborhood in Ürümchi. Her husband, a civil

servant, had suffered from a drinking problem in the past, but seemed to have it under control, and their daughter was happily living in the Netherlands, studying biology and married to a Dutchman. The Sidiks went to visit her twice, first in 2015 and then a year later, and they liked both the country and their new in-laws, as well as their new grandchild.

In 2016, the same seasonal migration of teachers from the provinces took place as summer recess began. A female colleague of Qelbinur's went back to her hometown of Aksu, an oasis town (Aksu means "white water" in the Uyghur language) close to the western border with Kyrgyzstan. When she came back, she said the villages around Aksu had been all but emptied of their inhabitants. There was a palpable fear in the region that just about anyone could be arrested next. In fact, this woman's three brothers had been detained and sentenced to long prison terms for the most trivial of things: the eldest and most devout brother was jailed for ten years for simply praying five times a day; the next oldest got eight years for attending weekly Friday prayers—known as "Jummah"—at his local mosque. The youngest also received an eight-year term, this one for attending several religious funeral services. Meanwhile, public gatherings were being staged in open-air stadiums where people were dragged onstage and publicly denounced for owning prayer mats or a copy of the Koran. Such wild stories started trickling in from other places too: a teacher who had gone home to Toksun in the center of the region had similar experiences, and even people from the hinterland of my hometown of Kashgar, in the south, heard of arrests and crackdowns.

Still, Qelbinur and others relied on their sense that such things wouldn't happen in the vast, modern metropolis of Ürümchi. One of the largest cities in Central Asia, it has its own modern metro system, and malls with Gucci, Dior and Chanel outlets. Qelbinur decided to focus on her teaching, and not worry about things she couldn't control. They were like frogs being boiled slowly in water, not yet aware of the mounting danger they were in.

But as the fall semester began that year, changes started to show in Ürümchi, too. Qelbinur lived in what was technically a gated community, though she had all but forgotten the fact because the gates were never closed, and had become rusted and overgrown. Now, though, the gates were suddenly shut, some of them permanently—people coming in and out were funneled through one building entrance. Strange, but a minor inconvenience. Then new surveillance cameras were installed, some with facial recognition devices. Razor wire suddenly topped the walls. A nearby community of lower-class residential homes was rapidly demolished and replaced almost overnight by apartment blocks, with guards, security cameras and locked front doors. Several years later, when Qelbinur saw the video footage of Chinese hospitals being built in just a few days in Wuhan as the coronavirus spread across the country, she was reminded of the speed at which these new neighborhoods had mushroomed in her hometown.

Most Uyghurs didn't know it at the time, but the reason for this sudden acceleration in security surveillance was that in August of 2016, Chen Quanguo had arrived in Xinjiang, with the aim of subjugating the Uyghurs in the same way he had crushed the life out of Tibet. His arrival was quickly felt across the region. Qelbinur, possibly because she is an ethnic Uzbek, would not feel its full impact for another six months. But for Zumrat Dawut, the Uyghur wife of a Pakistani trader and a mother of three, it resulted in a quick summons for her and her family—indeed, her whole block—to the offices of the local neighborhood watch committee.

These committees are all over Xinjiang. They are mostly made up of party loyalists or people trying to elevate their status in the community, but also by foot soldiers ordered to keep an eye on their neighbors, reporting any strangers in the streets or suspicious activity. They have existed across China for de-cades, but recently have taken on a more formalized, aggressive behavior: neighborhoods have been carved up into a tight grid pattern, with some fifteen to twenty households in each, and assigned a dedicated monitor to report back to the committee on everything that goes on.

"The basic task of the grid monitor will be to gain a full un-derstanding of the situation in the grid," a Communist Party directive sent out in 2018 and leaked to Radio Free Asia said. The monitors' task would be to snoop on their neighbors, in-tervene in any disputes and carry out "psychological interven-tion" if needed. And of course report anything suspicious to the committee.

Zumrat Dawut, a sturdy, savvy businesswoman in her late thirties who prided herself on knowing how the world works, knew that not all the committee's monitors were willing snoops or party loyalists, since her own brother was one of the unwill-ing conscripts. He made a decent salary working for the com-mittee (although much less than his Chinese counterparts), but he did not like it. Soon, as nightly house raids and arrests began, he would come to dread his work, but could not leave it or criticize it for fear of being denounced as "two-faced"—a state servant who dares to question his orders. Several high-profile Uyghurs ended up in the camps for being "two-faced," includ-ing the president of Xinjiang University, Dr. Tashpolat Tiyip.

Once summoned to the local committee offices that winter of 2016, Zumrat and her neighbors were ordered to hand over their phones for data scanning. This scan allowed the authori-ties to download all their personal data—call history, apps and the data these contained, personal photos, messages and emails, right back to the point of factory settings. This was unsettling, to say the least, but Zumrat knew she had done nothing wrong. What she didn't realize yet was that innocence would be no de-fense against punishment.

This quickly became clear to people who had bought their cell phones secondhand: data from previous users could get you locked up. That might include some long-deleted apps that Beijing had deemed unacceptable, such as WhatsApp or Facebook. The state wanted its citizens to use Chinese apps only, which it could easily monitor. For that same reason, iPhones were suddenly banned: they are too hard to hack. Many people started using "dumb phones," but even that simple change aroused police suspicion: What were these people trying to hide by using such outdated technology?

Zumrat's cross-border business with Pakistan and with China's bustling coastal cities had been doing well, and she had treated herself to a new iPhone for three thousand RMB, or around five hundred dollars. Now, she replaced it with a Samsung and tried to sell her old smartphone, but the ban had caused the iPhone market to collapse. She was lucky to offload it for just five hundred RMB, a fraction of what she had paid. Other people she knew, including some of her relatives, were unable to sell theirs and took the dramatic precaution of smashing the expensive phones with a hammer.

The data scan took hours to complete. People had to wait at the committee offices before their phones were handed back to them. When they got them, Zumrat noticed a new app had been installed. It was called "Clean Internet Security Soldier." This, she was told, was an advanced spying device that would log all her calls, text messages, internet browsing, online purchases and even her GPS position: if Uyghurs left their home, they were expected to have their phone with them so the authorities knew where they were at all times. It was also linked to bank accounts, so the state could see what they purchased and where. Two weeks after the app was installed, Zumrat casually greeted a friend with her habitual "Essalamu eleykum," a common expression across the Muslim world that literally means "peace be upon you" but mostly just means "hello." Shortly after, a security official approached her and told her the Arabic phrase now was banned. She had to stick to the "national language"—the new official term for Mandarin. Renaming it the national language was part of the government's attempt to create a monolithic society where the Han language, culture and way of life dominates. Next time, the official warned, things wouldn't be so easy for her.

While it was impossible for authorities to manually monitor every conversation, it was simple for an artificial intelligence algorithm to be on alert for specific trigger words or phrases that might signify religious leanings—"God," "Mohammed" or "mosque."

For most Uyghurs, that data scan was the first warning shot. Soon after came the second. Sudden, unannounced house raids began, seemingly at random from early 2017. State security forces and neighborhood watch members would show up at an apartment complex, usually later in the evening after families had had their dinner, rushing through the front and back doors to sweep entire buildings for banned materials: prayer mats, Korans, long dresses for women, but also axes and any extra knives. Since the spate of deadly knife attacks in 2014, Uyghur households had been allowed only two knives each: one chopping knife and one smaller one for preparing vegetables. Both had to be fitted with QR barcodes so their users could be traced, and the larger one had to be affixed to a kitchen counter with a chain. Failure to comply, or possession of other knives, could suddenly land you in prison. These raids became known as the "Strike Hard Campaign," and triggered the first wave of widespread arrests in Xinjiang.

How were people to know what was banned and what was still permitted? That vital information was transmitted through the Monday-morning flag-raising ceremony in Xinjiang, which quickly became a weekly ritual for the Uyghurs. These long-standing ceremonies began at 8:00 every week, and attendance was obligatory, come rain or shine. In Ürümchi, the temperatures can plunge to forty degrees below (Fahrenheit) in winter, and the people standing in the snow for two hours were forbidden from wearing any form of head covering that could be taken as a sign of religious devotion.

The Uyghurs were issued little booklets in which their attendance was stamped each week: these are a pretty pink, adorned with postcard-like images of the Great Wall and Beijing's Forbidden City on the cover. But the pretty cards could get you interned in a "reeducation camp" if your flag-raising attendance record dipped below 90 percent.

As well as issuing instructions on what you could keep in your home or what you were allowed to say to your friends and neighbors, these gatherings also served as mass experiments in brainwashing, a foretaste of the camps that so many of the attendees would soon end up in. As the red flag of China was rising above the crowd, the neighborhood watch members would lead chanted slogans about the greatness of the party and its secretary-general, Xi Jinping, and the need for Uyghurs to abandon their faith in anyone but him.

Zumrat recalled with a shudder the first time she was forced to renounce her religion. The party apparatchik leading the meeting shouted out to the assembled Uyghurs, "Is there a God?"

The shocked crowd paused, before answering, "No." They had to—other members of the neighborhood watch were scrutinizing their reactions as they stood around the flagpole. Zumrat moved her lips without saying the words that first time.

"Who is your new god?" the meeting leader called.

"Xi Jinping," the crowd dutifully chanted back.

Later, when Zumrat got home, she prayed for forgiveness.

9

Not everyone had the opportunity to adapt to the looming crackdown. If Qelbinur and Zumrat were like frogs being slowly boiled alive, Mihrigul Tursun's experience was more like a lobster being plunged into a pot of scalding water.

Mihrigul had always been a bright student, gifted at learning languages and with a yearning to improve her family's lot. Her father, whom she adored, was a truck driver, her brother a reserve policeman, roughly the equivalent of a sheriff's deputy. They were a solid working-class family from the remote town of Cherchen, a river oasis on the southern rim of the vast Taklamakan Desert (which itself borders the more famous Gobi Desert), a barren mass that threatens to swallow up the ancient settlement with its vast dust storms. Her mother had died when Mihrigul was just a baby, and she had been raised for a while by her grandmother before her father remarried.

Her academic abilities had won her a place in a high school[3] in the Chinese metropolis of Guangzhou, close to Hong Kong, at the age of just twelve. She stayed in China proper until she was twenty-two. Mihrigul had always felt like something of an outsider there, a pale-skinned, blue-eyed girl whom her classmates treated as something exotic and slightly alien. In class, the other kids called her "Heidi" because she looked so European. Policemen would often ask this foreign-looking girl for her papers: the cops were amazed she could speak such fluent Chinese and were often confounded by the fact that she had Chinese identity papers. Most had little notion of where Xinjiang was, way out on the far western border, even though it is the largest region of China. "Chinese police are so dumb," Mihrigul often says in conversation, with an exasperated laugh. She looks a bit like the proverbial "girl next door," an attractive young woman with a bright manner, despite the antidepressants and sleeping pills she now needs to manage the horrors of what she endured in China's camps.

Her hometown of Cherchen—which is also known in Chinese as Qiemo—lies on what was the southern branch of the Silk Road, and thousands of years ago traded with the earliest Chinese dynasties and with Tibet, just to the south. Marco Polo passed through on his way to China in 1273. Today it is perhaps best known for the Tarim mummies that were discovered in Bronze Age graves near the city: they are remarkable for their European features. The most famous one, known as "Cherchen Man," sports a ginger beard and reddish hair. They died some three thousand years ago and their bodies were naturally preserved in the dry desert air—experts believe they are evidence of Indo-European peoples having migrated across the Russian steppes and settling in the oasis.

3 "Neigaoban," meaning inland high school. It is one of the earlier and ongoing ways of forced assimilation of Uyghurs by bringing young Uyghurs to get educated in Chinese, adopt Chinese culture and eventually marry an ethnic Chinese spouse.

Having grown up in the glittering business hub of Guangzhou—which was historically known in English by the name Canton—Mihrigul was in no hurry to return to her desert hometown. She was ambitious, and won a place to study for an MBA in Egypt. She was thrilled: her dream was to start her own import-export business and make enough money to eventually get her family out of China. When she told her father, he begged her not to go, but she was determined to follow her dreams. It took her nine months to assemble all the permits and paperwork a Uyghur needs to study abroad. Despite his reluctance, her father helped pay for the course.

So in 2010 she packed her bags and boarded a flight for Cairo. On that first flight, a good-looking young Egyptian man seated in the row ahead struck up a conversation. She didn't speak any Arabic or English yet, so she used her phone's translation app to chat. Like everyone else, Mahmoud too was surprised when she said she was Chinese. They hit it off immediately—he had been in China buying goods to sell in Egypt, exactly the sort of thing Mihrigul planned on doing. She was glad to have a friend in the strange, distant city she was moving to, and they exchanged phone numbers and email addresses when they landed in Cairo. She used to visit and hang out at his apartment, and as she learned Arabic with Mahmoud's help, she also made friends with his mother.

But less than two months after she landed, Egypt was plunged into an uprising that would come to be known as the Arab Spring, convulsing the entire region. The university was shut down as millions took to the streets to protest against the decades-old authoritarian rule of Hosni Mubarak. China dispatched planes to evacuate its students—partly for their own safety, but partly out of fear they would be exposed to the contagious ideas of revolution. It was nine months before Mihrigul returned to Egypt.

When she did, Mahmoud was delighted to see her again. He

always called her Mihri, which was easier for him to say than her full Uyghur name. They became very close. Gradually their friendship blossomed into a romance.

All was not well at school though. It quickly became clear that when the Chinese students and workers returned to Egypt, a large number of spies and police informers had infiltrated the Chinese community there. Some of them approached Mihrigul and ordered her to start keeping tabs on fellow students enrolled at Al-Azhar University, a religiously conservative seat of learning that held great sway over the Muslim Brotherhood, a long-banned Islamic political organization that had risen to prominence after the revolution. The idea of spying appalled Mihrigul and she tried to put them off. They told her that if she didn't cooperate, she would have visa problems with the Egyptians. Speaking to some friends about what to do, she learned that if she married an Egyptian citizen she would automatically get an extended residence permit. If she had children with an Egyptian man, she would be able to apply for citizenship. She and Mahmoud decided to have a "green card" marriage that would allow her to stay in Egypt.

Their parents objected. Mahmoud's parents wanted him to marry an Arab, while Mihrigul's father wanted her to marry a Uyghur—he said that Arab men were allowed to have numerous wives, while a Uyghur man would respect her and only have one. This resistance came partly because he was a conservative, working-class man from a remote town near Tibet, but also because many Uyghurs are conscious of the growing assault on their population by China. His son—Mihrigul's older brother—was a bit of a tough guy who had always dreamed of joining the police, but to do so, he had to change his name from the Uyghur "Ekber" to the Chinese "Wang Guo," and also change his official ethnicity in all his documents to "Chinese." Dozens of Mihrigul's friends who had found government jobs were forced to do the same thing.

Rather like Orthodox Jews, Uyghurs try to preserve the cultural integrity of their precarious nation as much as possible. Marrying outside the community is frowned upon. Mihrigul's father had already seen his daughter taken away to inland China for most of her life, her head filled with Chinese culture. Now he feared that she might never come home at all.

Mihrigul told her parents it was only a marriage on paper, but still they objected. Her father threatened to cut her off. After three months of marriage, Mihrigul and Mahmoud agreed that they would divorce. But her parents did suggest a workaround: they had a Uyghur friend whose son was also studying in Egypt and who had long-term residency. If she married him, Mihrigul figured she could stay in Egypt and continue her studies.

As an aspiring businesswoman, Mihrigul was a resolute problem-solver. She knew she couldn't ever turn her back on her parents—as she put it, "A man I can always find, but a father and a mother I can't ever find again"—so she agreed to her parents' plan. An Islamic wedding was arranged. Mihrigul's parents flew to Cairo for the celebration and stayed with their daughter for a week. Of course, Mihrigul told her new Uyghur husband about Mahmoud, explaining that she was in love with someone else. Her new husband was okay with that: his own parents had been pushing him to get married for a while too, and this took the pressure off him. He said they could be friends, and in that way keep all their parents happy.

Thus began a romantic entanglement that would lead Mihrigul into China's concentration camps, but which would ultimately save her from them, too.

A couple of months after this wedding to a Uyghur man, Mihrigul discovered she was pregnant. When she went to the doctor, he dropped the bombshell: she was not only pregnant—she was carrying triplets. So there she was, twenty-five and married to a man she didn't love and about to have three babies in a foreign country. She was overwhelmed. That was when her parents intervened again.

As it happened, her older brother Ekber—now Wang Guo—and his wife were unable to conceive. They would be happy to take on her three babies as their own, allowing her to stay and focus on her studies. So in May 2015, when her babies—Elina, a girl, and two boys, Moez and Mohaned—were two months old and able to undertake the eleven-hour flight, she boarded a plane for Beijing. She left without being able to say goodbye to Mahmoud—he had moved to Dubai seeking work. The Egyptian economy had been decimated by the upheaval of the Arab Spring, and the military coup that ousted the Muslim Brotherhood government sent more shock waves through society. Many young Egyptians found themselves poor, disillusioned and afraid. Mahmoud left without knowing he was the father of three babies. Crucially, however, she registered him as the father on the birth certificate, rather than her Uyghur husband: a minor bureaucratic detail that would one day save her life.

That was the point when what might have just been the sad tale of two thwarted lovers became a much darker story.

It started with what appeared to be a small gesture of kindness: at Beijing Airport, where Mihrigul and her babies changed planes for a connection to Ürümchi, a young Chinese man and woman came up and offered to help the overburdened young mother. "They are so cute! Where are you guys from?" the woman cooed.

One of them carried Moez and the other took Elina, while Mihrigul carried Mohaned. When they landed in Ürümchi four hours later, the Chinese couple again volunteered to help with the babies. Jet-lagged and exhausted, Mihrigul was grateful for the help, already looking forward to seeing her family again.

Then, as they walked across the arrivals hall, the Chinese man flashed a badge and hissed at her.

"Don't say a word. We are police. Come with us."

Mihrigul was too shocked by the whiplash change in attitude to say anything. Her whole body started shaking. Mutely, she followed the police agents to a room inside the airport. Her children were taken away from her and she sat opposite a police officer in front of a two-way mirror.

The officer started asking questions: name, family, which school did she go to, where was her family, why she had been to Egypt, did she speak to any other Uyghurs there? At no point did he tell her why she had been arrested, or what charges she might face. All Mihrigul could think about was her kids—they were still so small, they needed to breastfeed and have their diapers changed after the flight. She asked if she could see them.

"You don't ask the questions!" the policeman snapped. "You answer questions! You have no right to question me. If you don't answer the questions, you know what will happen."

The interrogation went on without pause, not even for a glass of water, for three hours. Eventually, the policeman said he was done and gave Mihrigul some water. Dazed, she turned to leave. But he said, "Wait, someone is coming."

Without warning, two other cops stepped into the room and grabbed Mihrigul. They put duct tape over her mouth and slipped a black hood over her head. Her hands were cuffed behind her back and she was frog-marched outside to a waiting van. As the cops shoved her inside, her face slammed into a metal door and broke her nose. She couldn't scream because of the tape over her mouth. It was a struggle to even breathe. She felt like her skull had been broken.

Inside the van, the guards removed the hood and she could see the city flash by through a small mesh-covered window. They pulled up at a prison on a cold, windswept hilltop. She later learned the place was a notorious jail known as The Black Mountain, where hardened criminals and political prisoners were said to be subjected to torture and beatings. But at that point, Mihrigul had no idea where she might be, or why.

She was led down a corridor lined with cells behind metal bars, then ushered into an interrogation room. This time when she sat down, however, her interrogator clicked a remote control, and wrist, neck and ankle straps bound her to the chair. This is what is known in China as the "tiger chair," a kind of entry-level torture for new initiates to prison.

This was one of the few rooms she saw in all her time in the prison system where there were no cameras monitoring her.

"You could die here, you know," said her interrogator. Despite that dire threat, the questions he came out with were the same inane ones as before, mostly things the authorities must surely have known already. Only this time they were accompanied by slaps from three guards, which hurt all the more for her broken nose.

"Did you do anything to harm China?" they said. She said she had no idea what they were talking about, so they took turns slapping her some more. "If your memory isn't good, we'll help you remember."

"If you want to live and see your kids again, cooperate with us."

This went on for two whole days. At times she drifted into unconsciousness in the tiger chair, and they threw water in her face. Every couple of hours, the three men would be swapped out for another team of interrogators. Occasionally, they got tired of slapping her and asking pointless questions, so they would just sit there and stare at her. Eventually, exhausted and unable to answer their absurd questions anymore, Mihrigul said, "Just tell me what to confess to and I'll do it."

But they didn't tell her what she was supposed to have done. Not yet. Instead, they put her in a very small metal-lined room, more like a box than a cell. There was no window, no light, just a small hatch at the bottom of the door where food and water could be pushed through. She had no idea how long she was in there for, but was later told it was seven days. It felt like seven years to Mihrigul, who is claustrophobic and suffered frequent panic attacks. On one occasion, she hallucinated that her children were in there with her. She prayed for death to come. To this day, she cannot sleep without a light on.

When they removed her from the tiny room, she was led to a more normal-looking prison cell. It had double doors—the outer one was a set of steel bars, the inner one a heavy metal portal fitted with a spyhole. When the doors opened, the guards barked out, "Everyone kneel!" and the inmates all knelt down, faces to the wall so they could not see the guards.

Mihrigul was very scared—like everyone else, she had watched plenty of crime movies where the newcomer has to fight for their space in a cell. When the doors were closed she started crying, but as the prisoners turned to face her, they were kind and friendly, although they were forbidden from talking to each other. There were several cameras and at least one microphone monitoring the cell, and if anyone spoke they would be ordered to shut up, or dragged out and beaten.

Still, an older woman dared to mutter softly to the new arrival, "Don't worry, we're with you. Calm down." Several of the women were older, probably in their fifties or sixties but looking much older because of the harsh conditions. One girl was clearly younger than Mihrigul. A couple of the women started crying when they saw her in tears. Mihrigul was shocked to recognize one of them as a popular singer she had seen on television. She couldn't remember her name, because she had spent half of her life studying inside China, and actually knew very little about the traditional Uyghur music scene. Her musical preference was Chinese pop.

The thought went through her head, "If they can do this to famous people, what can they do to me?"

10

Zumrat prides herself on being worldly-wise, an operator who can always find a way to beat the system and make sure her family comes through. But she also knew that her three children, the youngest of whom was just five, were her weak point. For many years, when the Communist Party had restricted the number of children that Chinese people were allowed to have to just one—a policy that has been rolled back since 2013—Uyghurs were allowed to have two. Even that policy was under lax enforcement, and a wily woman with some financial means could usually find a way to get around it and have what is considered in Uyghur tradition to be a proper-size family.

Even before the crackdown, a Uyghur woman who had given birth to two children—by law, the two births had to be spaced out by three years, otherwise the fetus would be forcibly aborted—was obliged to have an IUD inserted to prevent her getting pregnant again. Zumrat had done that, but she experienced bleeding and back pain. She persuaded a doctor to remove the birth-control device, and when she did get pregnant she knew which palms to grease to get the certificates necessary for her third child to have access to schooling and health coverage.

That is not to say it was always easy: her brother Mutallip had been killed in a car crash years before, and only after his death had his widow discovered she was pregnant. She already had one child, and was entitled to a second, but the requisite three years had not passed since her previous birth. She managed to hide her pregnancy for a time, but the regular checkups Uyghur women are forced to undergo as part of China's population control measures finally revealed her condition. The authorities forced her to have a late-term abortion, even though the child would be the last vestige of the man she had lost.

Now, with new restrictions being imposed every week, it was clear the situation had changed for the worse: Zumrat worried it was only a matter of time before someone questioned her larger-than-permitted family.

Every day, there seemed to be more surveillance equipment going up—security cameras every fifty yards on the streets, police checkpoints, mobile police stations, even gates in the streets to divide neighborhoods into local subcommunities. To enter a building, you had to pass through a turnstile like something you'd see on the New York subway, and which used facial recognition technology to only allow residents to enter. If a relative wanted to come and stay for a night, both of you had to go to your local police station and register the "event," even though the tracking device on your phone was already telling the authorities where you were. In the streets at night, there were trucks parked outside homes with sophisticated listening devices. People started to talk in whispers in their own homes, away from the windows.

Whenever Zumrat met someone she trusted in the streets, there was a little ritual each person would go through before exchanging tidbits of gossip: first, they would roll their eyes up, or to left or right, to indicate where the nearest surveillance camera was mounted, and then talk briefly, scratching their noses or mouths so that their words could not be deciphered by lipreading. As in other totalitarian states, paranoia became the watchword for survival, only more so, because China could use its cutting-edge artificial intelligence and high-tech monitoring to peer into the most private recesses of people's lives.

In the few private moments that Uyghurs could still find, they secretly blamed the situation on Chen Quanguo, wondering why Chairman Xi wasn't reining in this party official who was so clearly overstepping his bounds. It wasn't until Zumrat escaped China that she finally came to the conclusion that it was Xi himself who was giving him his orders.

The price of the smallest slip was "reeducation." That's what the authorities called it, as though having a Koran in your house marked you as an Al Qaeda sympathizer bent on overthrowing the atheist Chinese government.

The "reeducation" process might begin as a mandatory day of chanting pro-Communist slogans in a detention facility. If the "crime" was serious enough, though, the unwitting offender might be plunged straight into the shadowy gulags that were emerging on the edges of towns and cities across Xinjiang. Generally, it was preferable to be sent to a prison, because at least a person's family could find you there and maybe even visit. But the camps were a black hole where vast numbers of people vanished without a trace, sometimes appearing months later, a shadow of their former selves, or simply dropping off the radar for good. Those who returned were often treated with suspicion, held at arm's length; what had they promised the authorities in order to escape the camps?

In addition to the suffocating high-tech surveillance, ordinary Uyghurs were ordered by the neighborhood watch committees to start spying on each other. A group of ten people, maybe neighbors in an apartment complex, would be paired up and told to submit a report each week, slipping it into a red box at the Monday-morning flag-raisings. Everyone had to answer questions about their designated target: Had the person ever performed a noncivil marriage in private or attended prayers or religious recitals? Had the person ever criticized a Chinese restaurant for not serving halal food? Zumrat was obliged to write something—a blank report would in itself raise suspicions—so she was always careful to write something innocuous but close enough to the truth, because you never knew who else might be reporting on the same event. Yes, she would say, so-and-so shunned non-halal meat at the restaurant, but doesn't eat meat at all for health reasons.

The stress was constant: every few days, someone else would vanish into the camps, and every morning Zumrat would wake up wondering if this would be the day they came for her. That winter and spring, she learned to adapt to the new situation. When she avoided arrest, and no one raised questions about her extra child, she began to hope that maybe she could make it after all.

But things were about to get much worse.

That winter of 2016, Qelbinur and her fellow teachers at the Ürümchi high school were tested on their proficiency in the Chinese language. As a Mandarin teacher, this presented no problem for her. But for several of her colleagues with different specialties, the test was challenging. Several failed and found themselves swiftly reassigned to menial jobs at schools for Han Chinese students. Despite their professional qualifications, they were sent to work in mailrooms or as receptionists; some were ordered to serve in the neighborhood watch committee, where they were told to monitor mosques and report on who attended and how long they stayed. Others were sent to the new "reeducation camps" to work as support staff.

They were all replaced by Han Chinese teachers, and no more classes were held in the Uyghur language.

Qelbinur survived this first purge. She managed to keep her job until the spring semester started in February 2017, when she was summoned by her school principal. Several of her colleagues, including some Han Chinese teachers, were also there. The principal, a woman, was very polite and friendly. She informed them there was a new job for them, teaching the "national language"—Mandarin—to a bunch of illiterate, uneducated people. Under no circumstances were they to talk to anyone about what they might see or hear in their new workplace.

Qelbinur didn't understand the secrecy surrounding the new job, but assumed she was being reassigned because she had so much experience teaching Chinese to kids. But for some reason, the principal kept referring to her daughter studying in the Netherlands, and that made her nervous, as though her daughter was being dangled as a threat in case of noncompliance.

The next morning, March 1, she showed up as instructed at a bus stop in Ürümchi and called the phone number she had been given. A Chinese policeman showed up in his car and drove her up a winding hill to a large facility she had never seen before. It was a gray building, four floors high, and clearly not a school in any sense she could understand: there were guards with semiautomatic rifles at the gate and the walls were hung with razor wire. Her police escort swiped an ID card to enter the compound and Qelbinur entered a lobby where more armed guards registered her arrival. Then she was led to what she was told was her "classroom."

The room was a large cell, gloomy, with one overhead light next to a wheeled whiteboard. That was where she was to stand and teach. There were half a dozen prison guards with rifles standing around the walls, and iron bars separated her from the "students," who sat in the semi-darkness, perched on small stools. Spy cameras peered down on this depressing scene from numerous angles. Most of the "students" were men, still dressed in their own clothes and sporting the longer beards you'd normally expect in traditional rural communities. But there were also a half dozen women, in long, conservative dresses—some were in their seventies, Qelbinur guessed. All of them had shackles around their ankles and wrists. Clearly, these were detainees rounded up in far-flung villages. Several of the men appeared to be religious leaders, local imams maybe, and Qelbinur noticed how shy the women were around them—in a conservative society, women do not usually approach male religious leaders. There was a sound of sobbing coming from the murky depths of the room. In all, Qelbinur estimated there were around one hundred people in that first "class."

Trying to stifle her shock, she began the lesson. Their knowledge of Chinese was almost nonexistent: these were people who had had almost no interaction with the Chinese state, living their own reclusive, religious lives far from towns and cities and the Communist Party. Given their age and their level of fear—and the fact that Mandarin is, after all, one of the hardest languages to learn at any age—it took her a week to teach them just the basic vowels and elementary letters.

Then, at the end of the first week, she went into the same class and struggled to recognize the group: their civilian clothes and beards were gone and they were all wearing prison uniforms. Their heads had been shaved, even the elderly women, who seemed mortified to appear in front of their religious elders without their modest head coverings. But then, the Muslim elders had lost their beards too, and they too looked confused and lost.

At the end of the hour-long lesson, the guards escorted her to another floor, where she again faced a large class in a different cell. Here, the people seemed better educated and with more proficient Chinese. Some of the younger ones worked hard in her classes, apparently believing that study would win them their freedom. But when Qelbinur heard the guards speaking in the

canteen at lunchtime, she got the impression they had no intention of freeing anyone.

Every day, she would teach for four hours in the morning and
two hours in the afternoon, with an hour for lunch at midday.

Sometimes, as the prisoners were being herded into their
next session, chains clanking, she would catch a glimpse into
their fetid cells. The smell was overpowering since each cell
had only one bucket to serve as a toilet and the inmates could
never shower. Rolled-up mats lay on the floor, the prisoners'
only bedding. Although the inmates were hard to recognize
with their shaven heads and identical uniforms—and the sheer,
swelling numbers of them during the months she worked in the
camps—a few stood out.

One was an energetic man in his fifties called Osman. Before
prison, he had been a successful businessman, running his own
dried fruit company—a staple Uyghur appetizer, served with
tea—that supplied Ürümchi's hotels and restaurants. He spoke
excellent Chinese and stood out at first because of his positive
outlook. But sleeping on a cold concrete floor, with just a thin
mat as bedding, took a toll on his body. He started to limp and
grew thinner every time she saw him. Eventually, he vanished,
like several other of her students. One lunchtime, when she had
a chance to talk to one of the guards, Qelbinur asked what had
become of Osman. The guard said he had died of a urinary tract
infection, a common complaint among the prisoners, who were
only allowed to use the bucket three times a day, and then only
for a minute. She asked the guards what happened to the bodies
of "students" who died. They said they had no idea.

It is worth noting here that the most famous victim of the
Nazi death camps, Anne Frank, didn't die in the gas chambers.
The Dutch Jewish teenager died of typhus in Bergen-Belsen just
weeks before the camp was liberated at the end of World War II.
Even today, the exact date of her death is unknown. "One day

they simply weren't there anymore," recalled one camp survivor who became friends with Anne and her sister.

That was what Qelbinur noticed with her classes. People would just disappear. It was hard to keep track of them, especially as the spring of 2017 brought a new wave of roundups and the prison population swelled to somewhere around seven or eight thousand people. The top floor of the building, which had previously been office space, was converted into cells to accommodate all the newcomers.

As a teacher, and as an outsider forced to work in the prison system, Qelbinur had a unique insight into the behind-the-scenes workings of the concentration camps. That first week, one of the guards came up to her and started asking her how her "students" from the villages were doing. Despite the fact they were struggling, she didn't want to land them in trouble, so she commented on how hard they were trying and how difficult the Chinese language was for new students, especially elderly ones. The man warned her: "These people are so intoxicated and they try to intoxicate others. They have serious mental problems, they are crazy. If we release them, they'll be a danger to society."

She tried to find out what had really happened to Osman, her favorite student who'd vanished. She couldn't believe he had died of a simple urinary tract infection. She had noticed that every Monday, classes were delayed because the prisoners had to line up to receive an injection and take a white pill. She asked the woman handing out the pills what they were. "Calcium," she said. "Because they don't see much daylight."

While Qelbinur didn't buy that, it was dangerous to push that line of questioning. As a Muslim woman, she herself might already be suspect. Every day, on the drive to or from prison, her police escort would set little tests for her: he'd take a different route to the camp, and ask her if she thought they were lost, as though probing whether she was memorizing the route.

At other times, a second cop would ride with them and they would strike up a conversation: "These Uyghurs die hard, don't they?" one said. "Just like when you pour boiling water on lice, they refuse to die."

They would ask her if she, as an Uzbek, felt any sympathy toward the prisoners, or if the stress of teaching was getting to her, or whether her husband would have any issues with his fellow Uyghurs being locked up. She made sure to answer in bland, generalized terms. At night, she would tell her husband what was happening, just to avoid going crazy. She had trouble sleeping, and as the clock ticked toward dawn, she dreaded the sun rising and having to return to the camp.

11

In the Uyghur language, "Mihrigul" is a very poetic name. It means "flower-like soul." But in the camps, people don't have names, only the numbers sewn to their drab uniforms. If she made a slip and spoke out loud, a harsh voice would bark out on the intercom, "Nineteen, shut your mouth!" One time, shortly after being incarcerated, she was dreaming of her father, apologizing for not staying home like he'd wanted, and instead pursuing her own ambitions. She must have been sobbing because one of the older women whispered, "Nineteen, pull yourself together."

That, Mihrigul soon noticed, was an earnest plea. Quite often, one of the women would simply break down, or give up. Mihrigul had seen a woman start screaming hysterically, "I'm done with life, do whatever you want" before the guards came in armed with a pole fitted with a grabbing pincer at the end: they secured her by the neck with this device and dragged her off. Mihrigul never saw her again.

This was all incomprehensible for her. She had been out of the country for years in Egypt, after a decade of study in inland China, and had missed all the warning signs that her fellow Uyghurs had been nervously picking up. Suddenly finding herself in a small prison cell with twenty-eight other women, crammed so tight they had to sleep on their sides like sardines and in two-hour shifts because there wasn't enough space for them to all lie down at once—it was not only terrifying, but utterly unfathomable.

Every morning, they were woken at 5:30 and told to line up for the solitary bucket in the corner of the cell where they could relieve themselves. There was no toilet paper, no running water, and in all the months she was incarcerated, she never once got to wash. The place stank, and everyone was filthy. They had to fold the thin mats they slept on with military precision, then line up for the cell inspection.

Then they were marched out into a yard and drilled while chanting slogans about the greatness of the Chinese Communist Party. "The CCP gives us new life and prosperity!" and "If there is no Communist Party, there is no new China!" They would do this for hours before returning to the cell to sit in silence until 9:30 p.m., when the lights would go out and they would all take turns trying to sleep—two hours on the floor, two hours standing in the dark, and so on through the night.

The nights were the worst. There were two girls in the cell who were younger than Mihrigul, just seventeen and nineteen years old. They were often taken out at night and would come back later, sobbing and clearly in distress. Mihrigul was sure they had been raped, a story many camp survivors—including male detainees—have reported. One day during an interrogation, a guard started groping her. She told her captors she had a sexually transmitted disease, and they left her alone after that. But not everyone was so lucky: there was one strikingly beautiful young dancer, just a couple of years younger than Mihrigul. She looked like the American actress Angelina Jolie. Every night, she was taken out of her cell and would return an hour later in tears. Even if the women had been allowed to talk, it would have been almost impossible for her to speak to the other inmates about what was happening to her: the shame of a young unmarried woman being raped in the highly conservative society would have made it very difficult.

Then one night, the young woman didn't come back. Mihrigul never saw her again. She later heard that she had taken a letter knife from a police officer's desk and stabbed one of her rapists in the neck, unable to bear it any longer.

Mihrigul's imprisonment went on for sixty-nine days. Then, out of the blue, she was told to go with her guards. They went into an office where she was told to sign a confession that she had tried to undermine the Chinese government's efforts to "maintain social stability." She also promised never to talk to anyone about what had happened to her in prison. The guards informed her she had been blacklisted, now unable to travel abroad or even possess a phone. If she wanted to travel anywhere within Xinjiang, she would need permission from the police.

She signed immediately, and with that, she was released. Outside the prison gates her father was waiting for her. He'd been there for five hours, having been summoned early so he could pay his daughter's "bill" for being housed in a state prison—two dollars a night, almost one hundred and fifty dollars in total, a huge sum for a rural truck driver. It was the first time Mihrigul had seen him in years. There was no hiding the shock on his face.

"What happened to your hair?" her father asked. Mihrigul had always had long, beautiful brown hair, but her jailers had cut it off. At that point, she broke down crying.

"I was wrong, Daddy," she sobbed. "I should have listened to you. I'll be a good daughter. If I'd listened to you none of this would have happened."

Her father held her. "You are my life," he said. "I love you, you're safe now."

But she wasn't. Worse, neither were her children.

Her father told them Elina, Moez and Mohaned were in the Ürümchi Children's Hospital. They rushed there to find Mihrigul's mother and brother were waiting in the lobby. Her mother said they had seen Elina and Moez—the first time she had ever set eyes on her grandchildren—but the doctor would not let them see Mohaned. He was sick, the doctor said. Mihrigul had an emotional reunion with Elina and Moez. As she held them in her arms, she noticed scar tissue on their necks. The doctor said they had needed to insert feeding tubes to keep them alive. Mihrigul remembered what healthy babies they had been in Egypt, plump on a mixture of breast milk and biscuit mixed with formula.

She insisted on seeing Mohaned, but the doctor would only let her look through the window of the ward he was on. She could see him in his bed, from far away, and nurses moving around the room, but she could not see her baby clearly. Though she had a powerful urge to stay in the hospital that night, she yielded to her family's insistence that she go with them and get a shower and some sleep. She was filthy, beaten and shorn, and agreed to go with them, at least for one night. Her brother stayed at the hospital to keep an eye on the kids.

When she went back to the hospital the next morning, the real bombshell struck. The doctor she had met the day before told her Mohaned was dead.

Mihrigul started screaming. "I don't believe you!" she yelled. "I saw him yesterday!"

They took her to the morgue and opened a drawer. "They put them in a freezer, like an ice cream," she remembers thinking in that moment of utter shock. "You killed my son!" she screamed at the doctor. "Give me a blanket, I need to keep him warm! He's sleeping, he'll wake up!" She tried to wake him. After that, her memory is a blur, though she does remember the doctor calling security to escort them out. Then everything went blank.

Her family arranged the burial. Mihrigul carried the tiny coffin herself, cooing, "Sleep now baby, I'll bring you some milk." Somewhere beside her, she heard her father saying he was worried she had lost her mind. She hadn't, although given what she had been through—and the horrors still in store—she would have every right to lose her grip on reality.

The family was poor—her father had lost his job while she was in jail, as punishment for his daughter's alleged betrayal of China—so they had to take the bus back from Ürümchi to Cherchen, a distance of some seven hundred and fifty miles. It took a full day on the bus, a day that passed in a blur for Mihrigul. She struggled to get her two surviving babies to latch after their long separation. She needed to feed them after more than two months wasting away in the Ürümchi Children's Hospital, but they had lost the habit of breastfeeding.

When she arrived home in Cherchen, Mihrigul discovered a very different life from the one she had left behind. First of all, she had to report to a whole array of security bureaus: local police, state security, county police, as well as the neighborhood watch committee.

That was only the start, however. Arriving home with new babies, she had expected endless visits from her sprawling family, as is customary in Uyghur communities. Her father is one of seven siblings, her stepmother one of a staggering twenty-three. Normally, if someone has a baby, the whole family swarms by with food and gifts for the child. But for Mihrigul, now an object of state suspicion, no one came.

Worse, her own parents were oddly cold to her once they got home, despite the horrific ordeal their daughter had undergone. She quickly realized it was not indifference but fear that was holding them back. She soon came to understand why: there were security cameras everywhere in the streets, listening devices in vans parked outside homes, checkpoints everywhere. One day, soon after her return, she was standing in the kitchen cooking with her stepmother and felt overcome with grief.

"Mum," she said, "my heart is so full of pain. I need to talk to you."

Her mother didn't look at her. "Can you pass that jug, please?" she said, then carried on cooking. It was like living in the movie *Invasion of the Body Snatchers*: family members looked the same, but were no longer themselves. They simply couldn't afford to be.

While her blood relatives and neighbors were too afraid to visit, or even meet her eye when they passed on the street, the family was suddenly served up with a series of fake "relatives." One day in that summer of 2015, a Chinese man showed up with official paperwork declaring he was the Tursun family's designated "Becoming Family relative." Then he moved straight in with the family.

The Becoming Family program may sound innocuous, like some teenage student exchange where you take in a kid from France or Spain. But in China, it means a government-appointed spy will move into your home, act like a member of your family, and eat, relax and even sleep next to you and your family, often in the same bedroom. You are obliged to provide them with decent meals (the state gives out a tiny food stipend, not nearly enough to cover what they eat), clean bedsheets and blankets, a toothbrush and a bucket to wash their feet. You are to welcome them unquestioningly into your home as they quiz your children about whether you secretly pray, use the words "Allah" or "Mohammed," or ever say anything derogatory about the government.

Meanwhile, as they sit on the sofa in your living room enjoying your hospitality, they are constantly entering data in a notebook about the daily goings-on of your household: Is your daughter's dress a bit too long, indicating covert Islamic modesty? Is the man of the house's beard long enough to qualify as religiously conservative? Are there pictures of Xi Jinping on the wall, Chinese flags decorating the window shelves? This data will be fed into a computer program and can then form the basis for your arrest and detention in a concentration camp while your children are packed off to a state orphanage to be raised as good Chinese kids and indoctrinated against you and your religion.

Some of the Becoming Family "relatives" do make an effort to learn Uyghur, but only so they can spy on your family more effectively. Otherwise, you and your family are obliged to speak Mandarin to each other when they are around, so they can understand what you are saying. If your Mandarin isn't great, as some Uyghurs find, you will have to hold stilted conversations in your home, with your kids, in what is effectively a foreign language.

What Mihrigul found was that no one wanted to talk about anything anymore, for fear of being overheard. Having just suffered the death of her baby at the hands of the Chinese state, having been tortured and witnessed several suspected rapes, she had to keep it all inside her, and make nice with the Becoming Family "relatives." The Chinese snoops would each stay for around a week or two and then be replaced by some other intrusive stranger. "Another brother will be coming soon!" they would cheerfully announce as they left. She never found out where they came from, because Uyghurs are forbidden to ask.

Darren Byler, a sociocultural anthropologist at the University of Colorado who has closely studied the Uyghur dispossession, estimated in 2018 that around a million Becoming Family "big brothers and sisters" had been dispatched to live in Uyghur homes.

The first wave began in 2014 with an operation dubbed "Visit the People, Benefit the People, and Bring Together the Hearts of the People," which saw around two hundred thousand Communist Party members foisted on Uyghur villages for long-term stays. In 2016, that was followed up with one hundred and ten thousand civil servants being dispatched in a second wave, entitled "United as One Family."

Byler, a researcher at the university's "China Made Project" that studies the development of China's insfrastructure, managed to get to know some of these Becoming Family spies during a research trip to Xinjiang in the spring of 2018. These people—mostly Han Chinese, but also some from Muslim minorities—told him they had been issued with a manual instructing them how to get their "little brothers and sisters" to "let their guard down." They were instructed to show warmth to their hosts, and not to start lecturing them right away on party doctrine. They were told to bring candy for the kids and voice concern for the well-being of their hosts. The Chinese "relative" was always told to look out for signs of Islamic extremism, and were given things to watch out for: "When entering the household, do family members appear flustered and use evasive language? Do they not watch TV programs at home, and instead only watch VCD discs? Are there any religious items still hanging on the walls of the house?"

The Becoming Family "guests" tell their hosts that all their internet and electronic communications are being monitored, so they should not even think about lying about their religious views.

In January of 2016, the whole of Mihrigul's family—in fact their whole neighborhood—were ordered to report to the local police station and submit to a barrage of scans, tests and examinations. First, the police took retina scans and fingerprints. Then blood or hair samples were taken for DNA profiling. Everyone was told to read from a set text for forty-five minutes so their voices could be recorded and identified, so that the spies with listening devices parked outside people's houses knew who was talking. They had to walk back and forth so cameras could capture a person's exact gait and posture for identification on street surveillance cameras, in case a person managed to obscure their face. The facial recognition section involved not simply a snapshot but a whole variety of expressions they were forced to make—happy, sad, angry, looking up, looking down. Their phones were taken away at the beginning to be scanned for any forbidden apps—such as WhatsApp or Facebook—or suspect phone calls from abroad. The same surveillance app that was installed on Zumrat's phone, "Clean Internet Security Soldier," was also loaded onto their phones. For those who did not possess a phone, a cheap Huawei cell phone was distributed: they were ordered to never turn it off or let the battery die, so the authorities could snoop on them wherever they were. If a person left their house, they had to take it with them so it could record their movements on GPS.

So when the Becoming Family "relatives" told you that you were being monitored, you knew to believe them.

Some of the Becoming Family intruders were clearly apprehensive about their deployments—after all, they had been told by the party that they were on the lookout for religious extremists in a region that China portrays as a hotbed of knife-wielding Al Qaeda sympathizers. One of them told Byler, "I heard that initially a number of Han workers were killed when they went to sensitive Uyghur villages. When women went for a walk after dinner, Uyghur men grabbed them and slit their throats… There is a lot we, ordinary people, don't know about the seriousness of the terrorism problem… What we do know is something had to be done."

Mihrigul and other Uyghurs I spoke to had also heard that some of the "big brothers" had been attacked, but the reasons they gave were very different.

The "relatives" might come one at a time, or a Uyghur family might end up with two at once. Even children as young as five sometimes have their own designated person, an adult who is often the opposite sex of their target. There are plenty of pictures posted online of them sitting on beds with their families, because the government encourages Uyghurs to share these images to show how they are joyfully collaborating with the authorities. One government official, when questioned about the Xinjiang persecution, even claimed that the Uyghurs are the happiest Muslims in the world. And frequently a male "relative" will be billeted in a house where there are only Uyghur women: perhaps the husband has had to go to China proper to seek work or has been sent to the camps already.

That has led to numerous cases of sexual harassment and even rape. Mihrigul says that in 2016 she heard a widow in her neighborhood who lived with her twelve-year-old daughter stabbed her "relative" to death after the man sexually abused both her and her daughter. She could not go to the police to report the sexual abuse, because the state was complicit. So she stabbed the man, a defensive act that was likely registered as a knife-wielding religious extremist attack. The woman and her daughter disappeared without a trace.

Silently, Mihrigul and her stepmother thanked God her father was living with them. Even so, at times her father had to sleep in one bedroom with one of the spies while another "relative"—a man—slept in the same bedroom as her and her mother. One day the two women were cooking in the kitchen when her mother heard Elina crying and went to check on the baby. The "relative" came up behind Mihrigul and groped her, trying to kiss her. She managed to push him off, then her stepmother came back. The two women tried to make sure they were never alone in their own house with these strangers. It was hard for her father, too: he knew what was going on, but was also aware that if he did or said anything there would be what the police like to call "consequences." He had to swallow his pride and suppress his impotent rage.

For Mihrigul, it was all too much. She would go to the apartment's tiny laundry closet, turn on the washing machine to

130

mask the sound and cry her eyes out. She knew her stepmother was doing the same. But living in close quarters with a potential rapist was untenable. She told her father she had to get out, or she would either kill the Becoming Family molester or herself. This time, her father agreed that she should leave. Luckily, she had lots of friends from her school days in the metropolis of Guangzhou. They helped her find a job at a company that processed overseas orders for domestic clients, putting retailers in touch with buyers and processing the shipping of orders. It wasn't the business career she had planned when she went for her MBA in Cairo, but it was work and it was far from the horrors she had just experienced.

12

There are estimates that while at least a million Uyghurs were being led off to China's concentration camps, a similar number of Chinese Becoming Family "relatives" were moving into Uyghur homes, like a hostile army being billeted on a restive population in the old days of empire. No one, it seemed, was to be spared.

Certainly not Zumrat, who on those cold Monday-morning flag-raising ceremonies was forced to chant, "We love our relatives. We welcome our relatives. We don't need to ask our relatives any questions."

She still has the photos of these strangers in her home, arms draped around her kids, pretending to be family. One of them shows a woman who looks like a teenager but was in fact much older, seen smiling with Zumrat's five-year-old son. Others show men, seemingly at ease as they sit in the living room with the family, drinking tea and eating the large meals she spread out before them. "They seemed to be enjoying themselves," Zumrat recalled.

Needless to say, her family wasn't. Zumrat felt stripped of her dignity, insulted, as she allowed these people to take her kids off and quiz them about their most private thoughts, in their own home. One of the intruders in particular disturbed her: a nineteen-year-old young man who had been assigned to be the "relative" of her ten-year-old daughter, Iffet. One day, when he wasn't on duty living in their home, the youth phoned the house. He sounded drunk, and said he wanted to take Iffet away on a trip. Zumrat was furious, but had to remain calm—this was after all a drunken teenager who held the fate of her entire family in his hands. She told him Iffet had a medical condition that meant she couldn't be away from home. That appeared to be enough to deflate his plans for now, but she always watched him like a hawk around her daughter.

Zumrat made sure to take her kids to one side when the "relatives" weren't around to try to explain to them to not be afraid, but not to trust these Chinese visitors and certainly not to tell them too much about their family life. But how can you expect a five-year-old to keep any secrets? The kids were terrified that something they might say would mean their parents were taken off to prison. And at school, they also faced frequent questions from teachers, who used their authority to pry about their parents: Did they have a Koran? Did they pray? Grade school kids would have to deny the god they believed in to keep their parents out of harm's way.

Not even Qelbinur was spared the Becoming Family program, despite being an ethnic Uzbek who was at the time working inside a concentration camp. After a long, stressful day teaching prisoners the language of their oppressors, she would often come home and find one of these state-sponsored cuckoos in her nest.

One of them was particularly troubling: a thick-set man who

appeared to be in his forties and was quick to make himself at home, sitting around the living room in just his boxer shorts and undershirt. On one of his first stays, he asked her to show him how to make some of the region's culinary specialties. As she was chopping vegetables in the kitchen, he put his hand on top of hers, as if to help, then left it there. She tried to pull her hand away but he held it tighter, then grabbed her and started kissing her. Qelbinur is a small woman, and was almost fifty at the time, and the man was large, corpulent—she still has a picture of her together with him and her husband. He is pressed horribly close to her, and though they are all awkwardly smiling in the picture, she said she had tears rolling down her cheeks. As she recounted this story to me, sitting in an asylum seekers' refuge in the Netherlands, she was shaking and crying.

Then one night the man showed up with a bottle of liquor. This is a common technique used by Becoming Family spies to test whether a host is adhering to Muslim abstinence from alcohol. Offering cigarettes is also used to the same end: observant Muslims are supposed to refrain from smoking or otherwise abusing their bodies. Qelbinur doesn't drink, and her husband had suffered for years from alcohol abuse. But they felt obliged to take a glass, just to avoid receiving a black mark in their ledger.

As the man poured their drinks, Qelbinur warned her husband in a whisper: "If you fall asleep and he rapes me, I will kill you."

She went to the kitchen to prepare some food and the man followed. Her husband stayed in the living room. Despite him being just yards away, the man molested her. "He did everything but have sex with me," she recalled, shuddering with tears. The man—who had told her he had a wife and child back home, wherever that might be—also complained when Qelbinur would not have oral sex with him. He said all the other Uyghur women were happy to perform such sex acts on their "relatives."

He told her he wasn't fully satisfied, as though he were writing a Yelp review for would-be rapists.

Qelbinur told her husband, but he was terrified and insisted there was nothing they could do. "It's just a week. What have you got to lose?" he said.

She was furious. "What's the purpose of your life, if you can't protect me from this bullshit? What happened to your manhood? If I were you, I'd kill him!"

Her husband blanched. "You're crazy!" he said. "It's only one day a week. You can suck it up. This will pass." She felt disgusted by his stance, and kept asking herself what happened to the brave Uyghur men who would sacrifice anything to protect their women. But the Chinese had broken the dignity of this Uyghur man, to the point where he was unwilling to protect his own wife, the mother of his child.

From that point on, there was little intimacy between Qelbinur and her husband. Their marriage was effectively over.

Zumrat survived for almost two years as her neighbors, friends and acquaintances vanished from the city around her. During the fasting month of Ramadan, if there were no "relatives" staying at the house, she and her husband would rise early and take their predawn meal in the bathroom, which had no windows—anyone who had their lights on so early during the holy month was instantly suspect.

She was careful to always buy the same amounts of food at the same shops: if you bought more or less than usual, the shopkeeper had a button he could press to alert the authorities. What extra mouths might you be feeding? Likewise with gas for your car: if you used more, it looked suspect, like you were driving somewhere new. If you used less, you would get a phone call from the neighborhood watch after a few days asking why you were lurking at home. Lots of the family photos and selfies on Zumrat's cell phone from that time were in fact snaps she had been ordered to take when the committee would call her while she was out and demand to know where she was, accompanied by photographic proof.

One day as she was walking down the street in Ürümchi, she noticed a work crew cleaning out a blocked drain. As she drew closer, she was shocked to see what the blockage actually was: the workers had extracted a pile of soggy, soiled Korans and prayer mats that people had been forced to flush down their toilets when the police or the neighborhood watch committees carried out their raids. Zumrat knew how painful it must have been for her fellow Muslims to treat the holiest of books with such disrespect. But it was a matter of survival.

What the Chinese authorities didn't seem to realize was that for Zumrat, as for many other Uyghurs, the brainwashing and oppression was in fact counterproductive: she found herself turning to her god more and more for solace and guidance during these terrifying times.

Then, on a Saturday morning in March 2018, her cell phone rang. It wasn't a number she knew but it ended in "110": that meant it was the police. It was the phone call everyone dreaded. Some Uyghurs were so scared of the summons phone call that even if it came during the hot summer months, they would put on winter clothes just in case, because they did not know when they would be returning.

She answered, and a voice on the line addressed her using the Chinese version of her name, Zaomure. The man ordered her to come at once to her local police station. Her husband was at the bank that morning, but the kids were somewhere in the house, playing or watching TV. There were so many police stations in Ürümchi by this point that the nearest one was only three hundred meters away. Feeling oddly confident that she had gotten this far without being arrested, she slipped out the door in her slippers, without saying goodbye and worrying the kids. She told herself the police probably wanted to do an update of their biometrics or another phone scan.

And indeed, that was how her visit started. When she got into the fortress-like building, the first thing the police did was take away her phone. But after a while, another policeman came in and told her to follow him. He had a big yellow envelope in his hand, and led her downstairs. By now, most Uyghurs knew that Chinese police stations have underground detention cells: being led there was definitely not a good sign. In the basement area, she was led past piles of confiscated Korans and prayer mats. The police officer occasionally kicked one of the holy books, either out of spite or because there were just so many they were spilling onto the floor.

Zumrat was led into an interrogation room. In it were a toilet and a tiger chair: the toilet had a metal bar screwed into the wall next to it, so the prisoner being interrogated could be handcuffed while they relieved themselves. She was strapped into the tiger chair and the questioning began.

They started with her cell phone records. In 2017, she had received a phone call from the United States. She said it was her Pakistani husband, on a business trip, visiting electronics trade shows. Simple to explain: she even told her interrogators they could check her husband's passport for the US visa. Instead, they started asking her if she had links to Uyghur separatists living in the US. This went on for at least an hour.

Then they came in with another envelope. This one contained banking records and wire transfers, including payments from overseas. This too was an incredibly pointless discussion— Zumrat and her husband ran an import-export business, and one branch of the business was registered under her Sinicized name: Zaomure Export Import Limited. Zumrat looked at the amount—around four hundred RMB, a trifling sum—and remembered it had been for some sunflower seeds that produced a high-quality oil, which she sold in several Chinese cities.

Several hours had passed by now, which was worrying, but Zumrat clung to the fact that she was able to defend every charge they brought against her. Next, they asked her about her foreign travel, usually enough to sink most Uyghurs. But even there she had been cautious in her holiday planning: she had always avoided traveling to any Middle Eastern countries, to avoid any hint of Islamic sympathies, and had been meticulous about booking her trips through Chinese government–sanctioned travel agencies, even attending the pretrip workshops where they instructed tourists on where to eat and who to avoid—usually Uyghur restaurants and Uyghur expats. She had been to Europe, Japan, Singapore, Bali and had even managed to secure a US visa for her and her family just before the crackdown began. That prompted the question every Uyghur with any connection to the US—no matter how slight—has to face: Did she know Rebiya Kadeer?

Needless to say, Zumrat knew who the famous Uyghur dissident was. But since Rebiya had disappeared into the Chinese prison system some twenty years earlier, and then escaped to the US, Zumrat had never met her, nor tried to. Nevertheless, they kept asking her if she knew Rebiya Kadeer. Zumrat was getting increasingly worried by this point: she had been in the room for hours, and had noticed dark stains on the walls. Were they dried blood, or paint designed to look like blood and frighten the prisoner in the tiger chair? The guards started tightening the straps on her wrists and ankles until the blood circulation was cut off, leaving her in agonizing pain. She begged to be allowed to go to the toilet to try to escape the pain for a moment: they allowed her to use the bowl in the same room, watching as she relieved herself. Then she was back in the tiger chair, and they started slapping her about the face with the documents they thought were so incriminating. The paper cut into the skin around her eyes.

So it continued, for twenty-four hours, with no breaks, no food and no water.

Early the next morning, more police came for her. They put a black hood over her head and bundled her first upstairs and then outside, into a van. She had no idea where they were going, or why. She wondered if they were going to shoot her in the head.

13

Mihrigul was allowed to travel to Guangzhou in July of 2016. She had to check in regularly with the local police and have frequent video calls with the security forces back in Cherchen. Although she missed her babies, she felt much better living in the huge coastal metropolis, where she had spent her high school years. Historically, it had long been the only port in China where foreigners were allowed to trade. Mihrigul now lost herself in this vast bustling city, using her language skills to place orders for things like cotton sheets from Egypt for Chinese clients, sending her wages back home to her parents to look after Elina and Moez. She worked long hours at an import-export company to exhaust herself, and when she got back to her apartment she would just collapse into bed. She still had Chinese friends in the city from her school days, and she told them about the things the state had done to her and her family in Xinjiang: Guang-zhou is a quite liberal city, just seventy-five miles from Hong

Kong, and her friends believed her, though to them Xinjiang felt almost like another country.

Even the local police were not so bad—she could meet her liaison for coffee rather than at the police station, and she sometimes bought them beer or cigarettes so they would back off a little.

Then, on April 1, 2017, the authorities launched a fresh wave of detentions of the Uyghur population. They did not announce it publicly, of course, so when Mihrigul received an order from the police in Cherchen telling her to report in person immediately, she hoped it was just for another round of biometric screenings and fingerprints. Telling her boss she'd be gone just a few days, she booked a return flight from Guangzhou to Cherchen. When she landed at 2:00 p.m., she intended to go straight to the police to get the scanning over with, then go home to see her kids.

Instead, she was arrested the minute she got off the plane and taken to an interrogation room. They strapped her into the now familiar tiger chair, shaved her head and put electrodes on her scalp to give her electric shocks. Oddly, they also gave her a pill that seemed to dull the pain, and which also made their voices sound distorted and distant. Other women who have been given similar pills believe it may be a type of date-rape drug. The police hit her so hard about the head that the hearing in her right ear was permanently damaged. To this day, she often cocks her head to hear better in conversation.

From the interrogation room at the airport she was handcuffed and taken to the Cherchen hospital. Ominously, they took her to the OB-GYN department. She was ordered to sit in an examination chair with stirrups, and a small curtain was pulled over her midriff so she was unable to see what the doctor was doing to her. The exam lasted around fifteen minutes and was intensely painful. Afterward, she felt shaky and weak, her stomach bloated. For two days she had bleeding but received no medical attention, because after the examination she was taken directly to yet another prison.

There, she was forced to strip naked in front of three male guards and change into a prison uniform. Handcuffs were snapped on her wrists, attached by a chain to shackles around her ankles. It was an absurd amount of restraint for a hundred-pound woman who only just topped five foot one. Still shaking from the painful examination, and fearful they might have somehow sterilized her, she was led through winding corridors, the guards barking instructions at her because she was blinded by a black hood over her head.

The hood was pulled off as the guards shoved her into a cell. At first, Mihrigul thought there must be some mistake: she was in a room full of men. But on second glance she saw the gaunt, shaven-headed figures were all women. They stared at the new-comer with hollow eyes, filling her with fear. She started crying as the cell door slammed, and a voice on the loudspeaker snapped out the number of another prisoner. "Number twenty-three, do you have any bread? Give it to her."

The woman surrendered her tiny nub of bread. It was hard as a rock, all but inedible. Then the same disembodied voice on the loudspeaker ordered everyone to sleep—as before, in shifts, lying on their sides on the hard floor—and the lights went out. In the darkness, a woman behind her whispered gently, "Don't cry, you are okay."

This time, there were forty women crammed into the cell. As the days passed, familiar faces started to emerge from the dehu-manized wraiths around Mihrigul. She recognized her old his-tory teacher from her lower school days in Cherchen; there was also a well-known local doctor who had studied in England and had gone on to become manager of the town's hospital. Some-times they could exchange a few whispered words: her former teacher said she recognized her, and said she had heard from her father that she had left China.

"Why did you come back?" she asked. She said she had been in jail for thirteen months. No one ever asked why you might be in prison. They all knew they were there simply because of their ethnicity.

Mihrigul also had whispered exchanges with a twenty-six-year-old woman who had a beautiful face but constantly bleeding hands: she had to scrub the cell floor every day and her skin had become cracked and infected from the caustic detergent. The woman whispered that she herself had been in the United States and had given birth there, to an American baby. When she came home to show her parents their grandchild, she assumed that with a child who was a US citizen she would be safe. Instead she was thrown in jail and had been there five months. She did not know what had become of her baby. If ever she got out of prison she wanted to get to the nearest US consulate and seek help. This time, it was Mihrigul who was surprised.

"If I ever got to the United States, I would never leave!" she told the young mother.

With the big roundup of spring 2017, the prison population had quickly expanded. Soon there were sixty-eight women crammed into the one room, and inmates were being swapped out every day. Some had clearly had the same OB-GYN "examination" that Mihrigul had been subjected to: they arrived with blood leaking from between their legs. Two of them did not stop bleeding and died soon after their arrival. But most of them, having been forced to swallow the mysterious pills handed out by the prison nurses, never had a period during their entire stay.

In the three months she was locked up this second time, Mihrigul saw a total of nine women die. She discovered one of them herself: one morning at the dawn wake-up call, the woman sleeping on the floor beside her wouldn't open her eyes. She had been ill, often asking the guards if they could give her the medicine she needed for her condition.

"Prison is your medicine!" the guards would shout at her.

That morning Mihrigul urged her to get up, warning that she risked a beating otherwise. The woman didn't move. Mihrigul nudged her with her foot. She wasn't breathing, and her face was cold to the touch. She was dead. The prisoners left her as they were marched outside to sing songs to the glory of the Communist Party.

China calls these prisons "reeducation camps" but in reality, they are designed to brainwash or break the spirit of the people inside. Mihrigul, a fluent Chinese speaker, would spend her days shuffling around the overcrowded prison yard, in step with hundreds of women, often just counting in Chinese, "One, two, three, four..." for hours. Other prisoners recount being forced to sit next to university professors, doctors, lawyers—clearly people in no need of "vocational training"—as they recited hours of kindergarten Chinese. The lessons they learned were mere slogans in praise of Xi Jinping, a throwback to the brainwashing of Mao's Cultural Revolution.

The food was abysmal, barely enough to keep them alive. Breakfast consisted of a piece of steamed bread the size of an egg—otherwise they mostly ate xi fan, a kind of rice porridge with no salt or vegetables. Everyone had a plastic bowl but no spoon. The first three days, Mihrigul couldn't even bear the smell of this watery slop. The first time she forced herself to drink some she threw up, but within two weeks she was ravenously slurping it down, and it was never enough. If the guards thought the prisoners were too slow responding to orders, or couldn't recite their propaganda chants accurately, they would cut the food rations.

The prisoners were so hungry, tired and dirty that all they could think about was food, sleep or a shower. In the whispers in the darkness, those were the fantasies shared as the women stood awaiting their turn to sleep. The outside world receded: Mihrigul never thought about her family this time around. Her dreams were about bread, a cup of clean water, a shower or a real bed in which she would sleep for a year, two years, or just never wake up again.

Then one day in July, after almost three months in jail, she just blacked out. When she opened her eyes, she was in a hospital. One hand and one foot were handcuffed to the metal frame of the hospital bed. She had an IV drip in one hand. From the clean, orderly surroundings, she guessed this was not a prison ward. After a while, a woman in a white coat came in. She had a beautiful face and spoke softly as she held up an array of small bottles.

"Mihrigul, I am your doctor," she introduced herself, but Mihrigul does not want to disclose her name for fear that she, too, could end up in prison.

"Listen to me," the doctor said. "You have your morning pill, this one, your afternoon pill and your evening pill." Then she left. When she came back again later, she repeated the exact same words, giving her name again. This strange routine went on until Mihrigul spoke up.

"Are you crazy?" she asked the doctor. "You told me your name three times, said you are my doctor and what pills I have to take."

The woman silently went to the door and closed it, then walked back over and gave Mihrigul a hug. Then she started to silently cry.

"I need you to be strong, Mihrigul," she said. "You are in Ürümchi Mental Hospital. If any other doctor comes in and gives you medicine, don't take it. Pretend to take it, then hide it."

Mihrigul nodded, confused and suddenly scared. The doctor asked her if she had any idea how long she had been in the mental hospital. She shook her head. "About two weeks now," the doctor said. "Listen," she added, "I want to save you, but the police are outside and no one is allowed to come in and see you. Don't tell anyone what I did for you."

Mihrigul promised. There was one other bed in the small

room she was in. In it was a woman who had been in a con- centration camp in Kashgar, and who screamed and cried in- cessantly. Whenever the door opened, she recoiled in terror. Mihrigul had no idea what had happened to her in the camp, but she would reach out to hold her hand and try to reassure her. Meanwhile, she did as her guardian angel told her: when- ever she was given pills by other doctors, she would pretend to swallow them, then spit them into the toilet when she was al- lowed to use the bathroom.

Eventually her father was allowed to come and pick her up. The doctors attached a plastic strap to her wrist with a label: "Lost memory." Mihrigul looked at her guardian angel doc- tor, who shook her head very slightly: *say nothing*. Mihrigul ac- cepted the tag and went with her father to catch the bus back to Cherchen.

This time, though, they were accompanied by two policemen on the long overland journey. The police kept all her documents with them. At the numerous checkpoints they went through, when local police would board the bus and check passengers' documents, her escorts would explain she was a "dangerous criminal in transit who has lost her memory."

As they rolled over the vast terrain of East Turkistan, her father offered her some fresh fruit. It was something she had craved in prison on those hungry, sleepless nights. But now, looking at the policemen sitting by her side, she had no appetite. Their pres- ence meant for sure this was just a brief reprieve, and that she would soon be back in the camps. Far from losing her memory, she could never forget what awaited her there.

14

After six months of teaching in the first camp, Qelbinur's initial contract expired in August of 2017. She was exhausted, suffering from insomnia and living in constant dread of her Becoming Family rapist's next visit. Despite that, her superiors told her that the police and the camp were pleased with her performance: she had not told anyone about the horrors she had witnessed. However, her former school's administrator informed her that since the syllabus had now been made exclusively Chinese, with all classes held in Mandarin, her old job was obsolete. In its place, she was offered another six-month posting at a "reeducation center." She was not given a chance to say no.

The routine was the same—she was picked up at the Chugong bus station at 7:00 a.m. and driven to a windowless box of buildings near the Ürümchi Medical University. Oddly, the six-floor block had "Senior Retirement Apartments" stenciled in large red letters on its facade. By now though, she knew what stood behind these fake signs.

When she was escorted inside, Qelbinur quickly realized the prison population here was very different. Many of the inmates were highly educated young women who, like Mihrigul and Qelbinur's own daughter, had been studying abroad. They had mistakenly believed they could return safely to see their families during the holidays and had been picked up at the airport and interned. Trying to warn your kid not to return by phone or email could land a Uyghur parent in jail. On occasion, Uyghur parents asked Han Chinese acquaintances to make that risky call for them. In at least one documented case, the kindly Han friend who did so ended up with a short jail sentence while the Uyghur parents disappeared into the camps.

Once again, the scene was a classroom from hell. There were hundreds of young women, heads shorn, lined up on benches, although in the darkness she could only really see the first few rows through the bars that separated teacher from "students."

The women, some of them young mothers, were well-educated, having won places at universities in Europe, the United States, Japan, Kazakhstan and South Korea. Normally, they would have been absorbing knowledge and skills that would help their country grow: now they were being endlessly drilled in mindless Communist Party propaganda. Qelbinur recalled one particular "class" in which the young women were called upon to express their love of the Motherland.

"I love the Motherland so much," said one, "that even though I was studying in South Korea and having a good education, I returned and am getting more education about the Motherland."

Another woman had her turn. "I love the Motherland so much that I could even leave my infant child that I was breast-feeding and who was only forty days old to come here and love the Motherland even more, by learning what I did not know and becoming a better person. I volunteered to come here and love the Motherland more, and so did my husband."

Qelbinur wanted to ask where the infant was, but couldn't. In any case, the young mother probably had no idea herself.

A third said, "I love the Motherland so much that I was about to get married but I postponed my wedding because I realized that my knowledge about the language, the law and country were not sufficient, so I volunteered to come here and be a better person."

Qelbinur was stunned by these responses: she couldn't believe the women actually meant what they were saying. Instead, it sounded like a bold and very dangerous act of defiance, a sarcasm that risked their very lives. They were, after all, surrounded by gun-toting guards, with overhead cameras recording every step of the proceedings. Whether the young women received extra punishment for their act of resistance, she never knew: the classes were huge, the inmates were mixed up every day and, with their washed-out faces and shaven heads, their skinny figures in blue-gray uniforms, it was difficult to keep track of them.

Sometimes the young women were late getting into class, and would come in sobbing or walking with difficulty. It was clear they had been sexually abused, but there was no way to ask them in front of the guards.

Then, one day, she saw someone she recognized: a Uyghur policewoman she knew was walking down one of the corridors of the camp. Qelbinur greeted her, and they exchanged a few pleasantries. She asked what the woman was doing there, and she replied that she had been sent to write a report on the facility. As they were talking in the hallway, a female prisoner was carried past on a stretcher. The woman was unconscious and deathly pale. Qelbinur quickly asked her acquaintance if they could meet up after she finished her "classes." The woman readily agreed.

That was when she learned the full horror of what was going on in the so-called "reeducation camp."

The policewoman told her she had been sent to look into reports of rampant and systematic sexual abuse at this particular camp. What she had learned made her sick to her stomach, as a Uyghur woman working for the Chinese police. It was not just that the guards and police were raping women for their own pleasure, though they were. It was also that they were inserting batons—even electric batons—into their vaginas, and in the case of men, into their rectums. Prisoners were forced to perform oral sex on their captors, who would violate any orifice on a prisoner's body—even their ears, the policewoman said. Because so many of the prisoners were young women, this camp had become a very popular posting with the guards. They had been bragging so much about how many women they had raped or abused that the police department overseeing the camp had gotten wind of it. Qelbinur's police acquaintance had been sent to look into it, but she realized her mission was a mere whitewash: the camp authorities had ordered her to conduct the interviews not inside an interrogation room or an office, but inside the cells where the guards themselves were monitoring the conversations. No prisoner in their right mind would confirm the stories. It was a cover-up, and she as a Uyghur woman had probably been selected to make the whitewash seem more credible.

Such horrifying reports of sexual abuse have been confirmed by another former camp language instructor, the ethnic Kazakh woman Sayragul Sauytbay, whose testimony in a court in Kazakhstan was the first wake-up call to the world about Xinjiang. She told the Israeli newspaper *Haaretz* that the police in the camp she was drafted into "had unlimited power. They could take whoever they wanted. There were also cases of gang rape. In one of the classes I taught, one of those victims entered half an hour after the start of the lesson. The police ordered her to sit down, but she couldn't do it, so they took her to the black room for punishment."

The black room, she said in an interview conducted in Sweden, where she had eventually escaped to, was where prisoners were made to sit on a chair of nails, or had their fingernails pulled out. They were hung from walls and beaten with electrified truncheons. It was called the "black room" because no one was supposed to talk about the horrors that went on inside.

"One day," she told the newspaper, "the police told us they were going to check to see whether our reeducation was succeeding, whether we were developing properly. They took 200 inmates outside, men and women, and told one of the women to confess her sins. She stood before us and declared she had been a bad person, but now that she had learned Chinese she had become a better person. When she was done speaking, the policemen ordered her to disrobe and simply raped her one after the other, in front of everyone. While they were raping her, they checked to see how we were reacting. People who turned their heads or closed their eyes, and those who looked angry or shocked, they were taken away and we never saw them again. It was awful. I will never forget the feeling of helplessness, of not being able to help her. After that happened, it was hard for me to sleep at night."

With rape and sexual abuse rife, it was no surprise that some of the women got pregnant, despite the white pills and the gynecological "exams." One day, as Qelbinur was waiting in the prison yard for her police escort back to town, she started talking to an elderly Chinese man who had also been seconded to the camp as a teacher. Since her driver had not yet shown up, he offered to drop her off. On the way, the man—who had previously specialized in law and politics—started complaining to his driver about the camp. As a Chinese man, he was more at ease to vent than Qelbinur, a member of a Muslim minority.

He complained about the absurdity of the situation, trying to teach law to well-educated people who had been illegally detained. "When I talk about law and order, they say, 'Why am I here? What kind of law justifies my detention?' How could I answer?" he said.

Qelbinur kept out of the conversation, just in case it was some kind of a trap. But she listened closely as the man, who must have been around seventy, started complaining that the guards were deliberately trying to make the taller, stronger and prettier women pregnant. When they became pregnant, he said, the babies were claimed by the state to be raised as pro-Chinese Uyghurs, who would think, speak and act like ethnic Chinese.

Could such a thing be possible? That's the thing about secretive authoritarian states: we just have no way of knowing. Who would have thought the Nazis were experimenting on twin children, injecting brown eyes with blue dye or removing organs from one child and then killing the other to dissect them for comparison, or immersing prisoners in tubs of freezing water until they died to study the effects of hypothermia on the human body. Certainly China has a well-documented and shameful history of harvesting organs from executed prisoners—some of them prisoners of conscience, or members of the oppressed Falun Gong spiritual group—and selling them to foreign patients in need of transplants. China said it had phased out that practice in 2015, but human rights groups and Falun Gong members insist that it still goes on, with many of the latter describing blood and organ tests similar to what the Uyghurs have undergone, to test for compatibility with ailing foreigners who can fly in to China for transplants timed to coincide with executions.

As the mother of a young woman herself, the stories of systemic rape in the camps were horrifying to Qelbinur. She vowed to kill herself if her own daughter ever returned to China. And as a woman who was being sexually abused by a stranger in her own home while her husband stood helplessly by, it was all too much.

A month after she started work in the second camp, Qelbinur collapsed.

★ ★ ★

In 1941, Nazi Germany opened a new concentration camp in Theresienstadt, just north of Prague in what is now the Czech Republic. An eighteenth-century Austro-Hungarian barracks town, Theresienstadt was retooled by the Nazis for two purposes: one was to serve as a holding station for Jews from Czechoslovakia en route to the Polish death camps in the north. The other was to be used as a propaganda tool, a "model" camp to show the world that Germany was caring for the Jewish people in the midst of the Second World War.

Conditions were bad, but not as deadly as in the other concentration camps scattered across occupied Eastern Europe. Masters of propaganda, the Nazis made a short film showing Jews living their lives: women milking cows, men working in a blacksmith's shop. The soundtrack of the film featured jaunty waltzes—there were enough musicians incarcerated in Theresienstadt to have two full symphony orchestras. The Nazis even allowed the Red Cross to visit once, in June 1944. For this carefully orchestrated trip, the houses were painted, gardens planted and the "residents," as they were called in the propaganda film, were given better clothes and posed in front of bakeries and shops whose windows were stocked with goods for the day. There were no armed guards, though German officials escorted the visitors.

A member of the Red Cross delegation even had the chance to ask one young woman—who ultimately survived the camps—about what life was like in Theresienstadt. Constrained by the presence of the German officials, she begged the visitor to "use your eyes and look around." Nevertheless, the Red Cross found the conditions to be acceptable, given the wartime hardships.

A month later, in July of 1944, the Red Army liberated the first concentration camp at Majdanek in eastern Poland and the outside world saw, for the first time, the reality of the camps. By that time, Theresienstadt had been "liquidated" and most of the people seen in the footage were on their way to the gas chambers.

In the summer of 2019, Chinese authorities in Xinjiang invited a select group of foreign journalists to visit a designated "reeducation facility." Clearly by this point Beijing understood that the pictures they had issued of smiling Uyghurs sitting attentively in classes were not fooling enough observers.

Among those invited was a BBC crew, including the corporation's China correspondent, John Sudworth. They were shown what appeared to be freshly painted classes in campuses free of razor wire or armed guards, in which smiling Uyghurs dressed in tracksuits or yellow polo shirts studied on computers, staged dance shows or learned how to make a bed for their future employment in hotels. The journalists were even allowed to speak to some of the "students," although always with a group of Chinese minders lurking close by.

Sudworth asked one of the "students," a smiling woman wearing makeup, what crime she had committed. The woman responded, "I haven't committed a crime. I just made a mistake."

A young man in the dance performance staged for the visitors explained with a rather stiff smile that he had suffered from "a weak awareness of the law. I was influenced by extremists and terrorism. A policeman in my village told me to get enrolled in school and transform my thoughts." The young man had a large purple bruise over one of his eyes.

The BBC crew also studied satellite images of the camp they had been allowed to visit and found clear evidence of its preparation for the media: high fences of razor wire and guard towers had been removed prior to the visit, and the large exercise yard had been converted into basketball courts. The images, going back several years, also showed the shocking rate at which many of these facilities have been expanded since the first camps came to light in or around 2015.

Of course, these dance classes and bed-making courses were

not what Zumrat saw that March of 2018 when she was delivered to a camp from the police station where she had been questioned and beaten.

She hadn't slept for two days, nor had she been given any food or water. From the police station, she had been taken to a hospital that looked like a military fortress, where she and hundreds of other Uyghur women were subjected to a variety of different medical exams and biometric screening—blood tests, DNA sampling, an intrusive OB-GYN screening, voice recordings where she had to read texts for forty-five minutes—and a mysterious room where she was forced to stand on a moving platform in front of a black mirror. The platform lurched in all directions, approaching the smoked glass mirror and then receding. To this day, she has no idea what it was for.

From there, she was driven to what appeared to be a hastily converted building, perhaps a school or a hospital whose windows had been covered with metal bars. As she was bundled out of the police van and the hood pulled off her head, she could hear a man screaming, begging the guards to kill him. He was clearly being tortured.

The guards—one woman and two men—handed her a prison uniform and ordered her to get changed right there in front of them. Zumrat had been married at a very young age and no man except her husband had ever seen her naked. She hesitated before obeying the order, but the woman guard got angry and told her that if she didn't strip she would tell the two men to rip off her clothes. As Zumrat finished undressing, the woman picked up her civilian clothes with two fingers, as though they disgusted her. Then one of the men put on rubber gloves and roughly searched inside her mouth.

Shackled and uniformed, she was led to a large room with around thirty-five women inside. Despite their shaved heads and drab fatigues, she recognized some women from her neighborhood: the wife of a local baker and the wife of a restaurant owner she knew. It was late, and the women were ordered to sleep on their right sides, because it was so crowded. They lay down like sardines, one arm stretched above their heads and the other on their sides to avoid touching each other.

"I wish I could say I slept, but it was impossible," she recalled. Instead, she lay there worrying about her family and about what might lie ahead for her. The women were woken up at 6:00 a.m. and lined up for the toilet bucket and a minute at the faucet to wash their faces in cold water. That was followed by repeatedly singing songs to the glory of the Communist Party to earn their breakfast, a soup that tasted of rotten vegetables, together with steam buns that were full of insects or flecks of paper or sponge. Once a week, they would be served meat that had so much fat on it they knew it must be pork, a test to see if they were "extremists" who refused to eat it.

After breakfast, they marched out of the cell to "class," long hours of chanting propaganda slogans in Chinese, a mind-numbing routine that lasted late into the evening. As they left their cell, a guard asked them if they believed in God and the Prophet Mohammed. Everyone received a blow the first time they were asked, because it was so hard to deny their faith.

The brainwashing session itself was in a large auditorium, like a cage with a blackboard, where they were taught Chinese by some press-ganged teacher like Qelbinur. They had to sit on the concrete floor and memorize Xi Jinping's thoughts on Communism or the agenda or the 19th Communist Party Congress. Even though none of the women were menstruating—they were given the same suspicious white pills that so many others reported—Zumrat noted that due to the lack of hygiene, the bucket toilet and the constant sitting on cold concrete floors, every one of the women had a crust of dried fluid on the seat of their prison uniform. One young woman had the same stains on her top—she had been breastfeeding her infant when she was dragged off, and was still lactating. Her husband had been arrested shortly before she gave birth by C-section. Then she too was detained, and the infant was left with a member of her family. Her caesarian wound became infected in the camp, and she cried in pain every night. The "crime" for which she had been arrested? She had a sister who had studied in Germany, and was therefore deemed to be a suspect.

It wasn't long before Zumrat was singled out for extra beatings. Soon after she arrived, she discovered that one of the women in her cell was diabetic and was not being given any insulin. She was fading fast, so one day Zumrat slipped her one of her steam buns to help keep her blood sugar stable. This small act of charity was spotted on a surveillance camera, and the guards came in to thrash her for noncompliance with the rules. Sharing food was not allowed. As they hit her, Zumrat instinctively cried out, "God help me!"

"You can call Allah to help you," one of the guards sneered. "Sounds like you're a radical piece of shit!" She was regularly beaten with plastic clubs for three days after that, on her legs, back and body, and also her arms where she held them up to protect her face. She knew she was now a target, and wondered how long she could last in the camp.

15

After her discharge in July 2017 from Ürümchi Mental Hospital, Mihrigul spent the rest of the summer at home. She was deeply depressed, and four months passed in a semi-daze of sleep and bad memories. Whenever someone spoke to her, she was reminded of the booming voice in her prison cell: if a door was slammed, it was enough sometimes to make her black out again. Months later, when she was in the United States, I helped her prepare to testify before Congress about her experiences, walking her through the questions she would be asked and the senators she would meet. Senator Marco Rubio of Florida came up to her and said, "Don't worry, you are safe now." But she didn't feel it, even in America. It would be a long time before she could feel *anything* again.

It was October when they came to get her. As the police led her from her home one last time, her father hugged her. Perhaps he knew they wouldn't see each other again, because he held on to her. "I love you," he said. "If you ever get away from this prison and can leave the country, promise me you'll never come back."

This time, they didn't bother beating or torturing her. She was forced to sign endless papers, then told to change into a prison uniform. Only now, it wasn't the same gray pants and top she had worn before: the uniform she was given was orange. This, she was told, was the color of death row inmates. One of the guards mocked her. "Special order for you, you look so beautiful in it."

In the following days, she was moved from cell to cell at the police station, as if they were deciding what to do with her. Eventually, the police took her to another prison, where she was placed in solitary confinement in an underground cell with no windows. Her guards gave her some paper and a pen and told her to confess whatever she might still have on her conscience. There were no more beatings, but they said she should write a farewell message to her children and her parents.

This, she knew, was the end. The guards asked her what she wanted for her last meal. She told them all she wanted was her mother's cooking. So they served up watery rice porridge and said, "Here, this is your mother's cooking." She didn't eat it. Neither did she write anything on the paper: she had nothing to confess, and she knew that no message from her would ever get to her children. The pages remained blank.

The bland routine of incarceration was interrupted one day when her guards informed her that she was going to be executed in a month, and was allowed to choose the way in which she died. She could be shot, but that would take three bullets to make sure she was dead. Each bullet would cost her family a staggering six hundred RMB, or ninety dollars. Or she could choose to be hanged, or to die by lethal injection: in the latter case, she was informed matter-of-factly, "You'll be contributing to the medical doctors who can study your body." It was unclear if they meant her organs would be removed and used for transplant, or whether her body would be dissected and studied.

It was too hideous a choice to make, and choosing might even signify her own complicity. If they wanted to kill her, let them decide how. She refused to sign. Alone in her cell, facing a grim death, Mihrigul began to question every aspect of her life. She struggled to accept that she was about to die for no reason at the age of just twenty-six. After a few days she started to pray: the irony of China's attempts to stamp out the spiritual life of the Uyghurs is that it has prompted many ordinary people who weren't particularly religious to turn more to their faith for solace. Everyone who is born has to die, Mihrigul told herself: maybe God loved her and wanted her to be with him. She started having vivid, happy dreams of a light coming into her prison cell, the cell door opening and her father coming to take her away. In her dreams, they were flying together, over flowers and green, lush countryside. She felt she was ready to let go of this life, but the dreams gave her a secret sense of hope too—a foretaste of heaven or escape.

Then one day the guards burst into her cell. They were flustered and angry and told her she had to sign some new papers. These ones testified that her children were born in Ürümchi and had a Uyghur father. They showed her a fake birth certificate for both her surviving kids, which listed neither a mother nor a father. Mihrigul assumed they were planning to send her children to a state orphanage for kids aged under four years, what the Chinese state euphemistically calls a "Little Angels Garden." Again, she refused to sign.

"These documents are fake!" she said. "My children are Egyptian citizens, they have an Egyptian father!"

That sent the cops into an even greater fury. For all their brutality, they were slaves to a vast bureaucracy, and there is nothing that sends the bureaucrats into a tailspin like inaccurate paperwork. Her tormentors, members of the state security apparatus, appeared to be enraged that the local police might have faked the birth certificates, creating a paper trail that could land them all in hot water. Mihrigul had noticed in the past that the local police were quite capable of mistaking her kids' Egyptian passports for copies of the Koran, so poorly educated were they. It struck her as quite possible that the local Cherchen police had not known what to do with her children's real IDs and had tried to bypass the problem by issuing new, but false, birth certificates. There was no way of knowing for sure. She later heard that the bumbling local cops who falsified the birth certificates were jailed for sixteen years for their forgery.

Mihrigul told the police that if they doubted her, they should go search her home and find her children's real passports. When they did, they discovered the kids' visas had expired. This posed another bureaucratic dilemma for them: the kids could not now legally remain in China, as their only legitimate documentation was foreign passports without valid visas. So they contacted the Egyptian embassy, and asked them to contact the children's father so that he could take custody and remove the problem. On their birth certificates, Mihrigul has listed Mahmoud, her Egyptian ex-husband, as the children's father, not the Uyghur man she had entered into a marriage of convenience with (and who had since disappeared into the camps himself).

And that is how Mahmoud, now working as a real estate agent in Dubai, found out not only that the mother of his children was in jail in China but that he was also the father of two small children. It was quite a shock, but he had always loved the woman he called Mihri. He couldn't abandon her or his kids.

A month passed, and the deadline for Mihrigul's execution came and went. Another two months of isolation passed before Mihrigul was abruptly summoned from her cell. Flustered guards started drilling her on what she was to say to the Egyptian man who was coming to collect her kids. For three days the guards cajoled, almost pleading with her: the same men who had been asking her to choose how she was to die were now suddenly friendly, telling her how smart she was, what great schools she had been sent to thanks to China's largesse, and asking why she had been involved with a "stupid Arab."

"Chinese people are better. If you do a good job and help the government, you'll have a much better future here. China is your home," they told her. "Don't tell him anything about what has happened to you in prison."

By this point, Mihrigul did not seriously believe she would ever leave her cell, and was reluctant for the father of her children to see her in such a sorry state—shaven-headed, wasted away and in a prison uniform—before she died. When she was led into the room in the police station where they were to meet and sign off the custody transfer of the children, Mahmoud did not even recognize the figure standing before him.

She spoke first.

"Mahmoud."

"Mihri?" he said.

She said yes, and they both started crying. Even the diplomats from the Egyptian embassy who had accompanied Mahmoud started crying. Despite the warnings to say nothing about her prison ordeal, Mihri immediately blurted out everything in Arabic. "I just came from prison, they want to kill me, they tortured me, and my children are yours…"

Mahmoud was furious. "Mihri, from now on and forever, I am with you. Don't worry. If anyone touches a hair on your head, I will kill them."

She begged him not to touch the guards, afraid they would kill him. "Please, be nice, take Moez and Elina and get out of here as fast as you can," she said. But he refused. "I didn't come for the kids, Mihri. Even though they're mine, I don't know them. I came for you. I won't leave without you."

From inside the police station, the Egyptian diplomats set up a conference call with their embassy and with the Chinese state's counsel for foreign affairs to discuss the situation. The senior Chinese official said they could take the kids but not Mihrigul. At that point, Mahmoud mentioned that his former wife had applied for Egyptian citizenship in 2015, when they were briefly married. The embassy confirmed it and said they would approve the application, effective immediately. The Chinese countered, saying that she could not legally hold dual citizenship. Mihrigul yelled at them that she would happily renounce her Chinese citizenship. The wrangling over the phone dragged on for five excruciating hours, during which the police—clearly terrified over this mess—tried to convince her to stay, arguing in Mandarin that China was her country, had paid for her education and that she would have a great life there if she played ball. They threatened her too, reminding her that China is a superpower and if she left they would still be able to reach her.

"We'll bring you back," they warned. "And you'll never see your parents again!"

Needless to say, there was no way in hell she was staying. The Egyptian embassy agreed she could shelter at one of its staff apartments in Beijing while the paperwork for its newest citizen was finalized. At Ürümchi Airport, waiting for the flight to the capital, Mihrigul said she needed to go to the bathroom. The Egyptian diplomats warned her not to go, nor to drink anything—they feared the Chinese might poison her. She stayed twenty-eight days in a cramped room at an embassy apartment with Mahmoud and the kids, who seemed malnourished. To this day she has no idea where they had been, since her parents had already disappeared into the camps after she was arrested that last time. On that count, at least, the police had not been lying: she would never see her parents again.

Meanwhile, the Chinese authorities kept delaying the paperwork needed to leave the country and throwing up petty obstacles. Four times she headed to the airport to catch a flight out of China, and the first three times she was denied entry to the plane on some technical excuse, losing money on each canceled ticket. They were running out of cash when they were finally allowed to board with her new Egyptian passport in early 2018.

She went to live with Mahmoud's parents in Cairo—he'd had to return to Dubai for work, to cover the huge expenses of getting Mihrigul out of China. But she was still not quite free. Police in Egypt are notoriously easy to bribe, and the government itself has been known to bow to Chinese pressure. Many Uyghurs have been arrested in Egypt, accused by the authorities of being illegal immigrants, while many more have fled the country to avoid being deported back to China. Mahmoud started getting phone calls from Egyptian police officers at his apartment in Dubai, telling him to control his wife, make sure she didn't speak to anyone, or ordering him to return. That made him nervous—the military had returned to power in Egypt after the revolution, and arbitrary torture and imprisonment were common. He warned Mihrigul she was probably in danger, so she applied to Turkey for a visa. It was denied. That was when she decided to tell her story to the world: she spoke to a journalist working for Radio Free Asia just in case she suddenly disappeared. Luckily, the journalist happened to have contacts in the US State Department, which was already on the alert for cases of Uyghurs facing persecution. After a few months, in September 2018 Mihrigul landed at Dulles Airport in Virginia with her two surviving children to apply for asylum. Mahmoud could not come with her—his visa to stay in Dubai had expired and he was afraid of returning to Egypt. In a legal limbo, he was stuck.

But even in America, China was not done with Mihrigul. In October of 2018, a year after she had been led away from her parent's house, she received a WeChat call from her family. Mihrigul knew they were in prison, but still the shock of hearing her parents denouncing her, asking her to return to the country that tortured her and tried to kill her, was a shock.

"You are no longer my daughter if you say anything bad about the country, our country is great," her stepmother said. "We raised you, we are your parents, please think about us at least, even if you don't care about anything else."

As they went on and on like this, Mihrigul realized they didn't even know where she was. Her stepmother pleaded with her to come home, not to stay in Egypt. Then, at one point, she heard her mother say to someone in the background, doubtless a policeman, "I told her. Yes, I already told her."

Eventually, Mihrigul couldn't take it anymore. She finally told them how she had been tortured, electrocuted and marked for death, and they hadn't even asked her about it. "You have no idea. If I'd died you'd never even know. If I returned to China, you'd never see me.

"I don't want to stop telling the world about what happened. Please forgive me. Forget me. Let me die in your minds. Consider me dead, but I will fight for my child that these people killed."

And that was the last she ever heard from her family. She doesn't know if they are alive or dead, although she heard a rumor that her brother—the one with the Chinese name—had been released and was working with one of the branches of state security.

But listening to those forced appeals for her to come back, she remembered the father she'd always adored, and what he'd whispered in her ear as she hugged him that last time, when the Chinese police led her away from her home.

"I love you," he had said. "I forgive you forever, and wherever you go, you are still my daughter. If you ever get away from this prison and can leave the country, promise me you'll never come back."

16

Fortunately for Zumrat, her Pakistani husband has always been a highly enterprising and persuasive person. As a businessman, fluent in Uyghur and several other languages, Mohammed had always cultivated contacts wherever he could. As such, the Pakistani embassy in Beijing had been happy to use him as a kind of honorary consul in Xinjiang. As soon as Zumrat was arrested in March 2018, he swung into action, flying to the embassy in the Chinese capital to report the arrest of his wife. The diplomats were sympathetic, but said he was not alone: there were "substantial" numbers of Pakistani men whose Uyghur wives or children had disappeared into the camps. They said they would raise it with the Chinese authorities. Mohammed dutifully waited several weeks, but when nothing happened, he and some other Pakistani men whose wives had disappeared started a media blitz right outside the embassy, telling the world what was going on.

That caught the attention of the Ürümchi police. They called

Mohammed and said there was a paid plane ticket waiting for
him at Beijing Airport. He should come back and "have a talk."
For Uyghurs, that expression usually means you are about to get
a warning, or veiled threat, from the police, but Mohammed
was fairly confident that as a Pakistani citizen, they wouldn't
touch him. When they met, he said he would not stop his campaign until Zumrat was released. The police made their usual
veiled threats of "consequences." Mohammed made it clear he
was not backing down. Sixty-two days after Zumrat was first
summoned to the police station, Mohammed was told to come
and pick up his wife.

But the victory was short-lived. Ürümchi—in fact, the whole
of Xinjiang—was by now a vast open-air prison camp for Uyghurs, and the state was far from done with Zumrat. A few
weeks after her release, she was back at the Monday-morning
flag-raising when the neighborhood watch announced that any
woman with three or more children had to stay behind after the
ceremony. The moment she had been dreading since the crackdown began had finally arrived.

Zumrat and scores of other women stayed: they were informed that they would all have to pay a fine for breaking the
law limiting them to two kids. The amount set for Zumrat was a
hefty 18,400 RMB, about three thousand dollars, roughly nine
months' salary for the average Uyghur. She was lucky in that
she had the means to pay it, and women with four kids or more
were having to stump up for even heavier fines. There was no
question that she would pay—the women were told that anyone
who failed to come up with the money would be sent for reeducation. Zumrat knew she could never go back to the camps.

Then, a few weeks later, the same ominous announcement
followed the flag-raising: all mothers of more than two kids
were to stay behind. This time, however, they were informed
that because of their infraction of the law, they would need to
be sterilized. In the coming weeks, they would have to stay be-

hind after the flag-raising and be taken in groups to a hospital for the operation, then brought back afterward. No family members were allowed to accompany them.

What went through Zumrat's head at that moment? She was remembering the Yugoslav war movies she had seen when she was younger (as a Communist country with a thriving film industry, Yugoslavia had been the go-to source for Chinese films on the European theater of World War II) in which Jewish women had been lined up by the Nazis and led off to the camps. She had no idea how sterilizations were conducted—would there be blood? Was it painful? She felt ill, and rushed home to tell Mohammed (as a Pakistani, he was not obliged to attend the ceremonies, just like the Han Chinese). He was livid and vowed to challenge the order: he dearly wanted a larger family. Despite Zumrat's objections, he stormed down to the neighborhood watch committee and tried every argument he could—his wife had a leaky bladder, he said, and the operation could make her incontinent. He promised to sign a document swearing not to have any more children. They told him to get out, and warned that if he caused any more trouble his visa would be revoked and he would be deported—and he would never see his family again.

The place Zumrat was taken to by public security officials a few weeks later was a government-run clinic designed primarily for quarantining people with contagious disease—as though Uyghur children might almost be considered a dangerous virus. The other women in the van with her were nervous. They were no strangers to government-imposed birth control—all Uyghur women were supposed to have IUDs inserted after their second child. Many, like Zumrat, had found sympathetic doctors to remove them, arguing that they caused bleeding or back pain. But this time it was different. This time it would be permanent.

The procedure itself was quick: she went into what appeared to be a delivery room and lay down on an OB-GYN bed, her feet up in stirrups. A doctor gave her anesthesia and when she woke up in the recovery room she felt an excruciating pain in her abdomen. The nurse told her she would be driven home after two hours. She would need to find a clinic to give her anti-inflammatory injections for a week.

She and her husband had already decided after she was incarcerated that they would have to leave China, even if it meant giving up their business and everything they owned. Now she started actively working to get her family out.

In April 2017, as Beijing became increasingly interested in Muslim women's reproductive abilities, Qelbinur was confused to receive notification that she had to report to the "Forever Happiness Medical Facility" in Ürümchi to have an IUD inserted. She was confused that a woman of her age would need a birth control device implanted, but saw that in fact, the order applied to all women from ethnic Muslim groups aged between eighteen and fifty. She dutifully went to the clinic and tried to explain to a younger Uyghur woman in charge of operations that she had an adult daughter, was forty-eight and had no plans to have any more children, even if that were physically possible at her age, which she very much doubted.

The hospital official was polite but unflinching. "I'm sorry, auntie, I'd do whatever you say but I might lose my job if I don't follow these orders."

So in July, she returned to the clinic and underwent the painful procedure. Immediately, she suffered from bleeding and abdominal pain. It was so bad that she found a doctor of traditional Uyghur medicine and persuaded him to remove the device, which was supposed to have remained in place for five years.

Less than a month later, however, another sweeping proclamation was issued: all Uyghur women between eighteen and fifty-five had to have the device inserted. She had to comply: the neighborhood watch committees kept tabs on whether women showed up to their appointments. In the clinic she saw scores of Uyghur women, lined up like sheep in the corridors to have the device implanted to prevent them from having more children. Again, she suffered pain and bleeding, but no one seemed to care.

Still it wasn't enough. Right on the day of her fiftieth birthday, May 5, 2019, she received an order that she had to be sterilized. Even though she had no desire to have any more children, it was a crushing intrusion into her private life, her body and her very essence as a woman. Like Zumrat, she was injected with a general anesthetic and woke to discomfort and bleeding. Back home, she felt numb. She and her husband were already estranged. Qelbinur decided enough was enough: she had to escape. Recalling her visits to their daughter in the Netherlands, in 2015 and 2016, right before all the horror began, she resolved that that was where she must go.

It took four months of traipsing from one government office to another to secure all the endless permits she needed to return to see her daughter. She told officials that she needed to seek medical attention abroad for the bleeding that had continued long after the operation. Eventually, the authorities conceded, but on certain conditions: she had to buy a return ticket and be back within a month. And her husband was denied permission to go with her this time: he would be held as a hostage against her return, in effect.

Qelbinur left Ürümchi on September 15 and spent three weeks in Beijing, getting the final stamps and permits. Like every other Uyghur trying to flee, she felt a rising fear that some hitch would arise that prevented her from leaving. But on October 9, she finally landed in the Netherlands. She couldn't quite believe it. Upon seeing her daughter, son-in-law and grandchildren waiting for her at the airport, she fainted. As she came to, her daughter was offering her a cup of coffee. She took it in a shaking hand and asked her daughter to pinch her to make sure she wasn't dreaming, that she wasn't about to wake up in China.

"I don't ever want to go back to China," she whispered.

"Even if you wanted to go back, I wouldn't let you," her daughter replied.

17

Zumrat also launched into a new flurry of activity, applying all of her inexhaustible energy to procuring permits and getting back the family's passports, which had been taken away in 2016, as had all Uyghurs' travel documents. She and her husband knew they were about to lose everything: their thriving business, the kids' friends, and ultimately they knew that their relatives would be harassed or thrown into the camps. But China was no longer safe for her, nor for any Uyghur who decided to stay.

Zumrat told the authorities she had to go to Pakistan to take care of her ailing father-in-law. For weeks, they threw up objections—didn't he have any relatives in Pakistan to care for him? Why couldn't her husband go alone? She argued that she, as a woman, was the one he wanted looking after him, not his two sons. Then another obstacle cropped up: the neighborhood watch committee accused her of not doing enough to promote "ethnic unity" in the region. It was an odd charge, but it soon became clear what they wanted—they "suggested" that if she wanted to become what they called "an acceptable citizen" and have a shot at leaving China even for a short period, she needed, as a suspect Uyghur, to help a Han Chinese person. They just happened to have one in mind: a woman who had once been a member of the Ürümchi neighborhood watch committee, a widow who was now suffering from bowel cancer and needed financial support to receive the best medical treatment. Escorted by a local policewoman, Zumrat was taken to meet this woman, who was indeed fighting cancer. They had the obligatory photos taken of them, sitting and smiling the forced smiles so common in Xinjiang selfies. They did not however take any photos of the twenty-four thousand RMB—approximately four thousand dollars—Zumrat was forced to hand over, yet another huge financial burden on top of the fine she had been forced to pay for having an extra child.

It was worth it though—now labeled a promoter of ethnic unity, she was allowed to proceed with the trip to Pakistan. They were permitted to travel for just one month, and were told to check in frequently with their local Ürümchi security contacts on their phone app: under no circumstances were they to delete the internet tracking app, and were under strict orders not to indulge in or go near any kind of religious activity. There was, of course, the obligatory warning of "consequences" if she failed to meet any of these requirements.

Zumrat was flooded with relief when their passports were returned. Just before the crackdown began in 2016, she had successfully applied for US visas for herself and her kids, so they could accompany Mohammed next time he went on a business trip. Their kids' passports with the visas in them had since expired, which is no doubt why the Chinese authorities thought she wouldn't flee from Pakistan: she would never leave without her children.

But Zumrat was one step ahead of them: she shipped the expired passports—the ones with the valid visas in them—ahead to her brother-in-law in Pakistan, together with the kids' new passports, and told him to get the visas transferred at the US embassy. Since the visas themselves were still valid, the US embassy complied. Then the brother-in-law shipped the passports back to her in Ürümchi. It was a high-risk gambit. If the authorities found out what she had done, she had little doubt she would be sent back to the camps.

As the departure date of January 27, 2019, loomed, there was one last requirement. To exit the country, she needed to show her household registry document. Zumrat's was a few years old and still had her religion listed as "Muslim." Like Mihrigul and Qelbinur, Zumrat believed in God, but wasn't a particularly religious woman. Uyghurs tend to be culturally religious, like the Turks they are related to, but broadly secular: they observe the holidays, fast during Ramadan and avoid eating pork, but Mihrigul, Qelbinur and Zumrat didn't wear headscarves like Muslim women in the Middle East. Zumrat had to go to the relevant bureau and get the new version of her document, which did not list a person's religious affiliation. At the office, a clerk asked if she was a Muslim, and would be practicing Islam when she was abroad. In order to gain her freedom, Zumrat had to deny her religion one last time: she knew deep down that her faith would not be judged by a piece of paper or what she said to some faceless bureaucrat. So she deleted her religion, and obtained the new document allowing her family to leave.

The hardest part was saying goodbye to her father: she could not tell anyone they were never coming back. He said goodbye, thinking he would see her in a few weeks. In fact, they never saw each other again. Predictably, he was arrested after she failed to return. A neighbor later told her he had died, although she could never find out where, or how.

It was just before noon when their flight landed in Islamabad, and the call to prayer was blaring from minarets across the city. Such an open and vibrant display of religion terrified her kids—they had been explicitly warned by their teachers not to expose themselves to any form of religion. When Zumrat was first arrested, a teacher had taken them aside and told them about "thought viruses" and how the camps would cure people who had been "intoxicated with the wrong ideology." To calm them down now, Zumrat and Mohammed told them they were never going back to China. Then she deleted all the phone numbers for the spies and snitches and police contacts from her WeChat app, and joyfully deleted the "Clean Internet Security Soldier" app.

But the real Rubicon was when she failed to board her flight home on February 27, her police-ordained return date. The authorities had already been onto her about the deleted app, but she had fobbed them off with a story about buying a new local phone, and saying that her Chinese phone wasn't working in Pakistan. Now she had an even better excuse: border skirmishes had broken out between Pakistan and India two weeks before and all airspace had been shut down across the region. That was enough to stall the Chinese police as the family counted down the days to their scheduled flight to Washington, DC, on April 1. Nevertheless, her brother—the one who was a reluctant member of the neighborhood watch committee—left several messages on WeChat, telling her to get in touch with the police "or they'll think you fled the country."

Their flight was scheduled for a stopover in Saudi Arabia before heading on to the United States. As they lined up for check-in, Zumrat was terrified that the authorities had canceled their passports. Sure enough, when they scanned her daughter's passport, the machine bleeped and refused to recognize it. The airline worker tried another machine. Again, the machine bleeped uselessly. Zumrat burst into tears. She knew they had to get out of Pakistan—China's influence there made it unsafe for fleeing Uyghurs to stay. Her husband, Mohammed, referred to his homeland as "mini-China," and they had heard plenty of tales of Uyghurs being deported back to China by the compliant Pakistani authorities. As a last resort, the woman at the airport manually typed her daughter's passport details into the computer. This time, miraculously, it worked: it had just been a technical glitch. Zumrat cried again, now with relief.

The family had a short stopover in Riyadh. When they boarded the Saudi Airlines plane for the final leg of their escape to Washington, Zumrat was amazed to hear Koranic verses playing softly over the intercom. There was even a small area dedicated for prayer on the plane. The contrast with China could not have been starker, or more reassuring. The very things her people were persecuted for en masse back home were here being celebrated and encouraged (although Saudi Arabia itself hardly encourages religious pluralism and, as we shall see later in the book, has a highly dubious record when it comes to confronting China over its abuse of the Uyghurs).

The flight was half empty, so they got to spread out and lie down, to finally relax after their ordeal. As they neared Dulles International Airport, Mohammed, being a seasoned traveler, warned his wife that as Muslims arriving from Pakistan via Saudi Arabia, there would almost certainly be a secondary screening by the Customs and Border Protection agents. Sure enough, they saw passengers in the line ahead of them being led off for additional questioning. When the CBP agent looked at Zumrat's passport, he said, "Chinese?"

"Uyghur Turkish," answered Mohammed, who speaks English well.

"Uyghur!" the officer said, apparently excited. "Welcome to America!" he said, and stamped her passport. It was the first time in her life that being Uyghur had ever caused her to be welcomed anywhere. Zumrat smiled at the officer, then led her family into the United States.

Escape can only ever be partial for the few Uyghurs fortunate enough to actually leave China. Some part of you has been forever lost inside the concentration camps—a trust in humanity, a certainty of who you are and where you fit in the world.

Mihrigul still has to sleep with a light on and take antidepressants to ward off the suicidal thoughts that prey on her: after arriving here, the self-destructive thoughts were so strong that she started the process of putting her kids up for adoption, so they would have a home and a new start if she lost her battle with depression. She changed her mind after learning that a couple had applied to take her toddlers. She just couldn't give them up again.

Zumrat is haunted by the loss of her father, who disappeared into the camps because she fled. Her father-in-law had to flee Pakistan after the Pakistani police came looking for Mohammed, saying they had a warrant from China accusing him of kidnapping his own wife and Chinese children. They now all live together in a cramped apartment in Virginia, where Mohammed, once a successful international businessman, has found a job through a Uyghur contact as a used car salesman.

For the first five months after she arrived in the Netherlands, Qelbinur, in poor health and still bleeding from her enforced sterilization at the age of fifty, was too afraid to tell the world what had happened to her. She lived with her daughter in Rotterdam for a while, but then applied for asylum and was moved to a shelter in Utrecht while her application was processed. That was when she decided she had to tell the world what was going on in China. She gave some interviews to the media. Pretty soon, her husband started contacting her on a regular basis. He was clearly being coerced by the Chinese police. Qelbinur had already lost respect for him when he sat by, watching the television in their home, while she was sexually assaulted by the Becoming Family spy in the room next door. Now, when she refused his entreaties to come back, he sounded desperate, hunted. At first, it seemed he was reading scripted messages and threats. But then things turned nasty.

"He called me a whore, he said, 'You are a horrible person, you betrayed me and the Motherland, the Dutch will not protect you, you are a traitor,'" she recalled, crying.

The next time they spoke, he threatened repercussions for her family still in Xinjiang. "I will be leading the efforts to have all of your family members locked up!" he said. Then he enacted a "talaq," an Islamic divorce—traditionally, a man can tell his wife three times that he divorces her, and their marriage is annulled. He did it by text message. But even then, the threats didn't stop. In January of 2020, he said to her, "The authorities just told me, and I'm very glad, that they are going to grab you from the Netherlands and bring you back home."

Then in February, he disappeared for a while. When he came back, he sounded even more angry and frightened. "The worst is yet to come," he said. "But you can change this. If you go to the Chinese embassy in the Netherlands and confess you have been spreading false rumors, that you've been trying to harm China, then you may change the situation."

He said he'd spent four hours with the authorities recording a video to testify that Qelbinur had been lying about the camps and about her forced sterilization. At this point she lost her temper. "You must be out of your mind!" she snapped. "Who was that guy who was complaining he could not have intimacy with me because of the bleeding? Have you forgotten about that?"

These days, Qelbinur is trying to put it behind her, but that includes writing off most of her life. Her asylum application has been accepted and she is scheduled to be able to leave the drab shelter and move in with her daughter and her family. But she still panics when she sees Chinese-looking people in the streets of Rotterdam—are they trying to abduct her and drag her back to China for speaking out?

Worse, she is often contacted by Uyghur women who have read her account of the camps, and send her pictures of their missing daughters, asking if she saw any of them, if they should stay hopeful or start mourning their loss. So far, she has recognized none of them: the bright, smiling young women in the photos they send look nothing like the gray shadows she saw in the camps. She cannot help them.

She has a lot of time on her hands these days. "What shocks me most is that in the face of these naked criminal acts people still seem to be indifferent, and people keep asking me, 'Are you serious? Is this true?' I feel like screaming at them, 'What more do you want to see? I'm not in the business of making stuff up, I'm telling you what I saw. Look at me, I'm a train wreck.' After these interviews, it takes me days to even collect myself. Why would I do this?

"I want to scream at the world, will you speak up once we're all gone? Where do you draw the line? Why do they hate us so much? What makes a person that brutal?"

PART 4

HOW TO DELETE A CULTURE

18

In May 2017, two years before Zumrat was forced to flee her homeland and as Ürümchi was just heading into the abyss, she had received a disturbing notice from the local authorities. She was told that the Muslim cemetery where her brother Mutallip was buried—the same one whose unborn baby had been subjected to an extreme late-term abortion after Mutallip died in a car crash—was being bulldozed for redevelopment. The family had to come and collect his remains, as well as the bones of Zumrat's grandfather, who was buried in the same plot.

When the family arrived at the Feng Tian cemetery near Ürümchi's Diwopu International Airport, they were ordered to wait until officials summoned them to witness the exhumation. Then they watched as men in white overalls and hard hats opened the graves with picks, before shoveling the mortal remains into canvas bundles.

They tried to pack the bundles as tightly as possible: Zumrat could hear bones cracking as her relatives' remains were crushed in. The family were then told to take the cloth-wrapped remains home and keep them there until they received instructions as to where they could be reburied. The only advice they received was to keep the bundles well covered "so that cats don't chew on them." As they left the cemetery, Zumrat spotted a truck being loaded with identical bundles that had not been claimed by relatives.

Clearly, the family had no place to keep human remains at home, so they wrapped them in plastic and stored them on the roof. Some neighbors kept their dead relatives in the basement, where people also kept sacks of vegetables.

"It was horrifying to think that there are dead bodies upstairs," Zumrat told me. "Whenever you heard a noise at night, it felt like they are tapping on the roof, saying, 'Why am I here when I should be in the earth?' It's strange beyond words, a nightmare."

It was almost two weeks before the authorities informed her that a new cemetery had been constructed on the edge of the city, in an arid patch of wasteland known as Liu Daowan. Unlike the leafy cemetery where her brother and grandfather had originally been buried under headstones marked with Koranic inscriptions, this was a barren no-man's land. The remains were put into small concrete vaults, stacked up in rows. Worse, the individual vaults were not marked: people knew the area where their relatives were buried, but not which tomb to pray over. They were given just ten minutes to say their goodbyes. When they left, they saw facial recognition cameras had been set up at the cemetery gates—anyone who visited regularly could be suspected of trying to recite Koranic prayers or observe other religious rites, a "crime" which could land them in the camps.

Expanding cities are often forced to relocate cemeteries and move graves, though usually with more respect for the dead than the authorities of Ürümchi showed. But what happened to Zumrat's family soon turned out to be part of something far

186

more systematic and disturbing. It fell into a pattern of Beijing's massive push to destroy cemeteries, mosques and holy sites across Xinjiang, in a calculated bid to erase an entire culture.

Uyghurs have always been discriminated against by their mainstream Chinese rulers, be it the colonialism of the imperial Qing dynasty or the modern Communist Party. There were uprisings that briefly won some semblance of liberation—the Uzbek adventurer Yakub Beg took advantage of the chaos of the late Qing period to set up an independent state in the 1860s and early 1870s—but mostly the resistance has been quiet, subtle acts of cultural defiance carried out in the privacy of people's homes, or in mosques or cemeteries. Instead of fighting, Uyghurs have pushed back against the encroaching Chinese culture by entrenching their own traditions, from wedding ceremonies to funeral rites, from pilgrimages to desert shrines to the observance of their own particular feasts and holidays.

Now, as part of the new drive to uproot their culture in its entirety, even these last threads of memory had to be severed.

While millions of Uyghurs were forced into camps to be indoctrinated in the ideology of the Chinese Communist Party, their past, their heritage, their very culture was being literally bulldozed. Uyghurs would emerge from concentration camps, full of fear and the endlessly repeated chants of "Chairman Xi thought," only to find the land they knew was gone, replaced by a bland Chinese simulacrum. This, Beijing calculated, would make them pliable, easier to control and reshape.

One of the intellectuals who disappeared into the camps was Qurban Mamut, the seventy-year-old retired editor of a journal called *Xinjiang Civilization*. Despite being sponsored and approved by the Communist Party itself, the magazine happened to cover cultural aspects of Uyghur life in Xinjiang. In the new climate, that doomed it and anyone linked to it.

Qurban was arrested at some point in 2018, possibly because his son Bahram Sintash lives in the United States and works for the Uyghur-language section of Radio Free Asia, a US-funded but editorially independent news outlet providing uncensored reports on the region. RFA's Uyghur-language service had been reporting on the oppression in Xinjiang. In retaliation, China arrested a slew of relatives of RFA staff at the time, one of the first signs of the coming storm.

A year before his detention, Qurban had visited his son's home outside Washington, DC. He stayed for several weeks, playing with his ten-year-old grandson and speaking of the worrying signs already emerging in Xinjiang since Chen Quanguo had been appointed as the region's new party boss. Bahram had begged his father to stay in America, at least until it became clear how bad things might get. But the older man felt a duty to return to Ürümchi, to stand with his fellow guardians of the Uyghur culture.

In 2018, Qurban suddenly dropped off WeChat, the popular Chinese social media app that Uyghurs in exile generally used to keep in touch with family still living in Xinjiang. Worried, Bahram asked his mother where his father was. She told him he was working on a home he had been building for the past ten years in the town of Kuchar, where his family originally hailed from.

A month or so later, Bahram contacted his mother again, and she repeated the same story. Then, abruptly, Bahram found that she had blocked him on WeChat, and all the other apps they used to communicate.

His entire family had gone entirely dark.

In desperation, he asked around among Uyghur friends who still had family living in Xinjiang, to see if they could find out what had happened. One of them delivered the awful news: his father had been taken off to the camps. His mother had lied to him, either to protect him or herself. The Chinese government often tells people that their relatives have only been taken off for a few months' reeducation, and if they comply, their family members will soon return. If they do not, their loved ones will never see them again. Uyghurs know that telling anyone outside the country about what has happened is tantamount to betraying state secrets, and that all social media conversations are closely monitored by artificial intelligence.

Bahram couldn't see his mother's WeChat, but friends who still could reported that she still occasionally posted on the app: never directly talking about her husband, just oblique allusions such as "Loved ones are so important." It was as though she was reaching out through the veil of censorship to her vanished family.

Even those glimpses of his mother quickly vanished, however—the friends who had supplied them now said their own relatives were too scared to relay even such innocuous tidbits.

Some information was leaking out of Xinjiang, though. Bahram came across online chatter that China had begun demolishing mosques across the region, including one particularly beautiful structure that he had himself visited in the town of Karghalik, when he was a twenty-one-year-old studying architecture and had traveled through his homeland to soak in the beauty of its historic buildings. He decided to investigate the matter for himself.

Since moving to the United States, Bahram has worked with graphic design (he did an internship at my wife's company), and knows his way around Google Earth, the site that shows satellite images of almost the whole planet. He located a satellite image of the four-hundred-year-old Kargalik mosque that was time-stamped August 31, 2018—around the same time his father had vanished.

From the satellite's perspective, he looked down on the sprawling compound, its dome and minarets looming over a crowded bazaar where the faithful and visitors bought food and refreshments. Behind it, a large courtyard was shaded by leafy parasol trees. It was a beautiful structure, showing off some unique examples of Uyghur design, such as the colorful bricks on the gatehouse, whose high arch was adorned with gilded verses from the Koran in Arabic and Uyghur calligraphy. Between its decorated halls and the square outside, the mosque could accommodate gatherings of up to ten thousand people.

The building was founded by Sultan Abdulrashid Khan in 1543, just a century after the completion of the famous Duomo cathedral in Florence. Kargalik had become an important waypoint for pilgrims and merchants on the road between the ancient cities of Hotan and Yarkand. Legend has it that during construction of the mosque, the wall that faced Mecca collapsed three times: when the foundations were dug up, a jar of gold and human remains were found. The body was that of a mullah, or religious scholar, from the city of Hormuz in Iran. He was given a proper burial in the mosque and the gold was used to finish building the shrine. From that point on, the mosque stood firm through the centuries.

With a sense of trepidation, Bahram scrolled forward on the Google Earth timeline. He found another image, dated January 10, 2019, less than five months later.

The mosque was gone, as though a huge eraser had rubbed it off the map. Just a huge, bare patch of dirt marked the spot where the Kargalik Grand Mosque had once stood for centuries, a building that had been listed by the Chinese government itself as a protected historic site.

After months of looking for his father, not knowing if he was dead or alive, the revelation was a gut punch. It was as though he had lost his father all over again. He had always been close to his dad—the old man had bailed him out so many times when Bahram got into fights with the police, who he would see picking on Uyghurs in the street. "If a Han Chinese gets into a fight with a Uyghur, the police arrest the Uyghur. I've seen it many times," he told me. Bahram is a very large and physically powerful man, and he always stood up for his friends. What ultimately saved him from jail was meeting a girl online who had gone to the same elementary school as him, and whose family had moved to Fairfax, Virginia, when she was eight. They fell in love on the internet, and he moved to the United States to marry her and start a new life. Otherwise he too would have ended up in the camps.

There is a terrible feeling of rage and despair among Uyghur exiles whose families vanish. They don't know if their loved ones are alive or dead, in the camps or maybe even at home, wishing they had joined the families overseas but too afraid to even send a text message. To this day, Bahram often dreams of his father. He sees the old man being beaten by prison guards and calling out to his burly son for help. It is torture. Bahram knew he had to fight back.

This time, instead of launching himself at a Chinese police-man, he decided to use his architectural knowledge and com-puter skills to track down every historical mosque that had been erased. It was a gargantuan task: while many mosques were de-stroyed in Chairman Mao's Cultural Revolution, thousands had survived in the desert and mountain towns of Xinjiang. Some had even been rebuilt during the brief Uyghur renaissance under Deng Xiaoping in the 1980s.

For six months, Bahram pored over satellite images, peer-ing into small towns for the telltale dome and minaret struc-tures that marked a mosque or shrine. He also put the word out on social media, asking exiles around the world to check up on their own local mosques on Google Earth. If they didn't know how to work the technology, Bahram would have them describe where the mosque was, like they were giving direc-tions to a newcomer in town. He would then follow these di-rections through the aerial images of their hometowns, setting the timeline back to 2015 when he was sure the mass destruc-tion had not yet begun. Then he would scroll forward to the present, and frequently find vacant lots, car parks, department stores or other buildings.

Most of the small mosques in provincial towns were not even marked on either Google Maps or its Chinese equivalent, Baidu Maps. Only local knowledge could pinpoint them, and given the blackout from inside Xinjiang, that could only come from the diaspora.

Some of the larger mosques had been stripped of all the symbols of Islam, such as their towers and domes and Koranic inscriptions. Many had been repurposed as municipal halls, desecrated with pictures of Mao or Xi (most branches of Islam, like Judaism, forbid the depiction of human images on religious sites). Instead of prayers and sermons, they would be resounding with the chants of Communist indoctrination or the minutes of local council meetings.

When Bahram approached the Uyghur Human Rights Project for help in getting the news out, the organization was able to give him an assistant, and later to publish his devastating findings as a report. By Bahram's calculation, as many as 80 percent of Xinjiang's mosques had been either destroyed, damaged or retooled as secular buildings.

"In the town of Changji, I found three mosques completely demolished and 12 mosques with their domes and minarets removed," he wrote in his final report, entitled "Demolishing Faith." "All of the mosques in this small city were affected. I believe that if you take a conservative estimate that 80 percent of the mosques around the Uyghur region have been affected, that would mean that as many as 10,000 to 15,000 mosques have been affected by the campaign."

The Australian Strategic Policy Institute (ASPI), which studies China closely, put that estimate slightly lower: it said that as of late 2020, at least 65 percent of the mosques in Xinjiang have been destroyed or damaged as a result of government policies. Of those, eighty-five hundred mosques have been demolished outright—the rest have been stripped of domes, Islamic symbols, or outbuildings and grounds. Despite the authorities' frequent claims that the land was needed for redevelopment, many of the plots now stand empty.

This has been particularly devastating in rural areas. When a village's mosque is demolished, the local population often lacks the means to travel to a far-off town where there might still be a surviving place of worship. They are cut adrift from their faith, just as the Communist leadership intended.

It was not just mosques that were vanishing, either. The imams who led the prayers and tended to their congregation's spiritual needs were also disappearing at a disproportionate rate. In the case of the Kargalik Grand Mosque, preacher Ablat Qarim Hajim was detained in 2017 and died in custody: no one knows what he died of. His body was later returned to his family. He had been the longest-serving religious leader of the mosque, and had initially encountered some antipathy because he held a government-issued religious diploma. Some Uyghur Muslims saw his sermons as "red activism," yet another sign that those being arrested are targeted simply because they are Uyghurs.

As far as my organization has been able to establish from court documents, at least 630 imams were sent to prison so far, of whom eighteen have died. More than a thousand have been held at some point in recent years. Almost all of them have received sentences of five years or more, and a quarter of them have been jailed for at least twenty years, with fourteen life sentences. They have faced trumped-up charges such as "gathering a crowd to disturb social order," "propagating extremism" and "inciting separatism."

There was another, perhaps even more sinister, side to the destruction. In many towns, all of the smaller mosques would be demolished except one, which would then be fitted out with facial recognition security cameras. As people turned to that one surviving mosque for their spiritual needs, the police could monitor every person who attended and arrest them for suspicious religious activity. The Uyghurs' own faith was being turned against them, so that even mosques that managed to keep their doors open were soon deserted.

Bahram's study of the mosques was so crucial because, as he himself says, "We can't see inside the camps, we can't see directly what China is doing to the Uyghurs inside their cells. But we can clearly see what they are doing to religious sites."

His startling report grabbed attention around the world. The *Washington Post* ran an op-ed comparing what China was doing to Kristallnacht in November 1938, when government-directed mobs in Nazi Germany attacked Jewish stores, beat up their owners and burned hundreds of synagogues, as well as smashing up cemeteries.

The destruction in Xinjiang didn't stop with mosques however: aside from the demolition of the graveyard where Zumrat's relatives were exhumed, Bahram's research showed some of the largest and oldest burial sites in Xinjiang have been entirely erased. Satellite pictures show a giant mud patch where the centuries-old Sultanim Cemetery once stood in the city of Hotan.

"My father and my grandfather were also buried in this cemetery," he was told by a Hotan scholar in exile he tracked down. "The cemetery was the most important holy place for millions of people to go and visit in Hotan every year."

Another very singular part of the Uyghur culture is the *"mazars,"* holy sites often found in remote desert areas that mark the presumed burial site of a saint or military hero.

Some of these are likely pre-Islamic relics from the time when the inhabitants of what is now called Xinjiang were Buddhists or Manichaeans, the latter subscribing to a belief that emerged in third century Persia about a world in a constant struggle between the forces of good and evil, light and darkness. The Uyghur Empire that ruled the region in the eighth century was defeated by the Kara-Khanid Turks, who had already converted to Islam and who spread their new faith as they moved eastward.

Rian Thum, an American historian and one of the leading experts on Uyghur culture, has spent years in Xinjiang and China. He says that pilgrimages to these shrines were a central part of the lore of the community. In premodern times, the people of the region didn't think of themselves as "Uyghurs," the name which derives from the long-lost medieval kingdom. Until the early twentieth century, they simply would refer to themselves as "Mussulman," or Muslim, or even "yerlik," which just means "a local." It was simply how they saw themselves: so many Indigenous names, like the Hadza of Tanzania, around the world just translate as "human being" or "local."

Many of the mazar shrines are simple in their construction, lozenge-shaped concrete burial mounds topped with a small dome and surrounded by colorful flags and banners planted by visiting pilgrims over the years. The tombs are often outsize, like a grave of a giant. Others are modest mudbrick and wood constructions, surviving over centuries thanks to repairs carried out by generations of pilgrims passing through, who group together to patch up a crumbling wall or replace weathered fences and the poles for prayer flags.

"Some of the most important ones are architecturally unremarkable in scale, they are not built of permanent materials," Rian told me. "They are impressive when you visit them partly because of their impermanence in these sandy terrains."

Because none had ever been excavated, it is not even known if there were actual bodies inside any of them. Some of the mudbrick and wood shrines have slowly migrated over time, as the sand dunes shifted beneath them and the pilgrims moved their shelters and flags to follow. Similar shrines can be seen in India and across Southeast Asia, perhaps marking a giant footprint of the Buddha, or a spot where a holy man once prayed.

They have a vital significance to rural Uyghurs in particular.

While most Uyghurs are Sunni Muslim, many are Sufis, the most spiritual and mystical branch of Islam, which is open to singing and dancing, things that other, stricter branches of the faith often frown upon.

"Just having been to a site can bring someone a kind of prestige and a connection to people who haven't been to the *mazar*. And when they come home, they have a little bit of a connection to the sacred and the supernatural and to the real that everyone can partake in," says Rian, who notes that many country folk tap into the mysticism or superstition that has accrued around a society that has lived on the crossroads of so many diverse cultures for so long. When he visited desert shrines, he saw women who hoped to get pregnant reaching with their fingers into a crack in a mazar's walls and then swallowing the first thing they touched, such as a small clod of dirt or mortar.

"Knowing that even if you can't visit a site that is hundreds of miles away, its presence is still very real—it can appear in your dreams, if you have been there you have a relationship to it, you can pray to that saint to intercede for you, or if you meet someone who's been there they have a little bit of the holiness that rubs off. These sites have a real presence in people's worlds, even when they can't access them."

Rian thinks that because of the Communist Party's absolute control of the information flow inside China, and the restrictions on travel, most rural Uyghurs have no idea that so many of their holy sites have been razed. But the satellite pictures show the blank spots where once these shrines stood, before the authorities trucked in bulldozers to destroy them.

What will the Uyghurs feel when they finally discover so much of their heritage, the scaffolding of their culture, has been deliberately swept away? Rian compares that shock to the outpouring of grief when a fire gutted Notre-Dame Cathedral in Paris in spring of 2019, as the whole world looked on in horror.

The cathedral was badly damaged, rather than destroyed, and

a multibillion-dollar reconstruction effort immediately swung into place: laser-cleaning for fallen stones, in-depth studies of the medieval building materials that scientists had been unable to analyze before. There were even anthropological studies of the emotional trauma that Parisians and tourists suffered.

Now imagine that it was not just Notre-Dame, but that the cathedrals of Chartres, Reims, Toulouse and Lourdes were all gone. And that the Père Lachaise cemetery, where Oscar Wilde, Chopin, Rossini and Jim Morrison are buried, had also been bulldozed. And imagine that the destruction was not the random work of an accidental fire, but the deliberate work of the government.

It is unthinkable, of course. But that is just what the Chinese Communist Party has done to the Uyghur culture. The only flaw in the analogy is that the CCP was too savvy to touch the most famous mosques in Kashgar and Ürümchi, aware that such violence would be glaringly obvious to the world, including to its own tourists who visit these exotic western cities but rarely stray off the beaten track. As we will see, one thing the Communist Party really fears is that its own people will find out the truth about what it is doing.

Instead, what it has done in Kashgar is slowly knock down the ancient buildings of the historic old city and replace them with modern, tourist-friendly replicas, while also installing mass surveillance equipment everywhere. It has turned what was once a unique jewel of Uyghur history into a police-state theme park.

As an act of cultural vandalism, what China has done far outstrips the Taliban's destruction of the Bamiyan Buddhas in Afghanistan in 2001, an act of wanton desecration that triggered outrage worldwide. The Taliban destroyed the graven images of another culture out of adherence to an extreme form of Islam: the Chinese Communist Party is destroying thousands of religious sites out of adherence to an extreme brand of nationalism and atheist Marxism.

Rian fears that the destruction of the mazars has been profoundly underestimated, and when Uyghurs find out the full extent of the destruction, the emotional impact will be devastating.

"When they know about this, their hearts are going to be absolutely broken," he said. Because unlike the charred timbers and stones of Notre-Dame that specialists can now analyze, there is nothing left of the Uyghur shrines to study or rebuild. Even the rubble has been swept away, in what looks like an attempt to lobotomize an entire culture.

In an interview in 2012, Rahile Dawut, a prominent scholar of Uyghur shrines, said: "If one were to remove these shrines, the Uyghur people would lose contact with the earth. They would no longer have a personal, cultural, and spiritual history. After a few years, we would not have a memory of why we live here or where we belong."

It is hard to know if Dawut knows of the tragedy that has befallen her beloved shrines: she too has vanished into the camps.

19

Culture is a fluid thing, a moving target that is an amalgam of communities clashing in wars, blending in trade, or moving over time to seek new opportunities or flee dangers at home. Gods, symbols and legends morph and merge over the years. It is a vaguely remembered historical artifact shaped by the hands of a hundred generations but also a vibrant, living thing that shapes the very essence of who we are today.

Take British history, for example: ask any schoolkid in Britain what happened in 1066 and they will tell you that it was the invasion of England by the Normans, when the French-speaking William the Conqueror defeated King Harold of England at the Battle of Hastings. Dig a little deeper though and you'll find that Harold was of recent Viking descent, half Danish and half Saxon, and his Anglo-Saxon army was made up of men whose ancestors had been Germanic soldiers brought to the British isles by the crumbling Roman Empire to prop up its far-flung territories, driving out the Indigenous Celts. William was also of

Viking heritage, the offspring of Norsemen—hence the name "Normans"—who had taken to raiding the monasteries in northern France a couple of centuries before and had gradually settled the land and adopted the language, itself a post-Roman creole of Latin. And a third of William's fighters came from Brittany, another region of northern France that in previous centuries had seen an influx of British Celts who had fled the Anglo-Saxon invasion and may have seen an opportunity to retake some of their ancestral lands from their old foes fighting under Harold.

Even the name "France" derives from the Franks, a Germanic tribe who settled in what had been known as Gaul when the Roman Empire collapsed.

Which is all to say, culture is by no means frozen in time. Just one hundred years ago, as Rian Thum noted, probably no one on earth referred to themselves as "Uyghurs," yet now most of the Uyghur-speaking people in Xinjiang do just that (although as late as the 1980s some people in rural areas still used *"yerlik"* or "Muslim," and some older people still might refer to themselves first by the specific town or province they hail from).

In his groundbreaking book, *The Sacred Routes of Uyghur History,* Thum uses the term "Altishahr" to describe the people who live in the region, a rich mixture of Uyghurs, Kazakhs, Mongols, Kyrgyz and Uzbeks. The name is an old Turkic description of the region that was intricately connected to the cultures of India, Pakistan, Afghanistan and, through the Silk Road, China, before modern politics cut it off. The people there had followed a variety of faiths and spiritual beliefs that shaped their civilization—the eighth-century Uyghur Empire was in fact the only Manichaean state in history.

When the Qing dynasty—itself Manchurian, rather than Han Chinese, in its ethnic origin—finally collapsed in 1912 after decades of strife and growing foreign encroachment, China was plunged into a prolonged spasm of instability, of warlord rule and civil war, out of which the Chinese Communist Party would ultimately emerge victorious in 1949.

Even before that, under the Qing emperors, Chinese rule of the Uyghur lands had been largely indirect, conducted through a series of local elites who governed Xinjiang's cities and provinces. The upheaval that engulfed China in the early twentieth century allowed these local elites to exert more independence: one of them, a brutal Han ruler called Jin Shuren, tried to run the region as his personal fiefdom, displacing the Turkic-speaking Altishahri from their land and replacing them with Han immigrants. That sparked a series of uprisings and led to the short-lived First East Turkistan Republic being set up in 1933. It had its own flag, currency and press, but no big power backing. It survived for less than a year. It was put down by a Hui (Chinese Muslim) warlord who became a de facto Soviet puppet and who was every bit as brutal and corrupt as his predecessor. He in turn fell out with his Soviet sponsors and tried to throw in his lot with Nationalist leader Chiang Kai-shek (who was himself ultimately defeated by Chairman Mao) but ended up being replaced by yet another Han nationalist whose resumption of Han immigration prompted the Turkic-speaking population to rise up once again.

That final revolt created the Soviet-backed Second East Turkestan Republic, which was established in 1942 and in which my grandfather served in a minor governmental role at the culture ministry.

It was during this tumultuous period that intellectuals from my homeland started traveling to the newly created Soviet Union, just across the border, and coming into contact with anti-colonialist ideas, including Lenin's version of national self-determination. The Soviets promoted the concept as an anti-imperialist tool, meant to encourage oppressed peoples to find their own identity and throw off their shackles. Lenin hoped that would lead them to join the Marxist struggle as autonomous ethno-national groups.

Casting around for a name for this burgeoning proto-nation, the intellectuals looked back into history and adopted the name of the pre-Islamic Uyghur Empire, which had fallen to the Muslim Kara-Khanid Turks more than a millennium before. The name had first been resurrected in 1910 by a local poet who dubbed himself "Child of the Uyghur," and although the historians could probably just as easily have found their antecedents in the Kara-Khanids, the name Uyghur stuck.

When Mao's Communists won the final victory in China in 1949, Stalin handed the territory back to Beijing, and the name was taken up in turn by the Chinese Communists. They lumped it together, however, with the imperial Qing name for its "new territories," and so the Xinjiang Uyghur Autonomous Region, or XUAR, was born.

Despite the new name—or rather, the revived *old* name—the culture of the people had not changed. Their beliefs and customs remained the same, along with their romantic and poetic nature. As happened after World War I in the Middle East, very old cultures were being repackaged in modern territories: "old wine in new skins," as one commentator put it at the time. And that is always a cause of historical friction, as the contemporary Middle East can clearly attest to.

The underpinning of any culture is, of course, its language, the medium through which we express ourselves in art, literature and everyday life. The Uyghurs speak a Turkic language that's not very different from Uzbek: if a Uyghur watches an Uzbek movie, they will understand 99 percent of it. With a Turkish film, they'd catch at least 80 percent.

Linguistically and culturally, Uyghurs have far more in common with Istanbul than Beijing. On my first-ever trip to Turkey, I was in a bookstore in Istanbul and an old man came up and asked me what I was looking for. I said I was looking for a Turkish history book—he could tell I was not from Anatolia and asked me if I was a Uyghur. When I nodded, he held my hand and gave me a hug, a kiss on my forehead, and said, "I have found my relative!" Then he took me through the Grand Bazaar and found me three books. "Read these and you'll be proud," he said. "There's no Turkish history without the Uyghurs."

But most Uyghurs have also had to become fluent in Mandarin because, like all colonized peoples, we have to learn the language of the imperial power in order to have a chance at getting ahead. When I was a student, being sent away to inner China and learning Mandarin were seen as gaining a foothold in the job market: only later did I realize that it was also a subtle way of peeling me away from my own roots. Immigrants feel this dilemma the whole time, of course. But we Uyghurs are not immigrants: we live on our own land. As the historian Gardner Bovingdon has put it, the Uyghurs are now "strangers in their own land."

That is why the Chinese authorities have tried to silence prominent Uyghur voices: they remind us of who we are. Beijing has also learned another lesson from Tibet—it is extremely bad PR to have an outspoken and respected spiritual leader like the Dalai Lama constantly reminding the world of the tragedy that has befallen his people.[4] So it had moved to silence us, and replace our voices with propaganda slogans chanted in Mandarin.

The most recent purge can be traced back to 2014 and the arrest of Ilham Tohti. The economist and political thinker had the temerity to call on China to actually allow the autonomy that is written into the Chinese constitution. In 2009, after the Ürümchi protests were brutally suppressed by Chinese forces, he told *Deutsche Welle* radio that "there have always been tensions between the Han Chinese and the Uyghurs. But they had never led to mutual hatred. I believe that the trust between the Uyghur minority and the Han Chinese is now destroyed. I also

---

4 In its efforts to control Tibet, the Chinese authorities in 1995 kidnapped the six-year-old Panchen Lama, the second-most important figure in Tibetan Buddhism, shortly after the boy had been named as the reincarnation of the recently deceased Panchen Lama. Since the Panchen Lama is one of the key figures in identifying the new Dalai Lama, that also was meant to give Beijing key leverage over the succession when the current Dalai Lama, now in his eighties, eventually passes away.

think that ethnic hatred has been taking shape. If Beijing can't bring the situation under control and continues to behave like a colonial power, we will continue to witness tragedies such as this one."

On the basis of that, China charged him with separatism, one of the most serious crimes in its books. Tohti was sentenced to life imprisonment. He has since been awarded the Sakharov Prize and the Václav Havel Human Rights Prize, but there is no sign he will ever walk free again.

Tohti was at least someone who had spoken out about the deteriorating situation in Xinjiang. Ablajan Ayup was simply a singer who drew heavily on Uyghur cultural themes, and became so popular among young people that he earned the reputation as "the Uyghur Justin Bieber." He told the BBC in an interview in 2017, just as the crackdown was taking off, that his dream was to build bridges between his community and the Han Chinese.

A year later, in February 2018, he was returning to Ürümchi from a concert in Shanghai when he vanished. As is often the case, his family had to assume he had been arrested, although the police said nothing at first. His detention was eventually confirmed, though the reason remained unclear at the time. Was it because he had once traveled to Malaysia? Because he had spoken to foreign journalists, even in the most mild-mannered way? The closest he had ever come to making a political statement was in 2014, four years before his disappearance, when the authorities canceled one of his concerts following the July clashes between Uyghur protesters and police that left one hundred people dead in Kashgar. Ayup had billed the gig as a display of ethnic unity between Han and Uyghur, but less than an hour before showtime the authorities pulled the plug. Ayup hit back by posting a picture of himself on social media with the caption: "I am not a terrorist!"

As we now know, it was all of the reasons above, and none of them: he was a prominent Uyghur artist, and that was enough.

20

As with just about every other aspect of human affairs, Marxism has a theory about minority languages. According to Communist theoreticians, minority languages will change slowly while remaining relatively stable, but will ultimately be replaced or assimilated by a common language.

They can be tolerated "as a necessary and temporary stage before their final integration," according to Communist dogma. That suited the leadership of the CCP, which from its founding in 1921 had adopted the Soviet model of recognizing ethnic minorities and even defending—on paper, at least—their right to secede from a federal China. In that, it hoped to distinguish itself from the imperial powers of the Qing dynasty, and from its rival Nationalists, led by Chiang Kai-shek, who was pushing a policy of Hanhua, or Sinicization. Mao removed the clause allowing ethnic minorities to secede in 1938, downgrading it instead to the right to autonomy, but the constitution adopted after the CCP's victory in 1949 still proclaimed that "all national minorities shall have the freedom to develop their dialects and languages, to preserve or reform their traditions, customs, and religious beliefs."

The fact that using the Uyghur language is protected by China's *own* laws—be it in education, commerce or daily life—was something that the poet Abduweli Ayup wanted to impress on every Uyghur. When he was a boy in the 1980s, Abduweli was enthralled by the Uyghur love of poetry, a tradition that has largely died out in the West. My own father, a mathematics professor, penned poetry and was enormously proud when one of my own compositions was featured on a radio show when I was still a teenager. There is a tradition in some homes of having a guest recite a quick line of verse as they arrive and take their seat. Abduweli remembered his father telling him of how he had once burned his fingers, because he had been given a cup of tea on his arrival and knew he wasn't supposed to put it down until he had come up with a line or two of poetry, but his mind went suddenly blank.

By the time he was in his teens, Abduweli was memorizing twelve-thousand-word poems and working on his own compositions. He gained a reputation as a young talent to watch, penning more work as he studied linguistics and eventually won a Ford Foundation scholarship to Kansas University, where his academic research led him into the field of children's language development. He discovered that poetry is an important tool in the teaching of a language, as the rhythm makes it easier for kids to remember: just think of the power of nursery rhymes. This got him thinking about teaching Uyghur to kids back home. Despite the rules of bilingual education set out in the constitution, all the kindergartens in Xinjiang taught exclusively in Mandarin: this was justified in official CCP jargon under the principle of Hanhua: "consolidating" language and thought to eliminate resistance. Translated in layman's terms, Abduweli says, it meant that "if kids couldn't speak Chinese, they couldn't even ask to go to the toilet."

While he was studying in the safety of the United States in the late 2000s, a number of his friends back home started complaining that they couldn't find anywhere for their young kids to learn their own language. Studies that Abduweli had come across in the US showed that if a language is not used in a country's education system, it will die out in just three generations. So, to the chagrin of his Kansas supervisor, who had just managed to snag him a rare thirty-eight-month scholarship to do his PhD, he resolved to return to Kashgar after he graduated in 2011 and set up the Mother Tongue kindergarten to teach small children in Uyghur, Mandarin and English.

Demand was high and the project was an instant success: he started out in 2011 with fifteen kids, but by the start of the second semester he had fifty-seven. The school was in an old administration building in the People's Park, which is dominated by a giant statue of Chairman Mao, but the kindergarten was also just one hundred yards from the tomb of the eleventh-century scholar, poet and statesman Yusuf Khass Hajib Balasaguni, who wrote *Blessed Knowledge*, a foundational work of Uyghur literature. Abduweli would take the kids there and tell them stories about his life and read them some of his works.

"Yes, the Arabs, Tajiks have a lot of books,
As for our speech, this is only the beginning.
Who is wise will appreciate this book with respect,
Who has matured with reason, appreciates knowledge..."

He would also take them to a nursing home where many elderly Uyghur intellectuals resided, so they could hear the old stories in their mother tongue. He showed them *Dora the Explorer* cartoons, with the Spanish parts dubbed into Uyghur and the rest in English. And his teachers also assiduously taught them

Mandarin, because when they went on to grade school, they would be taught in Chinese only.

Soon after he launched the kindergarten, however, the police came calling. Two Han Chinese and a Uyghur: they wanted what is known in China as "Hecha"—tea and a chat, which coming from cops in a police state inevitably comes with a side of underlying menace. Abduweli had traveled abroad before, so he knew the drill—there was always something slightly surreal about these encounters because the police are hoping to establish a connection between you and known troublemakers, so they can start leaning on you, even when you know there is no link there. Inevitably, they started asking whether he knew Rebiya Kadeer, the elderly dissident who had escaped to the US by that time, or whether he knew me—despite the fact we didn't meet until Abduweli finally fled China a few years later. So at this stage, he wasn't too worried, since he could honestly answer their questions in the negative. There was one alarming moment when they produced an email he had received from my organization, the Uyghur Human Rights Project—a mass mailing sent out to everyone who had subscribed to our lists. That could have been risky since the Communist Party sees the UHRP as some kind of separatist organization. Luckily Abduweli had never responded, so could argue he had only ever been a passive recipient. The police left him alone, for now.

Demand for his teaching services grew rapidly. A year after opening the school in the park in Kashgar, he applied for a permit to launch a second Mother Tongue kindergarten in Ürümchi. The request was immediately rejected. He applied in a different district of the city and was rejected again by the city educational authorities. It was clear he was being deliberately blocked, so he started posting the official rejection letters online, on a Uyghur website called Bagdax. People started following the saga of bureaucratic nay-saying in droves—at their peak, the website had more than five hundred thousand followers. Abduweli had clearly touched a nerve.

The young poet started to get invitations to deliver lectures on the importance of the Uyghur language at private training centers, places where young people were studying IT or English. There was huge interest in his talks: after the July 5 Ürümchi riots, people had woken up to the fact that their language was being actively eradicated. Crowds of up to one thousand people would pack into the lecture halls. In the question-and-answer period at the end of these talks, the depth of the problem became clear to Abduweli when young people would ask, rather shamefacedly, if they could pose their question to him in Mandarin because their Uyghur wasn't good enough.

Abduweli would remind his audience of Article 4 of the Chinese Constitution, which allows any ethnic group to have their education in their own language. And Article 36 that stipulates that people can choose the religion they practice. "I would tell them the Chinese Constitution already gave us this right, but it is our responsibility to exercise it," he told me.

As the movement grew, the poet knew he was increasingly in peril. He was tipped off that he would be arrested: some friends advised him to flee, but he had always criticized the people who chose to leave the homeland. After all, if the Uyghurs became immigrants in foreign countries, they would quickly be absorbed in their new lands and their heritage lost even faster than at home. So he stayed.

One night in March of 2013, Abduweli was in a Kazakh restaurant in Ürümchi with some friends, putting the finishing touches to plans for a gathering to celebrate Nowruz, a Uyghur New Year's festival, when the police came in. They warned him he had to call off the gathering, which was attracting visitors from across Xinjiang, Uyghurs, Uzbeks and Kazakhs. He said if they wanted it called off, they would have to announce that *they* were canceling it. They argued until 2:00 a.m., when Abduweli pleaded exhaustion and finally went to bed in the hotel he was staying at.

When he woke up the next morning, he found he couldn't make any outgoing calls on his phone. But he could receive them: in fact, his wife called him from Kashgar and told him that the police had just closed down the kindergarten. They had put up a sign saying it was shuttered because of "illegal activity." Shortly afterward, the police came and arrested him in his hotel. This time when they interrogated him, they started talking about Bangladesh. They said that in 1971, students at the University of Dhaka had organized protests at the Pakistani government suppressing the Bangla language, and that led to a bloody war of independence. They told him that this was not a language issue but a separatism issue. At that, Abduweli felt truly terrified for the first time: being convicted of separatism is a life sentence in China, if not a bullet in the head.

They held him for eight hours that time, then released him. He returned to Kashgar, but was soon detained again. As he was being interrogated in the police station, strapped into a tiger chair, he heard a strange noise behind him but couldn't see what was causing it. Then he felt a burning shock rip through his body. The police were using an electric baton, burning his rib cage.

When I spoke to Abduweli, he could not bring himself to talk again about what happened after that, on his first day in prison. He has written about it though, for PEN International, alluding to the sexual abuse he was subjected to by twenty prison guards who forced Abduweli—a small, slight man with dark hair and glasses—to strip naked in front of them.

"That evil-spirited 'man' ordered me to get completely naked and when I was, he had me bent down like a donkey and smacked my bottom. The anger of not being able to retaliate made me bite my lips until they bled. Although I have imagined the way the Chinese officers treat the Uyghur prisoners, I'd never thought that it would be this way. I immediately grabbed my bottom after several slaps, and I heard them laughing out loud. I was trembling with anger and humiliation. Their condescending sneers and tone were the only thing I could see.

"I was turned into a diversion and was being played like a monkey in a circus. The monkeys that surrounded me were riding me one after another."

It is too painful for Abduweli to talk about his ordeal more than once. Instead, he politely asked me to watch an interview he gave to Al Jazeera when he had just escaped to Istanbul. In that interview, he is asked if the twenty prison guards had raped him. He closes his eyes in pain, reliving that soul-crushing humiliation, and whispers, "Yes."

For simply daring to set up kindergartens for preschoolers and language training centers—all of it done legally, through China's own system—this soft-spoken poet had been gang-raped by state prison guards.

He was transferred to a jail in Ürümchi the next day. In the car, all he could feel was a red-mist hatred for his captors. He kept wondering how he could kill the policemen in the van, knowing that he would be killed himself but that would mean all this horror was over at last. But he couldn't even move, handcuffed and wedged between two state security policemen.

When he arrived at the new detention center in Ürümchi, he was led into a cell with a small cage in the center. Inside the cage was the obligatory tiger chair: above the tiger chair, a metal hook protruded from the roof.

"Oh," thought Abduweli. "This time they are going to hang me."

He was petrified, and sat shaking until two guards came in. He was immensely relieved to see one of them was a woman. He had feared he would be raped again.

The woman started interrogating him. This time there were no questions about separatism or whether the CIA had recruited him when he was in the US. Instead, she asked him about the investors in his kindergartens. When she was done, he was taken off to an actual jail cell where he was given a bunk with fifteen other inmates. He discovered they were a mix of Uyghurs and Han Chinese, and all had strange ranks—there was a "class president" who was Han Chinese and a "head of discipline" who was a very tall and very brutal Uyghur man, who slapped him when he spoke Uyghur and told him that Chinese was the only language allowed here. The irony that he was in jail for trying to preserve this man's language was not lost on Abduweli, but he had a new set of idioms to learn right now.

The "head of discipline" asked him if he liked dumplings. He said he did. The big man asked him how many dumplings he usually ate. Confused, Abduweli hazarded a guess.

"Five?" he said. So the man punched him in the stomach five times. Then he said, "Do you want to fly?" Again, Abduweli had no idea how to answer this. The big man told him to stand by the toilet: there was a hook in the ceiling and he suspended Abduweli by the wrists over the toilet for a long time, until he vomited and the cell boss ordered him taken down.

The "class president" ordered him to kneel in front of him, like some mini-emperor. He asked what Abduweli had been doing in the US, to which Abduweli replied that he had been a student there. "Well now I am the teacher and you are the student, you will follow me," he proclaimed.

On the wall of the cell, as if in mockery of the inmates, was a poster with thirty-six rules, setting out the inmates' rights: to call a lawyer, receive a fair trial and to have their ethnic language and religious faith respected. The cell boss told him to memorize them all. When he had, he then handed Abduweli a scrap of paper with the prison's real rules written on it, eleven in total. They flew in the face of the official guidelines—*You don't speak about God, you don't believe in God, there is no Uyghur and Chinese, everyone here is Chinese.* They were forbidden from covering their faces at night, even though the ceiling lights were on 24/7. The guards weren't to be called guards but "trainers."

The "head of discipline" told Abduweli that because he was a political prisoner, he had to eat his meals sitting on the floor and sleep on the floor next to the toilet. Because the prison was run on Beijing time, rather than Xinjiang time, they had to get up at 4:00 a.m. and fold their bedding with military precision, while a television in the cell played endless cartoons claiming that the Uyghurs came to the region a thousand years after the Han Chinese and that when Mao's troops marched in in 1949 all the Uyghurs turned out to greet them like long-lost brothers.

The days were long, a mixture of inedible food and endless hours sat cross-legged, reciting Chinese propaganda songs. Even though this was in 2013, several years before Chen's vast crackdown began in earnest, there were already cameras watching their every move, and the slightest deviation was met with shouts and punishment.

The authorities told Abduweli that if he signed documents admitting to investment fraud with his schools, he could be out in fifteen months: it is a common way for China to punish dissidents without attracting international attention and having them labeled as prisoners of conscience. If he did not agree, they told him, he would be considered a political prisoner and likely never see the outside of a prison again. Abduweli immediately signed the confession.

As grim as life was, he vowed to survive: he forced himself to eat the disgusting food and even to exercise on nights when he was forced to pointlessly "stand watch" for two hours over his sleeping cellmates. If the authorities wanted to kill him, fine, but he wasn't going to just waste away.

With no access to his beloved literature, the other prisoners became his books. He asked them endless questions about their lives, who they were and where they came from. He was especially interested in the stories of the Hui, an ethnic group descended in large part from immigrants who traveled into the region along the Silk Road some fifteen hundred years ago and had intermarried with the Chinese. They happen to be Muslim, although they speak Mandarin and are indistinguishable from other Chinese people. Listening to their stories of endless discrimination, he came to the conclusion that even if the Uyghurs really did everything the CCP demanded—gave up their language, their faith and their culture—they would never rise above the level of second-class citizens, just like the Hui.

To keep his mind busy, Abduweli also started writing new books. He had no access to pen or paper, so he composed and memorized three books in his head: one was for his elder daughter, about the time they had lived in America; the second was for his wife, and was about how to raise their two daughters without him, based on his studies in child development in Kansas; and the third was for his friends, a series of meditations on how to survive in a society that oppresses its own people. The training of his boyhood years, when he would commit epic poems to memory, was a huge help in retaining his own unwritten works purely in his head.

Although the sexual abuse never recurred, he was punished harshly for minor infractions. Once, he got into a debate with a Hui prisoner about whether the food served up for a spring festival was halal: because they were speaking in Mandarin, a Chinese guard overheard them and flew into a fury.

"I'll teach you about halal!" he screamed. He shackled Abduweli hand and foot, punched him, and then ordered the "class president" to drag him by a chain around his neck, like a dog, down the corridor. They stopped at each cell, and the cell boss warned the inmates that this would be their punishment if they ever discussed religious issues. Abduweli remained chained hand and foot for a week, barely eating or drinking to cut down on the need to use the toilet. The other prisoners would hold their noses and tell him that he was a dirty Uyghur and stank, but one elderly Chinese prisoner helped him clean himself, and he made it through the week.

He had been arrested in spring but was released in winter when Ürümchi was freezing. The clothes he had been wearing at his arrest were for warm weather, and he would likely have frozen had another Uyghur prisoner not donated a tracksuit to him as he left the jail. When Abduweli was released, he called his brother and emerged into a different world: he could not go anywhere because of his criminal record, could not visit anyone in their apartments because his ID card flagged him as a threat to any doorman. Alone and isolated, he ran the daily risk of being arrested again and disappearing forever into China's vast penal system. Twice he was detained at checkpoints—the first time was in Kashgar, where he only escaped because one of the cops at the police station happened to know Abduweli's eldest brother, who had himself been a policeman. The second time was in Ürümchi, where the police chief happened to know his poetry and took pity on him.

But it was enough: he knew he had to leave or he would die in prison. By luck, there was a delegation of Uyghur experts in herbal medicine heading to Turkey to start a hospital there. They needed a translator, and a friend introduced Abduweli to the head of the group. They agreed to hire him, but he only cleared the airport security thanks to a bureaucratic mix-up in his papers: his residency was still listed as being in Lengdu, a town in inner China where he had once taught at a university. He had left it there deliberately to avoid the usual discrimination that Uyghurs face. When the airport police called Lengdu to check his criminal record, it did not show up on the university's records for some serendipitous reason. Otherwise, he would have been caught and no doubt jailed for trying to flee the country. The police let him out on condition that he provide a contact number for them in Turkey, and to tell them if he changed apartments. He agreed, but once his wife and daughters had managed to join him in Turkey, he deleted all the police contacts and applied for asylum in Sweden.

Since then, Abduweli has become a leading voice speaking out against China's crimes against his people, telling his own story, and helping the Uyghur exile community to review leaked lists of people who have been herded into the camps. One of these leaked files was named the Karakax list, and gave the names of 3,000 people who had been detained and the reasons for their detention. Many of them were marked "suspicious" for having traveled abroad, or having a relative living overseas. For many Uyghurs who had no idea where their missing relatives had gone, this leak was the first confirmation they received that they had actually been detained.

Beijing was not happy. The police arrested two of his brothers and two of his sisters, who vanished into the camps, along with several members of his wife's family. He still does not know where they are, although Radio Free Europe recently confirmed that his niece Mihriay had died in the same Kashgar detention facility where Abduweli had once been held. She had been working as a researcher at Japan's Nara Institute of Science and Technology before being pressured to return home.

"I hate myself that I couldn't save anyone but lost my niece there," Abduweli wrote on Twitter after receiving the tragic news.

He has tried to turn away from the rage that once made him dream of killing his tormentors. In the end, his answer is in the language that the system tried to crush out of him: poetry, written in Uyghur.

Suffering, it is not you that I buried in my chest
My heart is filled with the luxuriant thorn of revenge
No answer has appeared, even though I die for it
One cannot wash away the blood of humiliation with blood.

PART 5

THE REINVENTION OF GENOCIDE

21

By a twist of fate, fifteen years before the poet Abduweli Ayup was arrested and sexually assaulted for trying to teach Uyghur kindergarteners in their own language, he had actually worked for one of the architects of his people's genocide.

Of course, back in June of 1998, Zhu Hailun was a relatively minor figure, a forty-year-old Communist Party boss in the backwater of Kashgar, a big fish in a small provincial pond. Abduweli was a fresh-faced twenty-four-year-old who had just finished a degree in linguistics in Beijing and was on his first job out of college. He was working as a translator for the administration of Doletbagh, a municipality on the edge of Kashgar. He wanted to earn some money while sitting tests for a master's at Xinjiang University in Ürümchi. A week after he started the job, Zhu came to his town during Ramadan, when all of the restaurants were closed for the Muslim month of fasting. The council invited him to have lunch at the municipal building instead, but the catering was not good and Zhu, a cold, unsmiling bureaucrat, felt no qualms about expressing his annoyance.

He turned to Abduweli and told him the Uyghurs were "fengjian," a Mandarin expression that roughly translates as "backward," or "primitive," but which can also be used as a derogatory term for Islamic. Hearing the phrase, Abduweli was shocked: the word would never have been used in the academic circles he had moved in back in Beijing. Maybe thirty years earlier in the violent days of the Cultural Revolution, but to hear it from a party boss of a city in the late 1990s was like a slap in the face. Zhu went on in the same vein: he said people were fasting for the holy month because they were "barbarians" who knew nothing of Chinese history.

Why did Zhu speak so bluntly to Abduweli? Probably because the young man had studied in Beijing—a city Zhu himself had never visited at that point in his life. "You are different from these people," he told Abduweli. "You are educated and lived in Beijing." It was a classic colonialist attitude, and could have been uttered by a British official to a London-educated Burmese official in the nineteenth century. Perhaps Zhu was also a little envious of his education and wanted to let him know that, despite all that, he was still of some lower social order.

They met again several months later, when Kashgar's farmers were in a dispute with the city authorities. The party had ordered them to grow cotton instead of the fruit and vegetables they traditionally cultivated, and which brought a much better price in Kashgar's markets. Farmers had to meet cotton production quotas set by the government, but they had also been allowed to maintain small, private plots of land to grow vegetables in their own time. Zhu had ordered these small kitchen gardens be razed, and the farmers were furious. Around a hundred of them drove their tractors to city hall and sat outside, holding up banners, and with babies' pacifiers stuck in their mouths, to show they were being silenced.

Zhu Hailun was furious at this act of defiance. He returned to Doletbagh and summoned all the local council officials, police and neighborhood watch leaders to hear him speak. These protesters were not simple farmers but separatists, he said, inspired by Uyghur intellectuals. They were, he fumed, barricading their mosques to be used as fortresses. He denounced them as "antirevolutionary," another jarring throwback to Mao's Cultural Revolution of the late 1960s.

Zhu ordered the town authorities to carry out two months of nighttime house raids, to search farms for illicit books, such as works on Uyghur history. One of the places they were ordered to search was in the underground pits where Uyghur farmers usually mulch wood into fertilizer.

Zhu was speaking in Mandarin, and it was Abduweli's job to translate his rant for the five hundred or so assembled officials, most of them Uyghurs. When he'd finished, Zhu turned to the young man and said in perfect Uyghur, "You missed a word."

Zhu, it turned out, spoke fluent Uyghur. Perhaps Abduweli shouldn't have been surprised. The stony-faced apparatchik had originally been sent to Xinjiang twenty years earlier, as part of his own "reeducation," when millions of young urban Chinese were forced by Mao to live in the countryside and labor alongside the working people, to bolster agricultural production and make proletarians of them. Even Xi Jinping, a so-called "princeling" whose own father had been in Mao's close circle before falling from grace, was sent to live among the peasants, something he now touts as a badge of honor, a bona fide man of the people.

Most ambitious young party cadres opted to return to their cities in inner China after their time spent among the far-flung masses. Zhu decided to stay on and study the Uyghur people, learning their language, culture and customs. Clearly, from what he told Abduweli, he had formed a very low opinion of his subjects. By that time, he had built a reputation for toughness and was known to be uncompromising. "One is one, two is two," he would say if any underling dared question his logic. He always kept to himself at functions and was never seen in the streets of Kashgar, living instead in a high-security compound near the People's Park, an area that was predominantly Han Chinese.

As the years passed, he rose through the regional party ranks and gained notoriety for his raids on Uyghur homes. By the time Abduweli worked for him, he was already a bogeyman for the Muslim communities. There was even a popular ditty sung about him, warning Uyghurs not to exhibit any sign of looking old or frail, lest they fall prey to the party boss who held them in such low esteem. The song was called "Zhu Hailun Is Coming."

Old lady, fix your eyebrows with mascara,
Old man, throw away your cane,
Kids, no breaks at school
Teacher, don't put on your headscarf
Clean up your bathroom
Zhu Hailun is coming!

The midnight searches started soon after that speech denouncing the farmers. Abduweli, as the official translator, found himself the target of ire from sleepy farmers roused from their beds in the middle of the night by squads of policemen. They were looking in particular for books by the historian Turghun Almas, one of the first Uyghur intellectuals to have his work banned. The farmers would shout at Abduweli, but he would have to pretend to the Chinese police it was nothing, they were just angry at something else. It was vital for him to talk the farmers down: if they attacked the authorities, it would end very badly for them.

The police would knock on doors after midnight, turn houses upside down and leave without apology. Not only did they not find any banned history books, they didn't find any books *at all.* Hardscrabble farmers in rural areas of Xinjiang are not big readers, it turns out.

Quite often, Zhu would show up for the night raids himself. Sometimes he was accompanied by a huge black police dog: this animal seemed to be the only creature that ever evoked any emotion in him, and it was only when playing fetch with this dangerous-looking beast—which terrified Abduweli and everyone else who came into contact with it—that he was ever seen to smile. He had a man in Abduweli's town look after the dog, a German or Dutch shepherd: the dog-sitter got paid better than Abduweli with his college degree.

Sometimes during these nocturnal operations, Zhu would feel the urge to vaunt his knowledge of Uyghur life to the minions around him. He would expound in Mandarin, and Abduweli would have to translate, no matter how denigrating his observations might be. One night, Zhu said he had read the Koran, which he dismissed as just an ordinary book, "nothing mysterious."

"These people like to think that God tells them to do this or do that," he said. "But your God is such a dick." There was a stunned silence: Uyghurs are very modest people, and even the most secular among them would have been deeply offended by that obscene remark. Abduweli wanted to punch him. Instead, he had to translate.

Even though the searches turned up nothing, the farmers who had taken part in the protest were tracked down and either arrested or fined. Those who were too poor to pay the fines had their fruit trees cut down on Zhu's orders.

Whenever Zhu visited a Uyghur village, the residents would be expected to spruce up their streets, turning even country tracks into city-grade roads. In one village, the students were ordered out of school before his arrival to clear a road that had become overgrown with weeds, and which was normally only used by farmers during the harvest season. As the official delegation was assembling on this gussied-up track and waiting for Zhu's arrival, a lone farmer came plodding along on his donkey cart. The flustered local officials were just ordering the confused peasant to get out of sight when Zhu's convoy sped up, a procession of black Toyota Land Cruisers with police escorts.

Zhu stepped out of his vehicle and asked what was going on. The village officials explained that the man had been trying to use the road. Zhu looked at the farmer in disgust. "How dare he?" he said. He nodded to his police escort. "Take care of him," he said. The policemen set upon the hapless farmer, beating him to the ground with their batons as the party boss looked on, a satisfied expression on his face.

Back in the late 1990s, Zhu would always ask two things upon his arrival in a Uyghur community: the first was about the crops the farmers were growing, and the second was how many women were pregnant or had an IUD contraceptive device implanted. Even then, he was obsessed with Uyghur birth rates. Every town in the area had a specially adapted ambulance that would drive to Uyghur homes and force women to have an IUD implanted. If a pregnant woman was found to have had more than the allotted number of children, the same vehicle would pull up, and the crew would perform an abortion. Even though Uyghur women were allowed to have more than one child, they had to wait three years between their first and second. After the first baby was born, women were obliged to have an IUD put in. If they got pregnant before the three years were up, they would be informed that the ambulance crew was coming to perform an abortion. Anyone who tried to resist the crew—and some did—was arrested.

Although Abduweli had no way of knowing it at the time, the seeds of the genocide were being sown right before his eyes: the enforced population control, the belief that Uyghurs were primitive "barbarians" whose minds needed to be exposed to China's glorious language and culture, the anti-religious fervor and the deep-seated paranoia about separatism. It was all there, just waiting.

Even before Chen Quanguo arrived from Tibet in 2016 to take over as Xinjiang party boss, Zhu had already laid the groundwork. He had risen to become the head of the powerful Political and Legal Affairs Committee. It was unusual for a local party cadre to rise to such high office—such positions are usually filled by potential highfliers from Beijing. But Zhu had cracked down hard on the Uyghurs after the 2009 Ürümchi protests, and his brutal efficiency had not gone unnoticed. By the time Chen arrived, there were already reeducation camps operating in Xinjiang, although on a smaller scale and for shorter periods of time, where people's "backward" minds were being filled with the glories of the Chinese Communist Party.

That meeting of Chen—Xi's hitman against ethnic minorities—and Zhu, who had spent decades studying the Uyghurs and dreaming up ways to crush them, was the touchstone for genocide.

22

On January 9, 2021, three days after a mob of Donald Trump supporters stormed the US Capitol, Twitter blocked the president from the popular social media app. That ban caused outrage among Trump supporters, who accused the tech giant of silencing an important political voice.

Just two days earlier, I had contacted Twitter myself to do exactly the same thing to the Chinese embassy in Washington.

The US president was accused of inciting a mob to attack the seat of US democracy and prevent certification of an election he had lost by millions of votes. The Chinese embassy, on the other hand, had shared a report from the website *China Daily* on the dramatic drop in birth rates among Uyghur women in recent years, what many critics in the West were already decrying at the time as a "demographic genocide."

But *China Daily*—an English-language website owned by the Propaganda Department of the Chinese Communist Party—wasn't criticizing the news: it was celebrating it.

The report trumpeted the fact that Uyghur women were "no longer baby-making machines," and said the decline in the birth rate had led to a drop in terrorism.

I requested that Twitter suspend the embassy's account. It declined to do the same thing it had done to Trump, but in the end, the company did suspend the account until the offensive tweet was deleted. It admitted that it had "violated our policy against dehumanization."

Think about that for a minute: an embassy tweet that reflected official Chinese policy toward Uyghur women was banned for being "dehumanizing."

Unfortunately, the factual content of the tweet was, in itself, accurate. Zhu Hailun's longstanding obsession with the reproductive organs of Uyghur women has finally brought Xinjiang's birth rate crashing down.

The *China Statistical Yearbook 2020*, which is compiled by the National Bureau of Statistics, put the birth rate in Xinjiang at just 8.14 births per 1,000 people. That is only a little over half the figure for 2017, when the birth rate was 15.88 births per 1,000 inhabitants.

During that same period, Xinjiang's population growth rate—which takes into account deaths as well as births—had plummeted even more steeply, by 67 percent.

In southern areas of Xinjiang, which are more heavily Uyghur-populated than the Han-settled north, that drop-off has been even more spectacular, according to data found online by the indefatigable German researcher Adrian Zenz. He dug up family planning budget documents from 2019 for the city of Hotan, the capital of a prefecture in the heartland of southern Xinjiang, that set out quotas for implanting IUDs and sterilizing Uyghur women.

In the kind of dry, bureaucratic language that has been used to cover up so many human rights atrocities in the past, the guidelines stipulated:

Performance targets:

Target 1: target population for intrauterine contraception device placement 524 people

Target 2: [target] population for sterilizations 14,872 people.

In Guma county, next to Hotan, the CCP's bureaucrats set themselves the goal of sterilizing 8,064 Uyghur, Kazakh and Uzbek women in that same period, with 5,970 women to be forced to have IUDs put in place. Between them, Communist officials in predominantly Uyghur areas like Hotan and Guma planned to sterilize roughly 14 and 34 percent respectively of women aged between eighteen and forty-nine, in just one year.

Applied on a massive scale, the CCP tactics appear to be working, bolstered by the incarceration of millions of people in prison camps, where wives are separated from husbands for months or years at a time, and where children are taken off to special schools where they cannot see their own families.

According to China's own statistics, birth rates in the predominantly Uyghur regions of Hotan and Kashgar plummeted by more than 60 percent from 2015 to 2018. Across the whole Xinjiang region, birth rates are plummeting, falling nearly 24 percent in 2019 alone.

Compare those figures to the nationwide decline in the birth rate across China of just 4.2 percent. That relatively modest drop-off has been enough to sound alarm bells in China that its own population is shrinking, and the government has launched a campaign to encourage Han Chinese citizens to have more children.

Extrapolating from these figures, Zenz calculated that the natural population growth rate in Kashgar and Hotan fell by 84 percent between 2015 and 2018, from 1.6 percent to just 0.26 percent.

It is, in essence, an updated version of the eugenics practiced first by European colonial powers and then by the Nazis, aimed at breeding out elements of society that were deemed "undesirable."

The Australian Strategic Policy Institute, which closely follows the Uyghur situation, said in its own report called *Family De-planning* that the "sharp drop in birth-rates…is proportionately the most extreme over a two-year period globally since 1950… and is more than double the rate of decline in Cambodia at the height of the Khmer Rouge genocide (1975–79)."

Zhu's own thinking leaps out from the official reports written across the region in recent years, starting with one written by Han officials in 2016 which lamented the still-healthy Uyghur birth rate and saw it through the prism of the party's anti-Islamic dogma. "It is undeniable that a wave of extremist religious thinking has fueled a resurgence in birth rates in Xinjiang's southern regions," the report said.

A year later, another paper in 2017, written by the head of the Institute of Sociology at the Xinjiang Academy of Social Sciences, warned that the growing Muslim population was becoming a hotbed of poverty and fanaticism which could "heighten political risk."

As we saw with Zumrat, in the years leading up to Chen Quanguo's arrival, it had been possible for families to get around the two-child limit for women living in cities, or for three kids in certain rural areas. But after Chen's arrival, officials started issuing directives to "contain illegal births and lower fertility levels" and to "leave no blind spots." That meant police started banging on doors in their hunt for families with more than the allotted number of kids, or for pregnant women. There were even rewards offered for people who reported unregistered births and, as we have seen, women were forced to submit to gynecological exams, enforced contraception and abortions.

"Test all who need to be tested," said one town's directive issued in 2018. "Detect and deal with those who violate policies early."

Many women who survived the camps have corroborated Mihrigul and Qelbinur's reports of female prisoners being forced to take mysterious pills or given injections in the camps. Most reported that they stopped menstruating shortly thereafter. Some who managed to have their fertility checked after fleeing China discovered they are now sterile.

The Associated Press reported in June 2020 that it had obtained slides from Xinjiang hospitals showing that the injections sometimes contained the hormonal medication Depo-Provera, a contraceptive that suppresses ovulation, and whose side effects include headaches and dizziness.

One of the women who was subjected to such injections and who later escaped is Tursunay Ziyawudun, with whom I have appeared in Congress to give testimony about the ongoing genocide in Xinjiang. Knowing the value of eyewitness testimony, I introduced her to various government officials to share her shocking account, including a visit with Samantha Power, whom President Joe Biden appointed administrator of the US Agency for International Development shortly after being elected. She met Tursunay just before Mother's Day, and was visibly moved. Tursunay, Power said in a tweet after our meeting, told her that "so many women are not going to be mothers… The world can't go on without mothers."

Tursunay, a tall, slender 42-year-old, was thrown in the camps for having the temerity to try to emigrate to Kazakhstan with her husband, who is an ethnic Kazakh. Inside she was given a series of injections, and guards repeatedly kicked her in the stomach during the interrogation sessions. She stopped having her period and has now discovered that she is now incapable of having children. She often suffers painful bleeding from her womb.

Tursnay was in a "class" with other women who were forced to listen to lectures on family planning, where a "teacher" informed the prisoners that any woman found to be pregnant during regular checkups would be forced to submit to an abortion. A woman in another group was found to be pregnant and promptly vanished from the camp.

The staggering drop-off in birth rates and population rates—the very thing celebrated by the Chinese embassy's tweet—has been widely labeled "demographic genocide" by critics and human rights groups citing Section D of Article II of the United Nations Convention on the Prevention and Punishment of the Crime of Genocide, which states that "imposing measures intended to prevent births within the [targeted] group" qualifies as genocide.

"The intention may not be to fully eliminate the Uighur population, but it will sharply diminish their vitality," Darren Byler, the expert on Uyghurs at the University of Colorado said at the time. "It will make them easier to assimilate into the mainstream Chinese population."

The 1948 Genocide Convention states that genocide occurs when specific acts are committed "with the intent to destroy, in whole or in part, a national, ethnical, racial or religious group." Beth Van Schaack, a professor of human rights at Stanford Law School, argues that this "intent" can include "conditions of life that are calculated to eventually destroy the group" that has been targeted.

In the past, intolerant regimes have dealt with "undesirable" minorities in their midst in a variety of brutal ways. In 1894, an anti-Semitic minister in Tsarist Russia, Count Konstantin Pobedonostsev, announced his "Jewish policy" to rid his country of its Jewish population, who largely lived in poverty and were subjected to frequent pogroms: "a third of Jews will be converted, a third will emigrate, and the rest will die of hunger," he stated.

Nazi Germany also tried to drive Jews out, at least in its early days, but when other countries refused to take in large numbers of them, it started locking them up and ultimately murdered millions. Even in modern Western states, such as the United States,

Canada or Australia, the children of Indigenous peoples have in the past been taken off to state-run schools and forced to abandon their own cultures and be shoehorned into the dominant white people's society. All these practices are rightly abhorred now.

China does not want to drive its Uyghurs outside the country: it fears they will stir up anti-Chinese sentiment abroad, and maybe find ways to reintroduce such dangerous ideas as democracy back home. So it locks up Uyghurs when they return home from foreign travel. Likewise, it appears they are not interested in Nazi-style death camps—so far, at least, although the camps it builds clearly qualify, as we shall see, as concentration camps.

Instead of outright extermination or expulsion, the Chinese Communist Party has devised its own multifaceted plan to eradicate and exploit the Uyghurs in ways that are both disturbingly new and shockingly familiar.

23

On July 1, 2020, US Customs and Border Protection made a grim announcement. Its agents at the Port of New York had seized thirteen tons of human hair products, worth an estimated eight hundred thousand dollars, that they said had been made by forced labor in Xinjiang.

The CBP said the shipment was "suspected to be made with human hair today that originated in Xinjiang, China, indicating potential human right abuses of forced child labor and imprisonment."

The implication of where the hair originated was clear to anyone watching what is going on in Xinjiang. Hundreds of thousands of Uyghur women with long, dark hair go into the camps and come out months or years later, shaven-headed.

The question is: How many women's heads would need to be shaved to produce thirteen tons of hair? And that was just one shipment that the border police actually found. How many others might have slipped through the shell companies and third parties that Chinese businesses use to hide their use of forced labor?

Black hair products are in huge demand in the United States, largely among the African-American community. The market is estimated to be worth around 2.5 billion dollars a year, and has come to be known as "black gold." Many Black women, cognizant of their people's own painful past with slavery, were horrified when the news broke.

Nothing screams "concentration camp" like human hair stolen from its owners. In the former Nazi death camp of Auschwitz, a huge display of hair shorn from the heads of exterminated Jewish men, women and children takes up half of a hall known as Block 4. The Nazis used human hair to make a kind of coarse fabric, samples of which are also on display as a warning to future generations in the camp-turned-museum just outside of Cracow, Poland.

By comparison to the thirteen tons of human hair intercepted by the US customs agents, after World War II almost two tons of human hair that had been rolled into fabric were found at a factory belonging to the German car parts maker Schaeffler, that is still in existence to this day. Historians estimate that this much smaller amount corresponded to about forty thousand people. Jacek Lachendro, a researcher at the Auschwitz memorial site, said the hair was tested after the war and found to contain traces of hydrogen cyanide, an ingredient of the Zyklon B gas used to kill Jewish prisoners. Schaeffler has denied the accusation.

If two tons of hair is the equivalent of forty thousand people, then thirteen tons would take roughly a quarter of a million people.

The very nature of concentration camps makes it difficult for outsiders to know what is going on inside them. They are designed to be secretive places, where torture, slave labor, rape and murder are carried out on an unthinkable scale and with no accountability. While the character of camps is ever shifting, depending on the time and place, in essence they share certain key traits: the mass detention of civilians without any real trial, usually on the basis of some aspect of their identity rather than some action they have carried out. This aspect can be race, ethnicity, religion, political affiliation, any kind of group identity that comes to be more important to the government or ruling party than actions the prisoners have or have not done. And it is frequently a preemptive kind of detention, with the ruling power arguing that the people being locked up need to be controlled because they pose some nebulous threat to the population in general.

Chances are you've never heard of the first-ever Nazi concentration camp. It was called Nohra, and it was located just outside Weimar, a pretty little town in central Germany that gave its name to the country's first, short-lived, democratic republic. Nohra opened about a month after Adolf Hitler's inauguration, in March 1933, shortly after the Reichstag fire had given the Nazis an excuse to suspend all civil liberties and detain people without evidence or charge.

Nohra was an ad hoc camp, built on the grounds of a military training school and housing political opponents of the Nazi regime: Andrea Pitzer, who wrote the definitive history of concentration camps, *One Long Night*, notes that the first Nazi prison camp had "no watchtowers or barbed wire, no striped uniforms or crematoria—just detention and interrogation under the almost maternal-sounding term 'protective custody.'"

Heinrich Himmler, the head of Hitler's SS, found his first permanent camp just weeks later at a former munitions factory that had once churned out shells for the Kaiser's army during World War I. It was in a Bavarian town called Dachau. Chances are you've heard of that one (although a recent Pew Research survey showed half of Americans did not even know that six million Jews were murdered in the Holocaust, a woeful failing in our society). Within weeks, Dachau was home to five thousand prisoners. In the twelve years of its existence, in excess of two hundred thousand prisoners passed through its gates. More than thirty thousand died in Dachau alone.

The world had known concentration camps before that, as we'll see in the next chapter. In their early days, concentration camps didn't always look like the grim pictures of watchtowers and barbed wire perimeters that we are so familiar with from the black-and-white photos of Auschwitz. In fact, the Communists who found themselves in Nohra in the camp's early days were actually allowed out for a day to vote at a local polling station, because they had not yet been charged with anything and the pretense of legal norms still lingered in Germany, like dew about to be burned off by the sun.

Germany's first camps were built in old breweries and abandoned textile mills or factories—one was even set up in a Renaissance castle. China faced a similar problem in 2017 as its AI program ordered mass detentions that left the police scrambling to find places to put all these people: that is why Zumrat found herself in what appeared to be an old college dorm and Qelbinur said one of the buildings she taught in still had a sign outside declaring it to be a home for senior citizens.

As it was rapidly expanding its network of some thirteen hundred camps in Xinjiang, China shut down all access to the region. The full details of what happens in these types of facilities usually only come to light after a regime falls, or following some shift in power at the top. Neither of these things seems likely in the near future with China.

What may have smoothed the ready acceptance of the camps among CCP cadres is the fact that, since its foundation in 1949, the People's Republic of China has always had forced labor camps, prison camps or black site jails where it locks up opponents of the regime.

Less than a year after declaring victory, Chairman Mao set up the notorious laogai, his "reform through labor" camps, as a pretext to herd tens of millions of Chinese into backbreaking agricultural work as part of his agrarian reform campaign. That coincided with a number of other campaigns ostensibly enacted to crack down on corruption, inefficiency and waste. The first purges are estimated to have killed between one and three million people, and were followed by a series of other crackdowns that culminated in the destructive frenzy known as the Cultural Revolution in 1968, the horrors of which are echoed in what is happening today in Xinjiang.

The Cultural Revolution was in large part a struggle for power between Mao, whose 1958 "Great Leap Forward" had led to a famine that killed as many as thirty million people and left him politically weakened, and saw the rise of more moderate figures in the party like Deng Xiaoping, who would ultimately succeed him and usher in an era of economic reform and more political freedom. Seeing his power slipping, Mao whipped up battalions of youthful Red Guard zealots to wreak havoc across the country, beating, tormenting and often killing their own teachers, as well as writers, artists and other cultural elites. They burned books and destroyed paintings, musical instruments and old manuscripts in their frenzy to erase the old world. After the wave of destruction had dissipated (Mao banished the Red Guards to the countryside when they became too powerful), five thousand of Beijing's seven thousand registered historical monuments were gone.

So China has a clear record on this: it is ruled by the very same Communist Party that carried out these horrors. Unlike Nazi Germany or the Soviet Union, the Chinese Communist Party never fell. And while Deng brought in a period of reform, if you compare the rhetoric of Mao and the words of Xi, there is an alarming sense of continuity.

For example, three years after the death of Soviet dictator Joseph Stalin, his successor, Nikita Khrushchev, denounced his predecessor's brutal excesses. That did not sit well with Mao, who had indulged in similar purges himself. But in 1957, Mao made a show of following Khrushchev's lead, and invited people to openly criticize the party. This, he said, would allow the CCP to learn from its mistakes. He called it the "Hundred Flowers Campaign." But it was a trick: behind the scenes, Mao was plotting to destroy anyone who spoke out. "How can we catch a snake if we don't let them out of their lairs? We want those sons-of-turtles to wriggle out and sing and fart," he said. "That way we can catch them."

Compare that dehumanizing language to Xi Jinping's own comments after a group of assailants with knives stormed a train station in Yunnan, killing twenty-nine people and wounding another forty, an attack China automatically blamed on Uyghur separatists. "Make terrorists like rats scurrying across the street, with everybody shouting, 'Beat them!'" Xi declared.

When he traveled a year later to Kashgar he inspected the police weapons on the wall of a station and commented that "none of these weapons is any answer for their big machete blades, axe heads and cold steel weapons," despite the fact the Chinese police are actually very well armed. "We must be as harsh as them, and show absolutely no mercy."

Communist Party cadres have been forced to swallow these types of proclamations and official propaganda for generations now. In fact, their very promotions depend on absorbing it. They may well have been blinded to the sheer scale of the incarcerations, as the camps mushroomed across Xinjiang. And that blind acceptance may have been eased by the fact that so many of the arrests were ordered by machines and AI programs.

In his groundbreaking book *Modernity and the Holocaust*, the Polish Jewish sociologist Zygmunt Bauman—who himself had to flee the Nazis in World War II, only to be persecuted by the Soviets when he arrived in Stalin's Russia—argued that modernity itself enabled the mass extermination of so many people in the war, and that it would continue to do so.

Bauman noted that the Nazi Holocaust was carried out by well-educated modern citizens of a bureaucratically organized society: this wasn't the frenzied bloodletting of the Rwandan genocide, when eight hundred thousand people were hacked to death with machetes. This was the smooth functioning of a cutting-edge modern bureaucracy where everyone fulfilled their small allotted role, and never got to see the result of their work as a whole, aside from the relatively small number of guards in the camps themselves.

Local police in Germany, or in occupied European countries, simply arrested the people they were told to arrest. The town council found the detainees temporary accommodation before they were shipped elsewhere by the schedulers in charge of train timetables. The train drivers simply drove their freight wagons to their designated destinations. The Holocaust was sliced up by bureaucracy into small, digestible bites that allowed the machine to be turned to its horrific purpose.

What Hannah Arendt called the "banality of evil," this cold efficiency is inherent in all modern systems, Bauman argued, but even more so in countries where the price for speaking up is harsh.

Even if not all the police and party apparatchiks carrying out the mass arrests, torture and sterilizations in Xinjiang were aware of the scale of the atrocity, the Communist Party bosses certainly knew exactly what was going on, because they had explicitly planned it.

And we have evidence of their planning.

24

It was supposed to be top secret, but in 2019 someone inside the CCP party apparatus leaked a trove of highly classified documents, first to Uyghurs in exile in the West and then to journalists. Whoever was behind the explosive leak said they wanted those responsible for these crimes against humanity to one day be held accountable.

Known internationally as the China Cables, the documents constitute an operating manual for the concentration camps, effectively a guide on how to detain an ethnic minority. That the authors were aware of how bad this would look is underscored by their insistence that no one outside of the system of repression ever finds out about the orders. Even the guards and other workers in the camps were to be forbidden from bringing their cell phones inside, for fear that some evidence might leak out. "It is necessary to strengthen the staff's awareness of staying secret, serious political discipline and secrecy discipline," the documents said.

Prisoners were to be kept completely isolated from the outside world, under round-the-clock "full video surveillance coverage of dormitories and classrooms free of blind spots" to stop anyone from trying to break out. "Prevent escapes while they are at class, dining, using the toilet, washing, receiving medical care or meeting with family," the documents said.

Inmates would be graded according to a strict scoring system on their behavior and compliance to determine when, or if, they were to be released. "Evaluate and resolve students' ideological problems and abnormal emotions at all times."

The directives covered the construction of the camps, the need for guard towers, for doors to be double locked and partitions set up inside to keep different groups separate, as well as the need to recruit informants to spy on their cellmates, just in case the all-seeing cameras missed some muttered words in the cells.

Depending upon their compliance in the indoctrination camps, the prisoners were given a score that determined when they might get out, or which part of the prison they should be kept in. The categories set out in the leaked documents were "general management," "strict" and "very strict."

"Break down scores and manage and individually assess the students' ideological transformation, study and training, and compliance with discipline," the manual said, essentially telling guards to monitor the inmates' compliance with their brainwashing and mastery of Mandarin.

Imagine, for just one minute, that your prison sentence depended on your ability to master the Chinese language—and remember that Uyghur is a Turkic language, in no way related to Mandarin. For city folk in Xinjiang, long exposure has made Mandarin at least a second language, if not a first one. But for many rural communities, and in particular older Uyghurs like those in Qelbinur's first "class," this task was tantamount to a very long sentence.

Every detail of camp life is set out in the documents, which explain that the point of the mind-crushing tedium of the in-doctrination sessions is designed to "promote the repentance and confession of the students for them to understand deeply the illegal, criminal and dangerous nature of their past behavior."

The documents detail how many meals inmates receive, when they can wash and what time they wake up. Even though Xinjiang is in a time zone two hours behind Beijing, most prisons use Beijing time, meaning the prisoners have to wake up at what is effectively four thirty or five o'clock in the morning.

Some of the directives almost seem to be mocking the inmates, given the actual conditions in the cells. "Strengthen the management of the students' hygiene," the orders said. "Ensure that they get timely haircuts and shave, change and wash their clothes. Arrange for them to have baths once or twice a week, so that they develop good habits."

In reality, as Mihrigul and Zumrat showed, prisoners can go months without washing, and "haircuts" simply mean shaving the heads of both women and men.

That same year, the *New York Times* received another batch of leaked documents, known as the Xinjiang Cables, one of the biggest leaks of Communist Party classified documents in decades. It included private speeches by Xi Jinping after the stabbing attack at the train station, in which the Communist leader orders his minions to launch an all-out war "against terrorism, infiltration and separatism" using the "organs of dictatorship," and showing "absolutely no mercy."

The same documents criticized Britain's response to its own (very real) terrorist attacks by Islamist extremists, saying that the British had failed to stem such strikes because they had put "human rights above security." Instead, Xi urged his security chiefs to model their response on the American "war on terror," the results of which I had seen in Guantanamo Bay.

Interestingly, the documents also reveal that some local officials were resistant to the orders coming down from Beijing.

They worried they would stoke up even more ethnic tensions than already existed, not to mention hampering economic growth. One county leader even went as far as to quietly release thousands of Uyghurs from the camps under his control.

In response, those officials were purged. The one who allowed inmates to be released was himself sent to jail.

The leaked documents also bore a signature, a stamp of authority from the top official behind this grand design of oppression.

The name was Zhu Hailun.

Unsurprisingly, Abduweli's time working for Zhu Hailun didn't end well. In addition to the constant nighttime raids on people's homes, Zhu had his teams working from dusk till dawn for six months, with no weekends, out in the villages around Kashgar, trying to get the farmers to produce more cotton. Eventually, Abduweli wrote a petition signed by himself and his team members, saying that the work practices flew in the face of Chinese labor law. When Abduweli handed his boss the letter, Zhu took it without a word. But at the next full meeting of two hundred council officials, he slapped the desk in front of him and ordered Abduweli to stand up.

"Who do you think you are?" he said. "You wrote and signed this, and this is anti-government and anti–Party! Growing cotton is one of the three unifications of agricultural policy! From today, you are fired! Go home."

Abduweli was unnerved, but also rather relieved. He hated the job and so it did not occur to him that he should be begging for forgiveness, as Zhu seemed to be expecting. That only infuriated the party boss even more. As he was leaving, Zhu shouted, "Stop! As a government official you made a *big* mistake. You incited other government officials to this anti-government act. You should be happy I didn't call the police!"

Abduweli left, cowed but hoping fervently never to see Zhu

again. But years later, when he was arrested in Ürümchi for launching his Mother Tongue kindergartens, one of his police interrogators leaned in and said to him, "This is from Zhu Hailun."

He had worked with Zhu for more than six months in the late '90s, translating his speeches and scores of his written orders. So when the Uyghur exile who had taken possession of the leaked China Cables asked him if he recognized the signature, it was immediately clear that it belonged to his old boss.

"Zhu," he said to himself. "Now it's my turn."

The term "concentration camp" comes from the tactics adopted by the imperial Spanish forces fighting an insurgency in Cuba in 1895. Rebel guerrillas were refusing to confront the superior Spanish forces in open battles, instead launching ambushes and raids and then melting into the local population again. So the Spanish decided to clear the countryside, burn all the crops, kill the livestock and move the peasantry into towns, to live behind barbed wire stockades guarded by watchtowers. No one could leave the urban areas without permission.

The Spanish military called this model "reconcentracion" and it proved disastrous for the people swept off their lands. Without any means of sustaining themselves, and lacking the skills to find work in the towns, they starved in droves. The enormous suffering—combined with a mysterious explosion that sank the *Maine*, a US warship anchored in Havana harbor to safeguard US citizens—triggered a war with America that led to a US occupation of Cuba and the Philippines. In the latter territory, the US soon found itself facing a guerrilla insurgency by rebels fighting for independence from their new occupier. To combat that resistance, US commanders introduced the exact same system of population concentration that had so repulsed the US public in Spanish Cuba.

Ever since the controversial and deadly system of mass camps for civilians was introduced, countries deploying it have sought to downplay or deny its use. They have usually done so by trying to call it something else—with the exception of Nazi Germany, which called its camps Konzentrationslagers, or KZs—or by saying the camps were there to improve "native" populations, what European colonial powers called their "civilizing mission."

Just as the insurgency in the Philippines was being crushed by US concentration camps, the British Army in colonial South Africa started herding tens of thousands of Boer women and children in what it called "refugee camps" as its troops battled settlers of Dutch origin in the autonomous regions of Transvaal and the Orange Free State. Both ministates had nominally been under British control before the war, but when gold was discovered in the territories, the British started exerting more direct control, sparking a rebellion. British forces under Lord Kitchener—who would later loom large as the commander on the Western front in World War I—copied the scorched earth tactics of Cuba and the Philippines, cutting Boer women and children off from their menfolk fighting the imperial forces. The reason they needed "refugee camps" was because the British had torched their farmsteads and shot their livestock.

The debate over what to call these camps, where women and children were dying in startling numbers of hunger and disease, came to the floor of Parliament. "There is no greater delusion in the mind of any man than to apply the term 'refugee' to the camps," thundered opposition leader David Lloyd George in the House of Commons. "They are camps of concentration, formed by the military as the result of military operations in the field."

In that respect, China is no different from these colonial forces of the past 120 years. At first, in 2017, it denied the very existence of the camps, but when the evidence became overwhelming a year later, it admitted that, yes, the camps do exist but insisted they were designed to help the poor Uyghurs. They would stop them from slipping into religious extremism or separatist thinking, while providing them with training for jobs and providing them with Chinese language skills to enter the work market.

So Beijing came up with the label of "reeducation camps," just as the crumbling British Empire had labeled its post-WWII camps (when the term "concentration camp" had definitely gone out of vogue) as "transit camps" for civilian populations driven off their land in Kenya, or the French who built "camps de regroupement" in Algeria as it battled independence fighters.

Sometimes, governments actually manage to keep a lid on these far-flung atrocities. Until recently, few British people were aware of the horrors of the British camps in 1950s Kenya, where around a million civilians were locked up as British forces fought the Mau Mau independence guerrillas. In these camps, men and women alike were raped using glass soda bottles filled with hot water, while men were castrated with shears, or used in forced labor projects on white settlements. When Kenya gained independence in 1963, the departing colonial administration hid many of the files they were supposed to have handed over, and it wasn't until survivors of the atrocities filed claims against the British government in 2009 that the full extent of the colonial brutality came to light.

One of the key differences between what happened in the last days of the European empires and what is happening in China right now is the political systems they each are embedded in.

True, British and French colonial governments were often racist and prone to breaking their own laws in the face of any resistance to home rule. But Britain and France are democratic countries, with a free press and governments that change, and with civil rights organizations and independent judiciaries. Such brutal policies are bound to come to light sooner or later, and public outcry will demand that they stop. Even in 1902, the tactics against the Boers provoked outrage and public debate, and an outspoken critic of the camps, Emily Hobhouse, was granted access to them to help alleviate the suffering and report on conditions there.

That is not the case in China, which does not even face any organized insurgency. True, there have been some deadly attacks, but most of them seem to have been random, carried out by individuals or small groups in response to longstanding discrimination against Uyghurs and the destruction of their holy sites. China is run by an all-powerful single party, one that has ruled unchallenged for more than 70 years now and which shows no sign of going away anytime soon. It has indoctrinated its cadres for decades, to the point that every act in Xinjiang is seen through the paranoid lens of radical Islamic terrorism, separatism or foreign interventionism.

One of the reasons that we, in the outside world, know about what is going inside China is because China itself has distributed images of the "reeducation facilities." It encourages Uyghurs to share pictures online of the Becoming Family "relatives" that are billeted on them. This is because China, much as it wants to hide its atrocities from the outside world, also very much wants the people who are being targeted to *know* they are being terrorized. If it is done in secret, bullying and intimidation don't work.

The fact that China's Communist Party is unlikely to face a reckoning anytime soon makes me extremely worried about the fate of my people. Because the Soviet Union shows us that these camps can last for decades, and inflict torture, starvation and death on millions. And as we saw in Nazi Germany, if such systems survive for a long period of time, they can mutate over time into something even more deadly.

There are already signs that China's system of oppression is evolving. As Andrea Pitzer noted, concentration camps emerged out of new technologies that became available in the late nineteenth century. The invention of barbed wire and machine guns allowed a very small number of guards to effectively control extremely large numbers of people.

Now, with new and ever more sophisticated surveillance technology at its disposal, China is able to monitor vast swathes of its population using cameras and artificial intelligence.

"You don't have to hold everyone the way you did in Nazi Germany now," Pitzer told me. "If you have good enough surveillance, and only have to track and bring in the people you are targeting for certain things and at certain times, whether it's for labor or interrogation. With this model you can torture a really small number of people, you can kill an even smaller number of people, even though it's still quite huge on this scale—but as a percentage of the whole you can terrorize a whole population through strategic just-in-time measures using modern surveillance."

In effect, you can turn a whole region into a vast, open-air camp.

Already, some of the large camps built in 2016 and 2017 are going dark on the satellite images. "Reeducated" Uyghurs are being moved out to work as forced labor in factories that supply vast amounts of goods and materials to the global economy. Some of the camps are closing, but the Uyghurs are no closer to freedom. In fact, they may be further away than ever.

Rian Thum, the scholar who has studied Uyghur culture and China his whole life, told me that what is happening in Xinjiang simply "defies categorization and historical parallels...because it both differs from previous atrocities, ethnic cleansing, genocide, crimes against humanity and because it has an overlap of elements of so many of the famous ones."

The North Korean police state, the Nazi concentration camps, the South African apartheid regime's passbooks for ethnic minorities to be allowed to travel around, as well as European colonialism and China's own Cultural Revolution, all have dangerous echoes in Xinjiang. All of these elements have come together in a way that Thum believes will constitute "a new paradigm for historians studying this kind of removal of ethnic groups."

PART 6

A MESSAGE FROM A SLAVE

25

By the summer of 2019, it was very rare for any Uyghur living in exile to receive a phone call from a relative still inside China. That was why Gulnur Idreis, a 34-year-old Uyghur woman who now resides in Melbourne, Australia, was so surprised to see her parents in Ürümchi calling her on WeChat in July of that year.

When she answered, she was even more shocked. Instead of her elderly parents, it was her thirty-eight-year-old sister, Dilnur, a nurse and mother of two, on the screen of her cell phone. Dilnur and her husband had been arrested for no apparent reason two years earlier, in the big roundups of 2017. In May of 2019, Dilnur had been transferred from a prison camp to live and work in a textile factory just outside Ürümchi. The trained nurse was now forced to embroider clothing and sweep the factory floor, an utter waste of her valuable skills. She was allowed home once a week to see her two children, who had been taken in by her parents since no one had heard from her husband after his arrest. Knowing the authorities would be listening in, Dilnur scribbled out a series of notes on paper and held them up to the screen so that her sister could read them and take screenshots.

"660 people are brought in shackled and handcuffed and it is big," she wrote. "They have no choice, they will end up in jail, if they say something... Tell them it has been two years, [I have] not been released."

She told her sister to make the dangerous move of telling the world what was happening, and then drew her finger over her neck to show that she was feeling suicidal despair about her fate.

"She said to me, please help me. If I can't [get] out of this place, you can tell the international [community], the government. Whatever you can do," Gulnur told Australia's ABC News.

Dilnur showed her sister her work badge, and Gulnur took a photo of it with her phone camera. Using that, the Australian reporters found that she appeared to be working in a textile factory called the Ürümchi Shengshi Huaer Culture Technology Co., which is located in an industrial park twenty miles north of the regional capital. Dilnur said she was forced to sleep in the factory dormitory, with one trip home a week to see her children and parents. After complaining that she suffered from poor eyesight, which made it hard for her to do the complicated embroidery her employers required, they made this trained nurse clean the factory floors instead.

As Shawn Zhang the Chinese satellite tracker noted, some of the camps have recently started going dark in images captured at night. The Communist leadership built these camps at huge expense, so it is unlikely that it will not seek to recoup its costs. And it seems it is doing so by sending Uyghurs who have been "reeducated" into forced labor at factories whose products—from the region's highly prized cotton and minerals to its vast production of tomatoes—reportedly feed into the supply chain of some of the largest companies in the world, such as Apple, Nike, Dell, Heinz, Campbell Soup, Coca-Cola and scores of others.

Sometimes, this is done hand in glove with the camps. By

chance, Shawn Zhang found an image taken as a satellite happened to pass directly over a known "reeducation camp" just at the moment when the inmates were filing out of the gates of the camp and into a factory that had been built next door. Some 135 camps have factories either inside them or in close proximity, researchers have established. It is rare though for a satellite to be in exactly the right place at the right minute: once again, the best evidence of China's policy usually comes from China's own online paper trail.

In October 2018, the chairman of the Xinjiang regional government, Shohrat Zakir, stated that "trainees" who had completed their time in the "vocational skills training education centres" would be placed in jobs with "settled enterprises" through a "seamless link between learning in school and employment in society."

Just as the CCP tried to rebrand its concentration camps as helpful vocational training centers, it has also attempted to whitewash its vast forced labor campaign as "poverty alleviation" for the Uyghurs. At least eighty thousand workers that we know of have recently been sent into forced labor, variously referred to as "surplus labor" or "poverty-stricken labor." The former term is a piece of CCP jargon that covers any unemployed person living outside of the camps, as well as anyone who is seasonally employed, works as a small-scale farmer or happens to be retired.

A report in March 2020 by the Australian Strategic Policy Institute (ASPI) noted that many Uyghur workers have been transported in special segregated trains to factories in China proper, where they live under what is called "military-style management." That means they are forced to live in dormitories segregated from the other workers, with razor wire, watchtowers and government minders assigned one for every fifty workers. After work—for which they are paid less than their Han Chinese counterparts—they are forced to continue with the Mandarin classes and Communist Party indoctrination that started in the camps. If they refuse to comply, they are reminded by local CCP officials that they will be sent back to the camps, or to a traditional prison, and there will be immediate consequences for their families back home.

One of the most shocking aspects of this forced transfer of workers is that local governments and private brokers are paid by the head for each Uyghur worker they pack off to de facto slavery in a factory in China.

"For every batch [of workers] that is trained, a batch of employment will be arranged and a batch transferred," reads a local government report in 2019 that ASPI found online. "Those employed need to receive thorough ideological education and remain in their jobs," it said.

Arranging "surplus labor" transfers can prove quite lucrative: a 2018 Xinjiang government notice said it would pay twenty RMB (three dollars) for every worker transferred to a plant inside Xinjiang—but for transfers outside Xinjiang, to plants in China proper, they would pay three hundred RMB (forty-seven dollars) a head. The Xinjiang regional government was also offering to pay Chinese factories one thousand RMB (156 dollars) for every Uyghur on a year-long "contract" and five thousand RMB (784 dollars) if they kept them for three years.

Again, the racism and colonial attitudes leap out from the pages of these reports. Some reports boast that the years spent in forced labor inside Chinese factories will transform Uyghurs into "modern" citizens, who will "take daily showers" and will even become "more physically attractive." Proximity to Han Chinese workers in these factories will reform their "backward qualities" and make them more Chinese: for this privilege, Uyghur workers are required to demonstrate "gratitude" to the Communist Party and their Han "elder sisters and brothers," according to the ASPI investigation, one of the most penetrating studies carried out so far.

This has led to some adverts that read like something out of the slaveholding past of the American South. A company called Qingdao Human Resources stated on its website it could supply one thousand Uyghur workers aged between sixteen and eighteen "who have already passed political and medical examinations.

"The advantages of Xinjiang workers are: semi-military style management, can withstand hardship, no loss of personnel... Minimum order 100 workers!" It said a separate dormitory was required for the Uyghurs, away from Han workers, "for easy management."

The advert was accompanied by a picture of a cartoon man and woman in some mimicry of traditional Uyghur dress, the man giving a "thumbs-up" gesture in apparent support of his own servitude and ability to "withstand hardship."

As an added bonus, the company said that factory managers could apply for Xinjiang police to be stationed at their factory twenty-four hours a day if they accepted the offer—they would even throw in a Uyghur cook as an extra incentive, and the Uyghurs could be delivered within fifteen days of the contract being signed.

Laura Murphy, a professor at Sheffield Hallam University in England and an expert in modern-day slavery, said that sometimes the camps, factories and labor transfer agencies are intentionally paired, so that a Uyghur might be sent for training in sewing, and once they are trained and "politically indoctrinated"—essentially broken in spirit—they can be shipped out for work inside a clothing factory. That is how trained nurses like Dilnur Idreis can be turned into factory floor drudges, and the Uyghur nation dispersed and diluted in China's vast, far-flung cities.

Not all the workers come directly from the camps, however: squads of CCP officials also tour Uyghur villages to pressure young people into signing up for factory work. Again, we know this because the Chinese government itself put together footage of these visits in 2017. The film was only meant to be seen by Chinese government officials, to show how the regional leadership was successfully thinning out the Uyghur population. But the BBC managed to get hold of a copy of the film and released it. It shows a group of government workers sitting at an open-air stall in Anhui county in southern Xinjiang. A loudspeaker blares out a call for workers, but no one volunteers, so the group starts going house to house, all handshakes and smiles at first, in an effort to push for Uyghurs to sign up for jobs in factories thousands of miles away in China's eastern manufacturing regions.

In one Uyghur home, they come across a young woman in a headscarf. Her name is Buzaynap. One of the male officials, identified in the clip as Zhang Bo, wheedles her to sign up.

"If you don't go, you'll end up like your sister. You'll soon get married. You'll never be able to leave this place." His assumption being that she actually wants to leave and has no desire to get married. Buzaynap stares at the ground, then shakes her head. She does not want to go away from her home and family to work in a Chinese factory. The official doesn't stop badgering her.

"If you feel bad, you can come back right away," he says, a statement we know not to be true, and which Buzaynap almost certainly also knows is a lie: once she is in a factory behind razor wire and watchtowers, she will not be free to go anywhere, possibly for years.

"They will buy you tickets, round-trip tickets," the man goes on. Buzaynap, who is only nineteen, covers her eyes at this point, as it appears to dawn on her that there is no ducking out of this. Eventually, she concedes.

"If others go, then I will go," she says, wiping a tear from the corner of her eye. "If no one goes, I won't go."

It is the best argument she can muster to try to avoid being transferred away from everything and everyone she knows, and being labeled as "surplus labor."

Aside from the browbeating, China could argue that there is no obvious form of coercion in the film: no guns, no beatings or any obvious threats. But there doesn't need to be: the knowledge of the camps is the gun being held to this young woman's head, noted Laura Murphy, who has led various studies of forced labor among Uyghurs. If you refuse to go, you will be labeled as "anti-government," separatist or extremist. That is a sure path to the camps, and the horrors that they hold.

Other officials have tried to lure recruits into signing up for the factory transports by telling them that their fathers, mothers or siblings in the camps will have their prison terms shortened in return for cooperation. In order to forestall women from making the excuse that they have to look after children or frail parents, it has set up children's nurseries or elderly care homes.

"If this is what you call poverty alleviation, you are sadly mistaken. It is poverty increasing," Murphy told me when we discussed her work. "It is much more likely that if you take a person's land and the thing they are skilled at, and take their families away and separate them from their culture, children, and their support system, they are far more likely to be impoverished. Nobody thinks orphanages are a route to riches."

The video dovetails with orders from Beijing to make sure that local governments identify all "surplus laborers" and do their best to make them take jobs in factories, be they close to home or thousands of miles away in China proper. As part of that directive, recruiters go house to house to evaluate each Uyghur or Kazakh person and put them into one of three categorizations—"controlled," "general" or "assured." The category then determines whether a person is placed near or far from home, or if they are assigned to "reeducation" in a camp.

According to the International Labour Organization (ILO), forced or compulsory labor includes "all work or service which is exacted from any person under the threat of a penalty and for which the person has not offered himself or herself voluntarily." It also forbids forced labor as "a means of political coercion or education or as a punishment for holding or expressing political views or views ideologically opposed to the established political, social or economic system." Beijing's practices clearly fall into that category.

Uyghur communities have always had their own economy. If you had gone to Kashgar when I was a kid, you'd see people taking raw cotton and smoothing it out on a wheel to make it into a blanket, or hammering out spoons, teapots, bowls, all stuff that reduces their dependence on the Chinese economy and its cheap, mass-produced goods that the rest of the world consumes so avidly. On my father's side, my family were shoemakers, and all the furniture in my house was made at my uncle's factory. China is taking the people off the land, turning farmers into factory drones who are forced to chant the praises of Xi Jinping at night; transforming university professors into makers of sneakers for the US market. Once they are gone, the state can take their land and reassign it to industrial-scale farms, ensuring they can never return to self-sufficiency.

And the United States is the fastest-growing export market for goods made in the Uyghur lands. The market grew by more than 250 percent between April 2019 and April 2020, and includes many industries such as clothing, footwear, hair products, metals and plastic.

The European Union was not far behind, with imports from Xinjiang rising year-on-year by 131 percent in the first six months of 2021 and totaling more than $373 million, according to the *South China Morning Post*'s calculations based on Chinese customs data. Britain was even hungrier for Xinjiang's products, with imports up by 192 percent for the same period. I have been desperately sounding the alarm about this in the media, in congressional testimonies, in public talks and by engaging with all sorts of firms that do business in China. I advise business leaders of the risk they run to their reputation as the world starts to learn what is really behind their brand-new sneakers, or when consumers find out whose hands made the ketchup they squeeze onto their fries. I also point out their legal liability, and remind them of the German industrialists who stood trial alongside Nazi leaders at Nuremberg after World War II, some of them for unwittingly using slave labor from concentration camps.

These companies have certainly started to take note, if only because of growing consumer awareness. Nike and Coca-Cola promised to root out forced labor in their supply chains using third-party audits. But when slavery is involved inside a police state that is itself the actual driver of the forced labor, a simple audit is completely inadequate. Authorities in Xinjiang have blocked auditors from carrying out their work without undue interference, and foreign companies have no say in the local hiring practices of their Chinese subcontracting firms.

Some Chinese partners try to assure US clients that it's okay, that *their* products are not made in Xinjiang. But many of these manufacturers do in fact have factories in the Uyghur region, which begs the question: Is it enough for a US company to argue, "Okay, they use slaves to make stuff for Europe but *we* are assured our stuff is clean?" Of course not. And in any case, as we have seen, tens—possibly hundreds—of thousands of Uyghurs have been shipped to factories in China's industrial hub along its eastern seaboard, making it nigh on impossible for Western consumers to know if coerced labor was used in the creation of their latest smartphone, laptop or the suit they are wearing to work.

Nike, for example, claimed that an audit confirmed that its Qingdao subcontracting factory had no Uyghur workers in 2019. But ASPI researchers took a closer look at Chinese state media— again, basic open-source information—and found that the factory still employed about eight hundred Uyghurs at the end of that year, and produced more than seven million pairs of shoes for Nike every year.

Were *your* sneakers made by slaves?

In a report in March 2020, the bipartisan Congressional-Executive Commission on China listed Nike and Coca-Cola as companies with suspected ties to forced labor in the Uyghur region. The list also featured Adidas, Calvin Klein, Campbell Soup Company, Costco, H&M, Patagonia, Tommy Hilfiger and others.

Think about that next time you go to a Nike store. I do it all the time, and believe me, it is a problem for me, too. My son loves Nike sneakers, and it is hard for me to explain to this little boy that he can't have them because I believe his people had been used as slaves to make them. Likewise, I love wearing Hugo Boss suits, but I have had to stop buying them because the German designer uses cotton from Xinjiang.

But Xinjiang cotton is hard to avoid these days. China provides some 22 percent of the world's cotton, and 84 percent of that comes from the Uyghur region. It is estimated that one in five garments produced globally contains Xinjiang cotton.

Many of the factories that Uyghurs are forced to work in process that cotton, which is then sold to other Chinese companies who sell it on in turn to multinationals. And China is such a global behemoth that multinational companies that have come to rely on its cheap labor and vast consumer market now find themselves unable to either push back against its criminal behavior or pull out of its economic orbit.

Those who speak up pay a high price. The Better Cotton Initiative (BCI), a collaboration between fashion giants such as H&M, Nike and Gap, together with farmers, human rights organizations and environmental groups, has been working for years to make the industry more equitable and sustainable. When the BCI publicly questioned the use of Uyghur forced labor in the cotton industry, and H&M said it would stop using Xinjiang cotton, China immediately declared total war on the Swedish garments giant.

Overnight, it erased all H&M adverts from leading e-commerce sites and even from its map apps. Suddenly, it was impossible to get a ride-hailing service to an H&M outlet: the drivers' maps simply couldn't recognize the stores as a valid destination. If a customer wanted to find one of the company's four hundred stores on Baidu Maps, the Chinese equivalent of Google Maps, it just wouldn't show up. Trying to buy online also drew a blank.

H&M, the second-largest clothing retailer in the world, was gone.

Chinese state television even went as far as blurring out the names of Western brands of clothes worn by contestants on reality TV shows when those companies have questioned the use of Uyghur forced labor.

At the same time, China led calls for a boycott of the boycotters, across all its social media platforms. It immediately whipped up users to rant against H&M and a host of other multinationals. As soon as companies publicly state they will stop using Xinjiang suppliers, celebrities started denouncing the big-name brands like Hugo Boss and H&M on Weibo, the Chinese Twitter, saying they would no longer endorse or wear their products.

Those stars included the A-list actress Yang Mi, pop idol Wang Yibo, and even famous performers from regions that China has targeted for crackdowns, such as the Uyghur actress Dilraba Dilmurat and Hong Kong's Cantopop singer Eason Chan.

In the face of such intense pressure, the Better Cotton Initiative made the controversial move of deleting from its website the statement raising concerns over Uyghur forced labor in the cotton industry.

Hugo Boss—which in 2011 was forced to apologize for having used Polish and French forced labor in its factories in World War II—tried to hedge. On its corporate website it insisted that it doesn't buy goods directly from Xinjiang. But on Weibo it was telling angry Chinese consumers that "Xinjiang's long-stapled cotton is one of the best in the world. We believe top quality raw materials will definitely show its value." It later deleted that comment.

These companies are in a bind: China, as I have noted, is a

massive market and only likely to grow in the future. Domestic consumption is set to double by 2030, according to Morgan Stanley, to 12.7 trillion dollars. That is pretty much what US consumers spend right now.

Some companies have risen to meet this challenge, either through consumer pressure or from the desire to do the right thing. One of the first was Badger Sportswear of North Carolina, which makes team clothes for US colleges. It cut its ties to a Chinese factory after the shocking news emerged that their supplier, Hetian Taida Apparel, was actually located inside an internment camp in Xinjiang.

Others have made less serious efforts, like Nike, which said its audits had cleared its supply chain when in fact its suppliers were still using Uyghur forced labor, according to ASPI.

What is worse, some of these global mega-companies like Nike and Coca-Cola went even further. According to the *New York Times*, as I was lobbying alongside members of Congress from both sides of the aisle to pass the Uyghur Forced Labor Prevention Act, they were reportedly lobbying to have some of its provisions watered down, arguing that the measures would overcomplicate their supply chain. Nike denied the reports that they were actively trying to muzzle the bill, which passed the House by 406 to just 3 votes, an unprecedented show of bipartisan support in these fractured times. But both they and Coca-Cola declined to even come to the Hill to testify in the hearings.

While I have zero sympathy for such behavior, I have advocated that the US government should help these companies to disengage from China. If they simply leave them to their own devices, the Chinese Communist Party will eat them alive. Beijing will exert relentless pressure on them and the outcome will likely be even more disastrous, for them and for the Uyghurs. I'd rather get the business community involved, to use whatever leverage they might have with the Chinese government to do the right thing.

Meanwhile, the US government simply has to pull the plug

on products made in China that are of vital interest to our national security or public welfare, as we saw with the shortages of personal protective equipment during the coronavirus pandemic. I was recently heartened to hear House Speaker Nancy Pelosi very publicly calling out the US Chamber of Commerce for lobbying against the Uyghur Forced Labor Prevention Act, after it disingenuously tried to argue that the legislation "would prove ineffective and may hinder efforts to prevent human rights abuses."

As with the vast network of camps, forced labor is nothing new in China. The CCP has long put political prisoners and other groups it considers suspicious, such as the spiritual movement known as Falun Gong, to work in either factories or labor camps under horrific conditions. The ways that some of these prisoners of conscience have got the word out to the world have been even more innovative than Dilnur Idreis's handwritten message on social media.

In October 2012, for example, a woman in suburban Portland, Oregon, was setting up a Halloween-themed birthday party for her five-year-old daughter and was dusting off some old decorations when a hand-written note slipped out of the packaging of a Styrofoam gravestone. It was an SOS letter, written in English, from the prisoner who had made the toy. The note said that thousands of members of the Falun Gong were being held without trial and forced to work fifteen hours a day, seven days a week, in a labor camp that had been around since the 1950s. The letter begged whoever might find it, out there in the free world, to alert governments and human rights organizations to the plight of the prisoners, jailed because they adhered to an organized spiritual group that the paranoid Communist Party had branded a threat to its security.

Quite often, lawyers representing companies with compromised supply chains in China reach out to me on their own initiative. Some are genuinely working to try to root out Uyghur forced labor, hard as that may be. Others seem to be merely trying to rehash the tired old excuses that they are doing "due diligence" and "auditing," hoping they can paper over any gray areas and cover their asses. But how can you audit people who can't even identify themselves as Uyghur, or even Muslim? How do you do due diligence checking on people who can't be themselves, and who are subject to a genocidal campaign? It is simply not possible.

I give them whatever advice I can, but recently I have found my temper growing short. That is partly because I barely sleep these days, kept awake by worries over the fate of my elderly parents and the enormity of the crime being perpetrated against my fellow Uyghurs. So when two reputable DC lawyers who represent US businesses in China recently reached out to me to get my perspective, I snapped, and gave it to them straight.

"You guys are fucked," I told them. "China is kicking your ass on the one side and on the other, US consumers all over the place are waking up to what is happening, and this is the one issue that unites Congress.

"Cut the crap," I told them. "Either pull the plug, or use your influence to change the Chinese behavior, and say, 'No, not in my name.' Tell China, 'You need my business and what you are forcing me to do is illegal, and I am under pressure at home.'"

They left that conversation deeply disturbed. A few weeks later, China hit back at the sanctions the US has started imposing, announcing its own anti-sanctions law that would punish any company that complied with the US sanctions. That has really plunged multinationals into a deep dilemma. They literally now have to choose which side they are on. No more fence-sitting.

And I doubt I will ever wear my Hugo Boss suits again.

26

The German data researcher Adrian Zenz has noted that keeping more than a million people locked up in camps was unlikely to have ever been sustainable for long. The news was bound to get out eventually, and Beijing, which styles itself as a global leader, has inevitably found it deeply damaging to its international standing. The forced labor program was the way in which the CPP could move Uyghurs out of the camps while maintaining a rigid control over them, continuing their brainwashing and also generating income to cover the costs of the camps.

But in doing so, China appears to have played its hand very badly. Locking people up in concentration camps is still rare enough—and extreme enough—that international conventions against it are limited and hard to enforce at a global level.

There are, however, countless laws and conventions prohibiting and penalizing the use of forced labor. And by using Uyghurs essentially as slave labor, the Chinese Communist Party has triggered any number of legal mechanisms that threaten to deal a painful blow to its economy.

One of those blows came in December of 2020, when US Customs and Border Protection announced a ban on goods produced by a Chinese corporate entity that few people outside China had ever even heard of: the Xinjiang Production and Construction Corps, or XPCC.

While obscure, the XPCC is one of the largest and strangest organizations in the world, a vast corporate entity that has its own sizable army and is often described as a "state within a state." It has some 2.7 million soldier-workers, governs ten cities and thirty-seven towns, and controls a chunk of territory that is larger than Ireland. It also runs its own health care system, schools and universities, has its own newspapers, radio and television stations, and owns an estimated four thousand enterprises, employing some 12 percent of the population of Xinjiang.

If you have ever eaten ketchup, it most likely had XPCC-produced tomatoes in it, probably picked by prisoners from the camps that it equips and oversees. By some estimates, it now produces 30 percent of Xinjiang's cotton.

The XPCC is known in Chinese simply as the "bingtuan," or "the Corps." Mao ordered it set up in in Xinjiang in 1954, with a variety of goals: it was principally a militia force that could defend the newly acquired territory from any future Russian incursion, but it was also meant to oversee the settlement of Han workers in the region to make the "New Frontier" more Chinese. At the same time, it was to build cities, farms and factories in the deserts, and furnish an entire infrastructure to this outpost region thousands of miles from Beijing.

Those first settler-soldiers had a hard time of it. Many of them were former troops of the defeated Nationalist Army of Chiang Kai-shek who had been press-ganged into service by the victorious Communists, and who lived for years in squalid mud huts with only one uniform provided per year.

While nominally under the authority of the Xinjiang regional government, the XPCC is a multibillion-dollar corporation that takes its orders directly from Beijing, and plays a key role in the enslavement and exploitation of the Uyghur people, whose land and resources it has expropriated for years.

Probably even the US lawmakers who backed the sanctions did not understand quite what the XPCC is: part army, part corporation, its closest historical analogy may, ironically, be the British East India Company, a vastly powerful trading company that maintained its own armed forces and became an agent of British imperialism in Asia and India. Ultimately, it was the East India Company that began China's descent into decades of chaos, when it launched a war in the 1840s to force the Qing dynasty to allow it to sell the opium it grew in India inside China. That trade, enforced by British gunboats, created a crushing addiction among ordinary Chinese people and opened the country up to foreign encroachments that ultimately led to the collapse and chaos of the early twentieth century, and the final takeover of the Communist Party.

Targeting the XPCC for sanctions, as well as leading Communist Party officials in Xinjiang—including regional bosses Zhu Hailun and Chen Quanguo—is an excellent way of punishing them, and making international companies shy away from any kind of financial involvement with them.

But there is one thing Beijing has done that will make it extremely difficult for the global community to exert its full pressure, and which is quite diabolical in its ingenuity.

The XPCC has in recent years become heavily involved in the production of solar panels, one of the keys to a sustainable future for our global civilization. As countries turn away from climate-damaging fossil fuels as a source of energy, solar panels have come to play a major role in slashing emissions from greenhouse gases. Yet the solar panel industry has been rapidly taken over by China in the past twenty years, and many of the firms at the cutting edge of that movement are located in industrial parks created and run by the XPCC.

As Professor Murphy notes in her report on Uyghur forced labor in China's solar panel industry, entitled *In Broad Daylight*, before 2005 almost all the companies that manufactured the key component of solar panels, polysilicon, were based in the United States, Germany or Japan. China had virtually no presence in the market.

"After only fifteen years in the industry, the People's Republic of China now dominates the global solar energy supply chain," she writes. "In 2020, China produced nearly 75 percent of the world's polysilicon (including solar-grade and electronic-grade). The four largest producers in Xinjiang alone account for around 45 percent of the world's solar-grade polysilicon supply. The journey to this extraordinary market share only took fifteen years, and it saw rapid acceleration in the last five."

Polysilicon is the solar panel industry's dirty secret: it is made from coal that is processed into ingots that are then sliced into wafers and used on the solar panels that so many environmentally conscious consumers are now putting on their rooftops to help save the planet.

How has China achieved this incredible leap forward, to sideline its international competitors and undermine the rest of the world market in solar panels? It has attributed its success to automation in the sector, but some experts point out that this is an industry that remains labor-intensive, due to the very fragile nature of the panels and the wafers they are made of. It essentially needs people to handle them.

Murphy's report details the extensive use of Uyghur "surplus labor" by the firms manufacturing solar equipment: eleven of the companies were engaged in forced labor transfers, another four were based inside the XPCC's industrial parks in Xinjiang and had accepted forced labor transfers, and a further ninety

Chinese and international companies had supply chains that appeared to be affected.

On the one hand, the production of cheap solar panels has been good news for the planet: the low production costs have allowed them to become a viable alternative to traditional fossil fuels, which are threatening severe climate disruption. But at what cost to the Uyghurs? Their cheap, mostly involuntary labor—combined with the below-market-price coal China produces and the government subsidies provided by Beijing—has allowed for the dumping of solar panels on foreign markets. And that has brought down the cost of this vital energy resource by as much as 75 percent in the past decade.

It has also allowed China to corner a vital market, throwing the West's plans for a green energy revolution into doubt. International competitors have been seriously undercut by the Chinese production, or completely driven out of business: in 2014, the Japanese solar panel manufacturer Sharp cut its workforce in Europe and the United States, while in 2021 another industry leader, Panasonic, said it was scrapping its own solar cell manufacturing because of the competition from China.

That has left the world largely reliant on China's solar panel production for the future. When President Joe Biden, or his climate envoy John Kerry, go to China to push their vision for a green energy transformation, Beijing will have the leverage to say, "You choose, between saving the world and turning a blind eye to Uyghur slavery."

It is not a choice we can allow ourselves to be forced into. Besides the appalling human rights crisis, what the Communist Party is doing is also strangling innovation within this vital industry.

The Information Technology and Innovation Foundation recently reported that "the decimation of PV [photovoltaic] manufacturing outside China drove many innovative firms out of the business, in large part because they could not match the predatory prices offered by government-subsidized Chinese competitors. China's new PV giants have innovated in important ways, especially through process innovation that moved the industry's dominant technology rapidly down a steep experience curve. *But the prospect of shifting to better, cheaper PV products with the potential for even greater emissions reductions over the long run, has been deferred or even lost."*

Fortunately, as of this writing, the Biden administration has responded with a firm hand. It has put five Chinese companies that produce polysilicon on the so-called "entity list," requiring US companies to apply for a license if they want to buy from them, and banned the import of solar products by Xinjiang Hoshine Silicon Industry.

Cotton slavery in the US South in the nineteenth century produced vast amounts of cheap raw material for the world's factories, from New York to London, but it ultimately led to a disastrous civil war and the brief breakup of the United States. Modern-day slavery in China is now posing a threat to the global economy in the same way, tainting almost everything we wear, the devices we get our information from and possibly even the means we will need to survive an era of climate emergency.

27

By this point, you may be wondering: How can the Chinese people *not* know about the genocide going on in their own country?

As we saw with the British concentration camps in Kenya, or the US camps in the Philippines, sometimes even a democracy can manage to cover up human rights atrocities for decades. As I was working on this book, Germany announced it was paying 1.3 billion dollars in compensation for its own previously unacknowledged genocide in Namibia. Many people may have found themselves asking: When had Germany even occupied Namibia? It was an obscure moment in the brutal colonial history of Africa, when German troops systematically exterminated the Indigenous Herero and Namib people who had rebelled against their loss of freedom and land in 1884. Tens of thousands of people were killed in what was then known as German South West Africa. It has aptly been called "the forgotten genocide" by historians.

China points to these historic examples as proof that its Western critics are all hypocrites, guilty of the same crimes and still unpunished for carrying them out. Whenever it is accused of using Uyghurs as forced labor, its official media publish cartoons of Uncle Sam whipping Black slaves. When the charge is genocide, they point out the annihilation of Native Americans in North America. Yet these are crimes from history, which a democratic society strives to learn from and not to repeat. They are not meant to be a model to be emulated by current great powers. And although Beijing may not quite realize it, by drawing the analogy it is tacitly admitting that they are in fact engaged in crimes that history will judge harshly.

But to truly understand how Chinese people in general could know so little of their government's crimes, the best example is actually the journey of the young Chinese woman who was principal author of the report *Uyghurs for Sale*, the ASPI investigation into forced labor in Xinjiang that I cited in the previous chapter.

Vicky Xu was a model student growing up in China, bright and talented and a loyal believer in the Communist Party. She decided to study media, and despite her humble family origins in a poor province in northwest China, she won a place in an elite media university in Beijing. There, she trained to become an English-language news presenter on state television, where she could use her talents to spread the Communist Party worldview of current events to a much wider audience.

But when she was nineteen, Xu took a year off and traveled to Perth, Australia, to work as a Mandarin teacher at a high school. She liked Australia, and enrolled at Melbourne University to do a course in political science and media. She was still a proud nationalist, and happily defended the system that governed her country.

One day, however, she saw a poster advertising a documentary about the Tiananmen Square massacre. This stumped her—she had been a top student at school, a class captain and she knew her history. She *knew* there had never been a massacre in Tiananmen Square in 1989. Puzzled, she went to the screening and for the first time in her life watched tanks rolling across the famous square, saw the bodies in winding sheets lined up on the ground, the Western journalists huddled behind walls as the bullets flew. Xu felt an overwhelming grief, but also a sense of betrayal: her parents and her teachers had all known about this, but no one had ever told her. Roughly two million citizens of Beijing had attended the mass protests on the square, yet no one had said a word to the younger generation about it.

Humans tend to rationalize anything that doesn't fit in with their long-held beliefs, something that has become ever easier in the age of the internet and its "news bubbles." After her initial confusion, Xu was able to find online claims that the Tiananmen Square footage was all a CIA fabrication, or other reports that downplayed its significance: even Henry Kissinger, that éminence grise of US foreign policy and a close friend of China for decades, had minimized the significance of the slaughter. She was able to apply some mental Band-Aids to her cracked worldview and carry on for a while.

When she started her new university course, Xu found she was the only Chinese student in her class and was bombarded with negative reports about her homeland, its atrocious record on human rights and democracy, its theft of Western intellectual property and the suspicions about its new leader, Xi Jinping. Far from undermining her belief in her country, the constant criticism made her defensive, stoked those old nationalist sentiments she had always held dear. Xu felt she had to explain her country to these people: she even caught herself trying to justify some of the human rights abuses, saying that with a country the size of China it was impossible to treat every single person with kid gloves. She went as far as getting the stars from the Chinese national flag tattooed on her ankle.

Then she began looking up Chinese dissidents in exile in Australia, hoping to expose them as frauds. But as she spoke to these normal people who had dared challenge the Communist doctrine, she started hearing firsthand accounts of a side of her country she had never encountered before. The most striking meeting was with a math professor who had been put into forced labor camps and persecuted for simply questioning the government, before fleeing to Australia.

The emotional truth of his story struck her, just as the personal accounts of the Uyghurs I take to testify at Congress never fail to bring home to senators and government officials the true human cost of China's abuses. The cracks in Vicky's worldview widened. The next time she went back home to China, she started using her newfound critical skills to report on real stories: a flooded village that was left to suffer with no help from the government, for one. As she was reporting, party officials quickly swooped down on her, trying to feed her the government line that everything was fine, even though it clearly wasn't. Meanwhile, police officers took her details and warned her not to do any independent reporting again.

Far from being cowed, however, the gutsy young Xu sold the story to the *New York Times*. Now, whenever she went anywhere inside her home country, she was stopped by the police and harassed. When she returned to Australia, she started to work at the *New York Times* and ABC television news, getting stories only someone with her rare skill set could access. The price for doing so was high: her parents were harassed and threatened, and she herself was bombarded by vitriolic attacks by bot armies and Chinese cadres who had been encouraged to vent their righteous rage on social media, even threatening her with death and sexual abuse and denouncing her as a traitor.

The frenzy of rage was so fevered that even her old friends turned on her: she said she could understand their viewpoint, since she had basically been in their exact same position until a few years before. Eventually, the last time she went to China to visit her dying grandmother, she was warned never to return. Xu went back to Australia, and with the zeal of the newly converted, launched herself into revealing China's human rights abuses, including the devastating report on China's factory slavery.

If it took so much to convince someone as bright and as equipped with critical faculties as Vicky Xu to escape the Communist Party programming, imagine what it would take to convince the billion-plus Chinese citizens still living inside the Great Firewall of China, where the party monitors who says what and only allows the official version of events to get out, and where speaking out will land you in jail or worse.

What happened to Vicky Xu was a microcosm of what happened in Germany in 1945. When US and British troops liberated Germany, they were horrified to find piles of dead and starving people inside the concentration camps strewn across the country. Yet the people living in towns right outside the camps professed to have known nothing of what was going on behind the barbed wire. Many times, the angry Allied troops would round up local civilians and force them to come inside the camps and see firsthand the horrors perpetrated in their names, on their very doorsteps. Most of the Germans left in utter shock, many of the women in tears. There is a famous photograph of German soldiers being forced to watch footage of the camps in a cinema. Many cover their eyes, look down or just stare blankly ahead of them.

But if those same American soldiers who forced the Germans to open their eyes had gone to a cinema back home in New York or Chicago, what would they have seen? *Gone with the Wind*, a nostalgic look at the United States' own slave system. The plantation of Tara is portrayed as an idyllic never-never land where enslaved people happily serve their white masters, whereas in reality the South's plantations were a series of privatized miniature concentration camps whose inmates were bought and sold, raped and murdered according to the whims of their owners. In the Jim Crow era that followed, tens of thousands of Black people were lynched, beaten, murdered, driven from their land or systematically denied their most basic human rights. It left a painful legacy long suppressed in American life, one that has occasionally erupted into riots that shook the country, most recently as I was writing this book in the summer of 2020.

The difference between a democracy and a dictatorship is in how they react to such unpalatable truths. Even Donald Trump, arguably the most authoritarian president in modern US history, did not order tanks to crush the Black Lives Matters protests, or mobilize army units to shoot dead thousands of protesters. Just as many Germans saw the horrors of the death camps for the first time after the US soldiers arrived, many white Americans were shocked to see live footage, shot on cell phones, of the racism their Black countrymen were forced to endure, not least the death of George Floyd, slowly suffocated under the knee of a white Minneapolis police officer.

That footage was seen on media across the country, and the policeman was found guilty of murder in a US courtroom. That is how progress is made in a democracy: it faces its flaws and strives to correct them, rather than saying, "Well, lots of other countries do bad things so we are allowed to as well," or throwing in jail whoever dares to show evidence of wrongdoing.

That is what George Orwell called "the memory hole." And China, as we shall see, has used the latest digital technology to perfect the art of collective amnesia.

PART 7

THE DIGITAL DICTATORSHIP

28

When the Berlin Wall came down in November 1989, East Germany's Ministry for State Security—more commonly known by its acronym, the "Stasi"—employed 91,015 people and had 173,081 informants on its books. Its archives, charting every aspect of the lives of some six million East Germans—one in every three citizens of the GDR—filled the equivalent of forty-eight thousand filing cabinets. By most estimates, it was the most effective and repressive secret police system that had ever existed.

That same year of 1989, a British scientist called Tim Berners-Lee, who was investigating the origins of the universe at CERN, the European Organization for Nuclear Research in Switzerland, set up a cutting-edge computer network to boost automated information-sharing between scientists in universities and institutes around the world. What he had invented, in fact, was the World Wide Web.

Those two events—the collapse of the Soviet Union and the birth of the internet—led to an explosion of optimism, that soon open borders and open technologies would help democracy conquer the world, as free-flowing information bypassed traditional gatekeepers and censors and landed in the privacy of people's homes. In 2000, Bill Clinton said that for China to try to censor the internet would be "like trying to nail Jell-O to a wall." The next year, with Clinton's backing, China joined the World Trade Organization and its economy started to skyrocket.

As late as 2011, when the Arab Spring uprisings were organized on Twitter, YouTube and Facebook and were toppling dictators across the Middle East, people still hoped that an open internet would herald a new era of global democracy.

But the arc of history is seldom so straightforward.

The tech boom that Tim Berners-Lee's invention spawned has reshaped just about every aspect of our lives, from how we work, communicate and shop to how we meet our life partners and view the world around us.

And the world first became truly aware of the darker side of the internet in 2016, when Russia managed to effectively shape the US elections on a tiny budget, using online trolls to spread disinformation through the very social media networks we had come to rely upon for so much of our daily news about the world. These poisonous lies were channeled through "bubbles," the online communities created by micro-targeting people according to the casual things they "liked" online, a tool developed to allow advertisers to more perfectly target their audiences.

That was when the world started to realize that the boom in artificial intelligence that had grown out of the tech explosion had also given authoritarian regimes tools that the Stasi could only have ever dreamed of.

Despite its ninety thousand employees, the Stasi didn't have the manpower to process all the material it had gathered. It therefore couldn't make full sense of the intelligence it might actually possess. And once it had acquired a target of interest— a dissident, say, or someone just expressing doubts about their government—it took an entire team of covert agents to tail them unnoticed through the streets. Hence the huge number of East German informants, otherwise known as "unofficial collaborators."

Not anymore. In 2013, Edward Snowden, a whistleblower at the National Security Agency, revealed that the NSA could collect five billion mobile phone location records in a single day, and forty-two billion internet records—things like emails or browsing history—in a month. A single US government server could store so much data that, if printed out, the paper would fill forty-two *trillion* filing cabinets. Artificial intelligence could then use keywords to sift the data to detect patterns in this bottomless ocean of information, allowing the agency to peer into people's lives in a way never seen before.

In addition, an all-pervasive system of surveillance cameras can likewise use artificial intelligence to scan vast numbers of people using facial recognition software, or using a person's particular gait to pick them out of the crowd even if their face is obscured. A handful of people can therefore keep tabs on millions. In 2018, the Chinese Communist Party's official mouthpiece, the *People's Daily*, claimed the country's facial recognition system was capable of scanning the faces of all of China's 1.4 billion citizens in just one second.

Snowden's revelations created uproar in the United States and around the world, as citizens and allies suddenly understood the degree to which they were being snooped upon. Fierce debate flared over the limits of privacy versus the value of AI for preventing crime and terrorism, or even just managing traffic flow in cities. That debate has led to some technologies, like facial recognition software, being banned in certain places such as California. It is a discussion being held all across the free world.

But in authoritarian states, the same technology has already snuffed out any such debate.

As Snowden was airing the NSA's cutting-edge spycraft to

the world, in China another document was circulating among Communist Party cadres. In typical party jargon, it became known as "Document No. 9" and bore all the hallmarks of Xi Jinping, who became General Secretary of the Communist Party and Chairman of the Central Military Commission in 2012, two ranks that combined make him China's de facto president.

The memo warned of the main threats to China's one-party system, the foremost being "Western constitutional democracy." That particular abomination was followed by such evils as promoting "universal values" of human rights, Western-inspired ideas of an independent media or of civic participation, and any criticism of the party's oppressive history.

Document No. 9 was essentially a blueprint for maintaining the oppression of the Chinese people by the Communist Party. It was a Gettysburg Address for a dictatorship, silently whispered on a carefully monitored internet rather than broadcast openly to the people whose lives it would shape. It also showed how much the paranoid Communist Party—which in July 2021 celebrated its one hundredth birthday—fears the values of an open and transparent society.

Western optimists—in policy debate, often referred to as "panda-huggers"—had long believed that economic reform might lead to a new middle class demanding their rights in China. To a certain extent, they had been right. Once the dead hand of the Communist Party got out of the Chinese people's way, the economy really started to take off, and concerned citizens did indeed start speaking up online, in blogs and articles and commentaries, chipping away at the once unassailable party that dominated their lives.

But those people who spoke out quickly found they were being targeted. In the summer of 2013, as Document No. 9 was landing on the screens of the party faithful, the Weibo accounts of the online critics were shut down. Some were forced to make televised confessions of their sins, while others were thrown in

jail on dubious charges. As the German journalist Kai Strittmatter details in his excellent book *We Have Been Harmonized: Life
in China's Surveillance State*, a billionaire venture capitalist called
Charles Xue, who had twelve million followers on Weibo and
had been calling for more environmental measures like cleaner
air quality in China's smog-choked cities, was arrested for "en-
couraging prostitution."

His arrest was televised, and the next time he appeared in
public was on state TV, in a prison uniform confessing how "irresponsible" he had been to ever question the party, and how
right it had been to clamp down on him and his fellow critics.
Afterward the Supreme Court ruled that anyone who spread a
"rumor" (i.e. criticism of the government) that was shared more
than five hundred times online, or which received five thousand
"likes," would be jailed for three years.

The extent to which Chinese censors were willing to crack
down became evident when a Chinese student was actually imprisoned for tweeting a popular meme comparing Xi to Win-
nie the Pooh, the portly children's character whose resemblance
to the Chinese leader had been widely remarked upon online
during a state visit to Washington. The twenty-five-year-old
student, who had been studying in the US, was arrested on his
return to China and sentenced to six months for posting "comments and inappropriate images insulting to the leader of this
country."

As Strittmatter points out, the CCP doesn't fear the internet
at all—it positively embraces it. More than 830 million Chinese
people are now online, most of them on mobile phones, and
the government is working to get even more hooked up. That
is largely because the internet is not the anonymous conduit of
free information that the optimists believed back in the halcyon
days of the early 2000s. Every email, internet search and instant
message leaves a telltale trail for anyone with the know-how
and the authority to follow. The very phones in people's pock-

ets can show the world where a person is or has been, which is why China hands them out to Uyghurs.

The other main reason the CCP loves the internet is that it has managed to "decouple" its own web from the rest of the world through what is known as the "Great Firewall," which not only bans a number of foreign companies like Facebook, Twitter or WhatsApp (Chinese people use homegrown equivalents, whose data can be accessed by the government) but also scans all incoming content for blacklisted content or words, such as "Tiananmen," and weeds them out before they can challenge the official narratives.

Combined with the very public examples of what happens if you speak out, the result has been an internet that looks almost exactly like the web in the rest of the world, with all its endless things to buy and fun things to watch, but it has a very dark side. It is not just advertisers tracking you with cookies: it is a paranoid party-state that sees all and imprisons millions.

China sells this heavily surveilled version of the internet with two powerful arguments: convenience and security. People may sacrifice their political freedom, but in return they are promised economic opportunity, less crime and the ease of having their entire lives just a swipe away on a mobile device. The WeChat device, once merely the Chinese equivalent of the banned WhatsApp, has incorporated elements of the Chinese versions of Facebook and Uber, online banking, money transfers, even court documents. As Strittmatter points out, while this is extremely convenient for the consumer, it is even more convenient for the authorities using AI to monitor every aspect of their lives.

The Israeli thinker Yuval Harari pointed out in his book *Homo Deus* that Google could probably predict the onset of flu season more efficiently than the CDC or other government health agencies, simply by scanning people's emails and web searches for keywords like "headache," "sneeze" and "fever." But they don't do it because it would be a massive breach of privacy. Health

concerns take a back seat to personal privacy. But that is not a debate that can be held in an autocratic society, where such decisions are taken out of the people's hands.

The technology itself is neutral: the algorithm behind an app that children can use to scan a pile of Lego bricks and then suggest to them what toy they can build can also be used to pick out ethnic minority faces in the packed streets of a city. China is actively working on facial recognition technology that will identify its ethnic minorities, like Uyghurs, Kazakhs or Uzbeks.

Some of the technology it uses has been purchased from Western companies, some of it extorted as the price of doing business in the People's Republic. The Chinese Ministry of Public Security even persuaded a Yale professor, Kenneth Kidd, an expert in how DNA can be used to identify which region or ethnic group a person is from, to allow one of their scientists to spend a year in his lab, studying his techniques. China provided him with DNA samples: they did not tell him they had been harvested from Xinjiang's ethnic minorities, but they did tell the American they had been collected with consent. Now China can use the obligatory blood tests to identify people by their DNA, and send them to concentration camps. There will be no passing yourself off as Han Chinese if you are a member of a Turkic minority trying to avoid incarceration.

As we saw in the introduction to this book, China has used its advanced technologies to develop a "social credit" system in which citizens receive a score ranked according to their actions. If you jaywalk, facial recognition cameras scan your face and flash a picture of you, together with your name, on a giant billboard by the roadside. This is not only a public humiliation: the misdemeanor knocks points off your credit score. If it falls too low—and you do not work to get the points back by doing something for the party or your local community—you can be banned from flights and high-speed trains, or have trouble getting a loan for a home.

There is another, deeper point to all this surveillance, one that China's former prisoners such as Abduweli Ayup know all too well: once people become used to the fact that there is always someone watching them, somewhere, the technology itself starts to become almost unnecessary. People feel they are always being watched, and automatically censor themselves.

"The idea is that the authorities are trying to put in place comprehensive surveillance and behavioral engineering on a mass scale," said Maya Wang of Human Rights Watch, one of the researchers who dissected the Integrated Joint Operating Program, or IJOP, that affords the Chinese police almost god-like scrutiny of the Uyghurs.

In fact, China calls its intensive spying on the Uyghurs "predictive policing." The idea, they say, is for its advanced AI systems to pick up on patterns of behavior and arrest people who are liable to commit a crime *before* they actually commit it. This absurdly dystopian idea has often been compared to the Tom Cruise science fiction movie *Minority Report*, based on a book by the king of tech dystopias, Philip K. Dick. In that movie, "precogs"—people with a mutant gene that allows them to see into the future—alert the police to a crime that is about to be committed. The police then arrest the person for a crime they didn't actually commit. In China's case, AIs stuffed with data from hacked phones and filled up with the observations of Becoming Family "relatives" play the role of these precogs.[5]

In fact, a better comparison would be to the early nineteenth-century pseudoscience of phrenology, in which physicians said they could predict a person's mental traits—including their propensity to crime—by measuring the bumps on the human skull. What the CCP's "predictive policing" does, in actual fact, is to

---

5   The CCP seems to be quite fond of science fiction in its security operations: its massive system of more than 20 million cameras fitted with facial recognition software in public spaces is dubbed "Skynet," the name of the future robot technology that tries to wipe out humanity in the 1984 Arnold Schwarzenegger movie *The Terminator*.

grant to a police state the carte blanche ability to arrest whomever they please, based on whether they have a long beard or refuse to drink alcohol.

Many China experts have noted that these repressive tools cross-pollinate from place to place in China. Some of the ideas, such as dividing neighborhoods up into grids to allow better surveillance, actually originated in China proper and were built out in Tibet, then refined and implemented on a massive scale in Xinjiang. Tibet, Xinjiang and Hong Kong have become testing grounds for these dystopian visions, where the techniques of repression can be honed and shipped back to inner China to maintain control of the huge Han Chinese population.

For example, Chinese security is reportedly testing on Uyghurs an app that purports to be able to detect a person's emotional state. Once perfected on the captive population, the technology could then be used on its own people as a kind of unsupervised, universal lie detector. With no ethical boundaries, huge technological advances can be made. It is worth remembering that Wernher von Braun, one of the architects of the Apollo moon shot, had developed much of his aeronautic expertise developing the V2 rockets that Nazi Germany fired at England during World War II, a project that used Jewish slave labor. Von Braun was captured after the war, and his murky history was airbrushed for years after he was reassigned to US research in the space race against the Soviet Union.

And the technology of repression is already being exported outside China.

When Zumrat Dawut and her family managed to flee Xinjiang for the United States, her children were at first surprised by how backward the technology appeared to be here; the internet was slow and spotty, and people still used credit cards, rather than their phones, to pay for purchases. In China, just about every aspect of a person's life is focused on their phone.

Just as Americans were stunned when the Soviet Union became the first country to send a man into space in 1961, it may come as a shock to many Americans that China is already far ahead in many aspects of AI development, which, in some ways, is to this century what the space race was to the last. In some Chinese cities, police officers are already wearing facial recognition glasses to spot known criminals; in others, the vast databases linked to ubiquitous networks of cameras—which have been used to round up millions of Uyghurs—are being used to pick known criminals out of crowds as they buy food from street vendors.

China is proud of these achievements—they are helping it meet Xi's stated goal of becoming a tech superpower and ultimately a world leader in artificial intelligence, something that will give it huge advantages economically and militarily. This is especially important since hacking has become the new front in asymmetrical warfare, avoiding conventional military confrontations (although China is also massively building up its armed forces at the same time).

Under Xi's leadership, Beijing in 2015 launched its "Made in China 2025" plan to push for dominance in global high-tech manufacturing in a decade. The plan uses government subsidies, a system of central planning combined with hyper-local implementation, and the mobilization of state-owned companies to try to make China self-sufficient in key areas such as computer chip manufacture. The goal is ultimately to surpass the United States as the home of the Big Tech platforms that dominate the world.

China's technology sector has already made massive leaps and bounds, in part because it has a staggeringly large market of 1.4 billion people, something that has spurred innovation in the sector, and partly because the CCP has locked out the big players that hold virtual monopolies in the West, such as Google, Facebook and Twitter. The CCP is also able to pick winners in its competitive domestic market, giving them structural advantages and compelling them to work alongside the government in data sharing and development.

The ambitious plan covers not only digital technology but a slew of other key sectors, such as agricultural technology, aerospace, emerging bio-medicine, high-speed rail infrastructure and maritime engineering. In short, China wants to carve out a lead position in what is known as the fourth industrial revolution, in which the integration of artificial intelligence into all aspects of our lives is set to transform the shape of society.

In one aspect, China has already become an AI leader: surveillance technology, a major global growth sector.

According to the Carnegie Endowment for Global Peace, at least seventy-five out of 176 countries are already actively using AI surveillance technology. Chinese companies are well ahead in this field, supplying so-called "smart city" packages not just to countries with authoritarian regimes but also to democracies like Germany, France, New Zealand and Canada. These "smart city" solutions offer integrated cloud-data systems that can be used to monitor a city's water and sewage supply, its traffic flow and infrastructure maintenance, but also—if the client so desires—to have surveillance systems keep tabs on its population. This makes sense from a crime-fighting perspective: if the mayor of Lagos in Nigeria is told by a Huawei spokesman he can sell him a system that can help manage his wastewater problems, but can also cut the city's crime epidemic by 80 percent overnight, he is likely to buy it. Many cities in democratic countries have also bought these, often because it made sense from an economic standpoint, and because the city officials were not aware, until the US sounded the alarm, of the potential for it to be used against political opponents.

Of the seventy-five countries using AI technology, sixty are supplied with technology linked to China: fifty of them are supplied by Huawei, now a giant in the field. Does China have back doors that allow it access to all that data? Possibly. When China donated two hundred million dollars to build the new African Union headquarters in Addis Ababa, it used Chinese designers and a Chinese state construction company. It was later discovered it had built into the sleek design a number of hacks to allow it access to what was being discussed inside the headquarters.

In a similar vein, the Reuters news agency reported in 2021 that a Chinese company selling prenatal tests worldwide is using them to harvest vast amounts of data from women that could be used to research population traits and to achieve leadership in the pharmaceutical industry. The company, BGI Group, developed the tests in collaboration with Chinese military hospitals to improve "population quality," a phrase sinisterly reminiscent of the days of eugenics, especially as one of the things they were trying to detect on their military supercomputer was indicators of mental illness in the pregnant mothers.

"The technology could propel China to dominate global pharmaceuticals, and also potentially lead to genetically enhanced soldiers, or engineered pathogens to target the US population or food supply," the report quoted experts as saying.

"If you look at China…the scale of the companies that are being built, the services being built, the wealth that is being created, is phenomenal," Eric Schmidt, the cofounder of Google, said in September 2018. He has predicted that the internet will split in two by 2028, with a Chinese-led internet and non-Chinese version headed by the United States.

Part of that will stem from China's ambitious "Belt and Road Initiative" to build infrastructure in seventy countries, from Asia to Europe. The vast project, launched by Xi in 2013, is expected to affect around 65 percent of the world's population in the coming years. Under the scheme, China bought up the controlling share of Athens's main port of Piraeus, right after the Greek financial crisis. It plans to build it up to be the biggest shipping hub in the Mediterranean, a bridgehead into Europe. The massive Chinese project, also known as the "new Silk Road," is supposed to help less solvent countries develop their critical infrastructure, having often been refused credit loans by Western banks looking for a return on their investment. But in reality, it often traps them in Chinese debt and pulls them closer into the Chinese orbit.

Not far north of Greece, in the tiny Balkan country of Montenegro, the government took a billion-dollar loan from China to have a Chinese company build a two-hundred-and-seventy-mile highway from its Adriatic port of Bar to Belgrade, the capital of neighboring Serbia. However, after building only twenty-five miles, Montenegro ran out of money, leaving the road unfinished and Podgorica owing China a sum equivalent to a quarter of its economy. As part of the deal, the Chinese state bank that granted the loan can seize land in Montenegro in case of a default. Final execution of the deal will be decided by a Chinese court of law, a serious blow to Montenegro's sovereignty.

In such a way—a combination of poor local leadership, Western reluctance to help and China's desire to spread its influence— the Port of Hambantota in Sri Lanka, located on a shipping lane between Asia and Europe that carries 80 percent of global maritime trade, fell under Chinese control. China has also taken control of the Pakistan port of Gwadar, at the entrance of the Persian Gulf, another vital shipping route.

For sure, most of the exports and loans are a case of China stepping into places ignored by the rest of the world. In some ways, it resembles the way the British built up their empire— securing ports in far-off lands to protect their trade routes, and then gradually taking over the hinterlands of these ports to ensure their overseas footholds, doing political deals with neighboring rulers who gradually fell under British sway and started becoming reliant on British weapons, trade or influence.

Sarah Cook, a China expert at the NGO Freedom House, told me she didn't believe that Beijing was exporting its smart city surveillance packages explicitly in order to make other countries more authoritarian. In fact, the CCP may prefer dealing with democracies, since they are more open and therefore more vulnerable to Chinese money and influence operations. What China wants is to become a world leader in the most important sector in the world: AI and digital technology. But the net effect is that countries will be using key infrastructure developed by an authoritarian system and designed to surveil their populations, and that in itself is a threat to democracy.

"There's a real danger that along with those products and services comes a different leadership regime from government, with censorship, controls, etc.," Google boss Eric Schmidt has warned.

Hence Washington's decision to bar US government agencies from using telecommunications equipment made by China's Huawei and ZTE to help build out its 5G networks, the next generation of high-speed communications. It would be a fatal flaw to allow your rival to control your country's central nervous system. The message has percolated around the world, although many countries have been slow to adapt, given their reliance on trade with China and Beijing's growing political muscle.

That clout has been clearly demonstrated by what China calls its "wolf warrior diplomacy." It is something of a contradiction in terms: instead of traditional diplomacy, Chinese envoys are now expected to take to social media and push back against any perceived insult from countries that are critical of China. These messages can be jarring at times, and very undiplomatic: when a condominium collapsed in Surfside, Florida, in June 2021, China's consul general in Rio de Janeiro, Li Yang, mocked the recovery efforts by tweeting pictures of rescue workers on the rubble pile with the English text, "'America is coming back!' But none of the people buried in the ruins are coming back!!"

Just as shockingly, when India was losing thousands of people daily to the coronavirus pandemic that had spread like wildfire from China itself, the CCP's Central Political and Legal Affairs Commission posted an image on Weibo showing a Chinese rocket launch alongside a photo of the bodies of COVID victims being cremated in India, a US ally which has strained ties with Beijing. The text beside the images read: "Lighting a fire in China VS lighting a fire in India."[6]

The term "wolf warrior diplomacy" itself derives from a Chinese blockbuster movie about a unit of tough soldiers from the People's Liberation Army sent to Africa to rescue Chinese civilians. The movie's tagline was: "Even though a thousand miles away, anyone who affronts China will pay."

This aggressive "diplomacy" is not confined to social media.

In June 2021, as COVID-19 was still claiming hundreds of thousands of lives, China threatened Ukraine, stating it would withhold deliveries of the Chinese-made vaccine that Kyiv was using to battle the pandemic if did not withdraw support for a push by more than forty countries for the UN Human Rights Council in Geneva to be granted more access to investigate what was going on in Xinjiang.

Ukraine, which had briefly joined the statement, withdrew its name. China's threat would have blocked a delivery of half a million vaccine doses to the country, which had lost some fifty thousand people to the disease by that point, diplomats told the Associated Press.

That kind of kowtowing is nowhere more evident than in the Muslim world, which purports to back all members of the Islamic faith. But when Mohammed bin Salman, the Saudi crown prince and de facto ruler of his country, visited Xi in 2019 he told Chinese media that "China has the right to take anti-terrorism and de-extremism measures to safeguard national security," a clear washing of his hands of the Uyghurs and the other Muslims of Xinjiang.

---

6   The episode ended even more embarrassingly for China when its ten-story, twenty-three-ton rocket booster made an "uncontrolled reentry" into the atmosphere, raising fears it could land on a built-up area. Luckily it landed in the sea.

Likewise, Pakistan's president, Imran Khan, refused point-blank to condemn what was happening in Xinjiang when pressed in an interview by journalist Jonathan Swan in summer of 2021. Khan, who in the same interview slammed Islamophobia in the West, said that China had assured him that the steady drumbeats of reports of genocide were not true, and that was good enough for him. "China has been one of the greatest friends to us in our most difficult times," he said. After that interview, the US publication Vox commented that "China is buying Muslim leaders' silence on the Uyghurs."

When 43 mainly Western states made a joint statement in the United Nations in October 2021 calling on China to "ensure full respect for the rule of law" in Xinjiang, the Communist leadership of Cuba managed to rally 62 other countries in support of China. Many were African countries that have come to rely on Chinese support, like Algeria, Congo, Eritrea, Ethiopia, Gambon, Ghana, Libya, Zimbabwe and Zambia, but the list also included wealthy Muslim states like Saudi Arabia, Iran and the UAE. China has found other unlikely allies, including the Swedish telecoms giant Ericsson, which actually stood to pick up some very large contracts after the US called for the company's Chinese rivals Huawei and ZTE to be locked out of Europe's communications infrastructure. But Ericsson feared it in turn would be frozen out of the Chinese market, so its CEO Börje Ekholm lobbied the government in Stockholm to reverse the ban, despite the obvious security risks to Sweden. He even went as far as saying that if the government didn't do so, his flagship company would consider leaving Sweden itself.

But perhaps China's greatest PR coup was in the aftermath of its bungled response to the outbreak of the COVID-19 pandemic in the city of Wuhan. It was desperate to paper over its initial botched response, when police had actually arrested Li Wenliang, the thirty-four-year-old doctor who had tried to raise the alarm about the virulence of the new disease (he was

accused of "rumor-mongering," and later died of the disease).
For two months—a vital period to respond to the crisis—China
failed to take sufficient measures as the virus spread out of control. Instead it constantly downplayed the threat, claiming the
disease was a form of pneumonia and offered only incomplete
data to the World Health Organization, which was itself trying
to formulate an effective response.

Yet the World Health Organization—which had privately
voiced concerns about China's opacity—was quick to sing its
praises publicly.

Kai Strittmatter, who has been a China observer for more
than thirty years, said this was typical of the way China had always acted domestically. It is not enough to simply cover up a
disaster: the CCP has to make the victims of its failings show
gratitude to the party for "saving" them, even when that narrative is a blatant lie.

After it had finally mobilized its huge resources to contain the
outbreak, the Communist Party actually launched a campaign
named "thank-CCP education" for having cleared up its own
mess. At the same time, it forced upon the world a narrative of
heroic sacrifice and courageous mobilization.

Why did the WHO cover up for China, even as the CCP was
refusing to share the virus's genome mapping for weeks? The
world body went as far as calling its commitment to transparency "very impressive, and beyond words."

Tapes later obtained by the Associated Press suggest that the
organization was indulging in such flattery to try to coax the
necessary information out of the Communist leadership, which
was, as ever, wary of sharing anything that could make the situation in China look bad—that is, the true picture of what had
happened.

Even though the reports of its stalling and missteps are now
public, inside China, the authorities can simply block them from
being shared. In their place, they can now cite the original words

of praise from the WHO, which in fact had the unfortunate side effect of undermining the WHO's own credibility around the world and made combating the disease even more complicated.

"It's amazing, but what is even more amazing is that it works," Strittmatter told me when I discussed the machinations of what China watchers called an "enforced national amnesia."

The CCP's attempts to rewrite the whole COVID cover-up were so egregious that even under threat of arrest, people vented their fury online at the "gratitude campaign." When Vice Premier Sun Chunlan visited Wuhan, residents dared to shout out, "Fake, everything is fake!"

But the propaganda machine is relentless, and huge, and speaking out carries great risk. The CCP simply used its mouthpieces to drown out the dissenting voices, which gradually faded under threat of persecution. Thus, the state-owned Xinhua News Agency had the gall in March of 2020 to say that the United States owed China an apology and that the world should be thanking Beijing. "Without the enormous sacrifices and efforts made by China, the world could not have gained a precious window of time to combat the novel coronavirus epidemic; one can say that China has, by its own strength alone, staunchly held off the novel coronavirus epidemic for a very long time."

As Strittmatter points out, if the CCP tells you black is white, it is not enough to simply agree. You have to then explain precisely *why* black is white, and in the process make yourself complicit in the illusion, and therefore compromised, which is, of course, how an authoritarian regime wants its people to be.

PART 8

FIGHTING BACK

29

The election of Donald Trump in November 2016 came as a shock to me and many others around the world. As an immigrant from a Communist regime, America has always been much more than just a place I live. It has been a moral authority and stood for the values of freedom, decency, democracy and respect for others. So when I heard the would-be American president using overtly racist language about Mexicans and my fellow Muslims, when I heard him boasting about sexually harassing women or denigrating disabled people, it pained me deeply.

In the run-up to the election, I had been asked by Kurt Campbell, who had served as Hillary Clinton's assistant secretary of state for Asia, to work on a policy paper for the Democratic presidential candidate. Although I have always been nonpartisan in my politics, I agreed because I had been disturbed by the buddiness shown by some in the Obama administration with the Chinese Communist Party. I wanted to delineate how Clinton could take a more human rights–based approach. In 1995, as

First Lady, she had made the risky move of delivering a highly political speech on women's rights at the UN women's conference in Beijing, when everyone was insisting she should just come out with the usual platitudes. She not only stood on the platform and told the world that "women's rights are human rights," but she also threatened to boycott the entire event if Beijing did not release the Chinese-American activist Harry Wu. As a result, Wu was freed the same day I first landed at Los Angeles Airport from China. He later wrote a letter in support of my asylum application. And of course, her husband, Bill, had essentially saved Bosnia's Muslim population from slaughter by the Bosnian Serbs that same year by launching NATO air strikes that ended the war in the Balkans.

But on the night of November 8, 2016, Trump won, and all that became purely academic. I have a photo that my wife took of me that night: it was 3:00 a.m. and neither of us could sleep. Neither could my baby son, who is perched on my back as I am slumped over my iPad, watching the shocking news slowly sink in.

True, Trump had promised a tougher line on trade with China, but he had not said a word about their appalling human rights record. Several years later, when Trump's national security adviser John Bolton published his tell-all book about the mayhem inside the White House, I had that same sickening feeling when I read that Trump had told Xi it was right to put the Uyghurs into "reeducation camps."

And yet under Trump, everything changed.

It wasn't directly because of Trump himself. Rather, his mercurial temper and bull-in-a-china-shop approach to governing provided the explosive charge that would allow others in his orbit—old China hands, many of them unknown to the broader public—to blow up the decades-old approach of expecting China to liberalize politically as it did so economically.

Many of these administration officials had come to reject this old hope, which dated back to the days of Deng Xiaoping in the 1980s, when some of this new generation of China hawks were still in diapers. By the early 2000s, it was clear to many of them that the Communist Party had zero intention of ever dropping either its ideology or its grip on power.

The CCP had adopted capitalism—the ideology of its foes— merely as a weapon to save itself from Soviet-style collapse, but had adapted it into a new model that an increasing number of authoritarian regimes now sought to emulate.

In his landmark 1985 book, *Amusing Ourselves to Death*, the American cultural critic Neil Postman argued that societies had largely given up their belief that populations could be controlled through the Orwellian system of oppression, brainwashing and state control. Instead, he said, they favored a model first advanced by Orwell's contemporary Aldous Huxley, whose *Brave New World* shows a civilization permanently distracted by mindless amusements, recreational drugs and sex.

These days, China has fused those two models into something altogether new. Its citizens can upload endless funny dance clips and cat videos onto TikTok, they can build up their own businesses and become extremely wealthy, all as long as they observe one core tenet of the new social contract—never question the Communist Party. Because then the Orwellian side instantly kicks in. Behind the glittering lights of Shanghai and Beijing, the thriving restaurants and robust annual growth figures, there is a grim world of prisons and gulags and torture awaiting those who challenge the absolute political authority of the CCP.

As Chinese novelist Yan Lianke said in 2018, "Living in China is confusing now, because it can feel like being in North Korea and the United States at the same time."

Inside the White House, the seismic events that were to revolutionize US policy toward China took at least two years to take shape amid the chaos and power struggles between various factions. *Washington Post* columnist and China expert Josh

Rogin notes that these factions were delineated into what he called the "superhawks"—Steve Bannon, Peter Navarro and Stephen Miller—who wanted to all but start a war with China; the "Wall Street clique" of Treasury Secretary Steve Mnuchin and Larry Kudlow, head of the National Economic Council, who wanted to cut business deals with Beijing; the "hardliners"— people like Matt Pottinger, a former journalist and US marine who served on the National Security Council and knew what China was really like; and the so-called "Axis of Adults" such as generals John Kelly, H.R. McMaster and Jim Mattis, the experienced military veterans who had decades of service under their belts but knew little of China.

As these factions formed and clashed behind the closed doors of the White House, I was worried and depressed. The neophyte Trump had hardly anyone on his staff who actually knew China or how to deal with it. After his campaign trail rhetoric about getting tough on the trade deficit, he appeared to be cozying up to Xi, just as the previous administration had done. The Wall Street clique of his administration was in the ascendancy in those early days, and friends of mine inside the government told me the financiers wanted nothing more than to make nice with the world's second-largest economy. In fact, Xi was the first foreign head of state to be invited to Trump's Florida club Mar-a-Lago, in April 2017. Looking back, the timing was highly significant: that was the month that the CCP launched its first mass roundups of Uyghurs into the camps. But in Palm Beach, the real estate mogul hoped to woo the Chinese Communist leader to push through a trade deal to close the US deficit, and was tweeting about the great chocolate cake the two leaders had been served at dinner.

But Xi was a cunning operator, a man who had survived the purge of his father, a onetime acolyte of Chairman Mao, and returned from his own "reeducation" in the rural hinterlands to work his way up through the ranks of the Communist Party, all while never showing his hand. It appears Xi quickly realized that Trump was a man who admired authoritarian leaders and knew little about the complex issues at play. He played Trump so well that even four years later, when China was unleashing the coronavirus pandemic on an unsuspecting world and trying to hush up its spread, Trump was still reluctant to turn on his old "friend."

"China has been working very hard to contain the Coronavirus," Trump said on Twitter on January 21, 2020, right before America was engulfed by the pandemic. "The United States greatly appreciates their efforts and transparency. It will all work out well. In particular, on behalf of the American People, I want to thank President Xi!"

Just as bad, Trump's new secretary of state, Rex Tillerson, the former head of the Exxon oil company who also had zero government experience, was playing right into China's hands.

At his Senate confirmation hearing, he praised China as "a valuable ally in curtailing elements of radical Islam" and even added that "we should not let disagreements over other issues exclude areas for productive partnership."

Tillerson made a trip early in his tenure to China to meet Xi, who used the old CCP trick of getting the Texas oil executive to exactly parrot Xi's own public talking points. Tillerson promised Washington was "ready to develop relations with China based on the principle of no conflict, no confrontation, mutual respect, and win–win cooperation." The statement was almost word for word what Xi had said when congratulating Trump on his election win.

As the first reports of what was happening in Xinjiang began to seep out into the wider world, people were still mesmerized by Xi. They seemed to think he might be the next Gorbachev, sweeping away the corruption that had plagued China before his ascent to power (he purged hundreds of thousands of people on corruption charges—it later became apparent this was also a tactic to intimidate and remove rivals). Trump called him a great leader who "loves his people," but by the time he said that, Xi's Communist Party had already begun locking up huge numbers of innocent Uyghurs.

I was very frustrated by all this. When Trump announced his ban on people from certain Muslim-majority countries from entering the US, I penned an article for the Asia Society news site *ChinaFile*, under the headline, "What Do Trump and Xi Share? A Dislike of Muslims."

I pointed out that shortly after the brutal crackdown on pro-democracy activists in Tiananmen Square in 1989, Trump praised Chinese leaders for the "strength" they displayed in quelling the protests, in which hundreds of student protesters died. Then, during the GOP debate in 2016, he had referred to those same democracy demonstrations as a "riot."

In an attempt to draw attention to what was going on, I helped to organize a Uyghur cultural gathering in Rayburn House, a government building right next to the US Capitol. I served as a master of ceremonies. We had men and women in traditional Uyghur dress, and a large spread of home-cooked Uyghur food. James McGovern of Massachusetts, the chair of the Congressional-Executive Committee on China, attended, and a number of Uyghur leaders, including Dolkun Isa, the president of the World Uyghur Congress, delivered speeches. As I was seeing one of the guests out, I spotted Jon Stewart, the comedian who hosted *The Daily Show* for years, leaving the building. I went up and introduced myself, saying I was a big fan. He said he had been talking in another committee room on behalf of New York firefighters battling for extra health care after suffering terrible side effects from inhaling toxic dust on 9/11. He was very friendly, so I asked him: "Would you do me a favor?"

As a celebrity, he probably gets asked that a lot, but he graciously listened as I asked him to say a few words to the assembled Uyghurs and their guests upstairs. Remarkably, he agreed, and delivered a short speech expressing his admiration for the culture on display, and saying he couldn't believe that China's Communist Party would want to eradicate such a rich heritage. For me, that generous display of kindness—in response to what was essentially an act of desperation on my part—symbolized all that is good about America. Jon left the gathering with a huge bag of Uyghur food that some of the women had pressed on him for his drive back to New York City.

Then, in May of 2018, Adrian Zenz's first report on the mass detentions came out. It was a bombshell, but the immediate re-action around the globe was one of widespread incredulity, both in the media and the corridors of power.

Since my organization, the Uyghur Human Rights Project, had been reporting for months on the crackdown, I was asked by the BBC to appear on one of their signature debate shows called *HARDtalk* to discuss what was going on. The format is one interviewer, one guest: the interviewer is supposed to throw unflinchingly tough questions at the guest—hence the name of the show. As the chairman of the UHRP, I was to argue the case that the Chinese authorities really had locked up a million people in camps.

The dominant narrative was still that the Chinese regime was cracking down on Uyghur terrorism, not trying to eradi-cate an entire culture.

At that point, no Uyghur had dared to speak out publicly on a major news outlet and accuse the CCP of crimes against humanity. Most feared for the consequences for their relatives back home. It was nerve-racking to be the first, and on such a combative program. No one had my back—I was essentially a nobody, just a Uyghur exile acting for a very small organization with no real political clout. I had no idea what might happen, though I knew the Chinese authorities would not react kindly.

In 2014, the Chinese authorities had tried to lure me to ei-ther Dubai or Mexico, ostensibly to "discuss" my activism and the impact it was having on my family. I suspected it was an attempt to kidnap me. I contacted the State Department when I traveled later that year to Turkey, and they took it seriously enough to give me a twenty-four-hour hotline to call if anything happened. With a rogue state, anything is possible, as a US-based Saudi journalist sadly discovered himself several years later in Istanbul.

But mostly I was worried about presenting my case in a way that would convince viewers that atrocities were being committed against my people. I prepared a huge binder of talking points for this televised clash. In the days before I flew to London, I barely slept more than a couple of hours a night, worried that by speaking out I would put my parents in even greater peril—or, almost as bad, that I would do a poor job of pushing back against the Chinese narrative that the presenter was bound to throw in my face.

Sure enough, when presenter Shaun Ley introduced me, he asked, "Is he being duped, or is China duping the world?"

"Imagine," I began, "that you go to church on Sunday, and the government stops you and makes you go through iris and body scans. And imagine that you get up one morning and the government wants you to marry off your daughter. Imagine you don't have anyone to confide with, even in your private life, and imagine that you are forced to denounce your religion and walk away from your centuries-old tradition.

"What is happening in the Uyghurs' home, East Turkistan, is the Cultural Revolution on steroids."

There. I had said it. There was no turning back now. The presenter made some attempts to present China's side of the argument, that the Uyghurs were dangerous separatists or Islamist terrorists who needed to be behind bars. But that is a fairly simple argument to rebut: I just pointed out that the United Kingdom, France, the United States, had all suffered far bloodier terror attacks on their soil, but none of them had gone out and built concentration camps and herded all their Muslim citizens into them without trial or knowing if they would ever be released. There had been no forced sterilizations of European Muslim women.

I felt relieved that at last a Uyghur representative had spoken out on a major global news outlet, but I was also deeply worried for my parents. The show aired the next day: as I arrived at the Heathrow departures lounge for my flight home, it was playing on the large television screen. An elderly Canadian couple was watching and recognized me from the screen, the first time that had ever happened to me. They came over and gave me a hug, which was very touching in that moment of awful stress.

As I flew back to the US, I kept wondering if my parents were being dragged off to a camp even as I cruised at thirty thousand feet over the Atlantic. The minute I got off the plane in DC, I logged on to WeChat. Relief flooded through me when my parents answered. Nothing had happened so far. But that was not to last long.

In those gloomy days of 2017, I approached an old friend of mine, Kelley Currie, a fellow lawyer who had long worked as a human rights advocate for Tibet. I asked her who in the new administration I should talk to about protecting my parents from the Communist Party's wrath. She suggested Matt Pottinger, a former journalist and Marine Corps officer who had just joined the National Security Council under Trump. I didn't know Matt at the time, but I soon would, and very well: in fact, I often joke with him that one day there will be a statue of him standing in Kashgar.

A sandy-haired and boyish-looking man in his early forties, Matt had taken a fascinating and unlikely route to the White House. Having studied Chinese at college, he was hired by the Reuters news agency to cover the country. With his fluent Mandarin, he rose to become a correspondent for the *Wall Street Journal*, where he got to know firsthand the country and its people, as well as its oppressive security apparatus. He was often harassed by the authorities and had to flush his notes down a toilet one time to avoid them falling into police hands. Another time, a government thug punched him in the face in a Beijing Starbucks and told him to get out of China.

But that wasn't why he eventually left journalism: in 2004, he came across a video of a hostage being beheaded by Al Qaeda in Iraq, one of a string of grisly murders in the US-occupied country at the time. Pottinger was already having doubts about the rise of the authoritarian state he was covering as a journalist, and realized, as he later put it, that democracy is "not inevitable and it shouldn't be taken for granted, but it is a form of government very much worth fighting for." Even then, as Washington was collaborating with Beijing in the fight against terrorism, Pottinger said he had a "sort of a sense of unease that China was not really going to converge with the more liberal order."

He wanted to be more directly involved in the fight for democracy, so in 2005, at the ripe old age of thirty-two, he quit his job and joined the US Marine Corps, barely scraping through the demanding physical fitness tests but quickly being snatched up by military intelligence once he was in. Serving in Iraq and Afghanistan and rising to the rank of major, his abilities came to the attention of Lieutenant General Michael Flynn. Flynn was impressed, and when Trump named the controversial general (who had quit the military under a cloud and became a cheerleader for the populist Republican candidate) as his national security adviser, Flynn tapped Matt as his China expert. Matt was working on Wall Street by then, but when his country called, he immediately answered.

Flynn himself only lasted a couple of weeks in the job before being forced out by scandal. He was later charged with lying to the FBI over contacts he had with Russia. Matt, on the other hand, rose to one of the top jobs in the agency and outlasted a whole string of national security advisers who fell afoul of

Trump's notorious temper. He was one of the few officials to last the whole term, quitting only on January 6, 2021, when Trump whipped up his mob to storm the US Capitol.

I first met Matt in his office at the White House in late 2018. The year before, I had made contact with Leah Bray, the NSC's China director who had previously served under the Obama administration, and briefed her about the disturbing news coming out of Xinjiang, and about how the CCP was harassing my parents because of my advocacy work. I asked her what she could do: they were, after all, the parents of a US citizen. She later told me that she had taken my request to Matt, and that when Trump met Xi in Beijing in November 2017, he had handed him a list of ten people the US government was concerned about: three names on the list were Uyghurs, my parents and Ilham Tohti, the economist and former professor at Minzu University in Beijing serving a life sentence for criticizing the regime. It was probably that list that kept my parents from being sent off to a camp for years, an experience they would probably not have survived.

As it was, my father—by now in his seventies—had been ordered to undergo daily "reeducation." It was Beijing's way of punishing me. Every day my mum had to drive him to a facility in Kashgar where he was forced to attend indoctrination classes in Chinese, despite his poor health—he is diabetic, and his hands shake badly. One day he spilled scalding tea on his leg, leaving second-degree burns that would not heal. Luckily, one of the people working at the camp happened to be a former student of my father's and took pity on him, arranging for him to see a doctor rather than sit in agony regurgitating the thoughts of Xi Jinping.

For the visit to Matt, I took along Dolkun Isa, the head of the World Uyghur Congress, whom China accuses of being a terrorist. Dolkun had never even been allowed in the White House before, and was surprised at how much time Matt gave us—aides kept coming in with reminders and notes about impending meetings or phone calls, but he just waved them away. When I told him about what was happening to my father, he swore like a marine.

"That is fucking brutal," he said. I'm sure much worse curse words have been uttered in the White House, but Dolkun was impressed.

"You two must be old friends," he said afterward.

"No," I said. "We have never met before." But we would again.

The wheels of change had started moving by this time: Steven Mnuchin's Wall Street clique had failed to come up with a trade deal to Trump's satisfaction, and the superhawks like Flynn and Steve Bannon had become mired in their own infighting or criminal investigations. That had led to the ascendancy of the hardliners like Matt, who knew China well and wanted to end Washington's kid-glove treatment. Behind the scenes, he was drafting new guidelines that would allow the US to push back against China's intellectual property theft and influence operations inside the United States.

Over at the State Department, meanwhile, the oilman Tillerson had been replaced by Mike Pompeo, who brought with him a bleakly realistic view of China from his days as head of the CIA.

Pompeo drafted another former *Wall Street Journal* China hand, Mary Kissel, whom I knew from her time as the paper's Asia-Pacific editorial chief, when I had written articles for her. Mary is razor-sharp and knows all of China's tricks, from the debt traps it uses to ensnare poor countries and seize up their strategic seaports and infrastructure, to the machinations of Beijing's Politburo power struggles. My old friend Kelley Currie had also started working with Nikki Haley on the team representing Washington at the United Nations, frequently clashing with Chinese officials there and confronting their brazen lies.

Kelley personally had to contact Interpol when China had my friend Dolkun Isa added to a red list as a terrorist in a bid to stop him from attending a UN conference in New York City: she swiftly made sure he was removed from the list, and then proudly paraded him around the UN, much to the annoyance of the Chinese delegation.

What these people understood was that China's Communists were not liberalizing. On the contrary, under Xi the party-state appeared to be headed back to the bad old days of Mao. And the news now coming out of Xinjiang only added urgency to their cause.

The change in attitude that had begun behind closed doors started to manifest itself publicly in October 2018. That was when Vice President Mike Pence delivered a stunning speech to the conservative Hudson Institute where now I am a senior fellow. The speech—largely written by Matt Pottinger—was a huge shot across the bow for Communist China, and it ripped up decades of the softly-softly, wait-and-see approach. Some even saw it as tantamount to a declaration of a new Cold War.

"America had hoped that economic liberalization would bring China into a greater partnership with us and with the world," Pence said. "Instead, China has chosen economic aggression, which has in turn emboldened its growing military."

Pence accused Beijing of abusing its economic power, stealing American technology, bullying both its neighbors and the very US companies that had helped it turbocharge its economy, and of reneging on its promises not to militarize the South China Sea.

He also noted, for the first time in a US major policy speech, that the CCP was persecuting religious minorities.

"And in Xinjiang, the Communist Party has imprisoned as many as one million Muslim Uyghurs in government camps where they endure around-the-clock brainwashing. Survivors of the camps have described their experiences as a deliberate attempt by Beijing to strangle Uyghur culture and stamp out the Muslim faith."

When I heard the speech, I knew the relationship between the West and China had fundamentally changed—that people were finally starting to wake up.

Congress had started to rouse itself to the challenge, too. In September of 2018, I was invited to testify at the House Subcommittee on Asia and the Pacific, alongside the unflappable German researcher Adrian Zenz. It was the most significant thing I'd done in the US up until that point, and it was there that I first made recommendations that would eventually lead to the historic Uyghur Human Rights Policy Act, a bill that shared an acronym, UHRP, with my own organization. The act included measures such as using law enforcement to push back against harassment of US citizens and the use of the Magnitsky Act to sanction human rights abusers in the Communist regime.

Later, in October 2019, Adrian and I along with two other experts testified on Uyghur forced labor before the Congressional-Executive Committee on China. This hearing compelled the members to introduce legislation, the Uyghur Forced Labor Prevention Act that Biden signed into law right before Christmas 2021. This bill included recommendations that I made in that hearing.

"Just talking to you could cost the lives of my parents," I told the committee convened to discuss the issue of Uyghur forced labor in China. I was told afterward that Senator Marco Rubio was moved by that statement, and he would later become a staunch ally in battling for recognition of China's atrocities, something for which he was ultimately sanctioned by Beijing.

One of the commonly asked questions at the 2018 hearing, my interviews, and public speaking was: Why are we the only ones talking about China's persecution of the Uyghurs? Where is the rest of the world? I decided, with Matt Pottinger's backing, to go to Australia to find out.

Why Australia? First, I had heard of Australian Uyghurs being swept up into China's camps: the news had been made public by Graham Fletcher, the head of the North Asia Division in the Department of Foreign Affairs and Trade. He went on to become Australia's ambassador to China in 2019. And second, I knew that Australia had found itself on the front line of China's attempt to shape the politics of Western democratic powers. It is, to quote one of the country's foremost experts on China, John Garnaut, "the canary in the coal mine of Chinese Communist Party interference."

The CCP calls its overseas influence operations the "United Front." The policy stems back to the days of Mao, when the fledgling Communist party-state was still recovering from decades of war and mayhem, and it needed to enlist its allies to attack its foes. As its economy and power have grown, so too have the united front operations. In Australia, with a large Chinese-speaking population, the CCP makes extensive efforts to shape the narrative and use unwitting citizens to act as its mouthpiece. This is aided by the fact that many older Chinese-Australians still feel more comfortable getting their news in Mandarin, which allows the party to exert an even more direct influence: they can intimidate China-based advertisers to stop sponsoring Australian outlets that criticize the regime, or work through front organizations with harmless-sounding titles such as the China Association for International Friendly Contact, or the Australian Council for the Promotion of Peaceful Reunification of China. Sometimes, these groups can be used to funnel money to politicians and get them to rehash China's talking points, often without them even realizing they are doing so.

China's security chief Meng Jianzhu even meddled in Australian politics, warning the Labor Party during an election campaign not to block a bilateral extradition treaty. *The Australian* newspaper reported that Meng said that "it would be a shame if the Chinese government representative had to tell the Chi-

nese community in Australia that Labor did not support the relationship between Australia and China."

If anyone tries to criticize these Communist Party tactics,
they are accused of being anti-Chinese. John Garnaut, another
former journalist who had lived in China, realized that the best
way to combat this was to raise awareness of the issue, starting
with Australia's own ethnic Chinese community.

Such influence was already on display when Beijing hosted
the Olympics in 2008. The CCP "astroturfed" thousands of
red-flag-waving Chinese-Australian students to march to the
Parliament building in Canberra "to defend the sacred Olym-
pic torch" from demonstrators who were legitimately protesting Beijing's brutal crackdown in Tibet.

Sometimes the intimidation is more direct, and blunt: one
journalist who dared to criticize a Chinese state-owned company operating in Australia told Garnaut he had been lured to
a karaoke bar and roughed up.

I organized a delegation to visit Australia for a week, doing a
whistle-stop tour of four cities: Canberra, Sydney, Melbourne
and Adelaide. The delegation included Dolkun Isa, Louisa Greve,
former vice president of the National Endowment for Democracy who has also served as UHRP's government relations director, and the UHRP executive director, Omer Kanat. We met
with Graham Fletcher's successor and senior diplomats at the
foreign ministry and Parliamentarians who work on China and
foreign affairs, and I spoke at public forums, including the Lowy
Institute at an event hosted by Richard McGregor, the former
Financial Times Beijing bureau chief and author of a book on the
Chinese Communist Party. We lobbied the Australian Parliament to impose sanctions along the lines of the US Magnitsky
Act, originally set up to punish Russian officials involved in the
killing of an anti-corruption whistleblower who died in prison.

After the BBC appearance, my congressional testimony and
the visit to Australia, I was starting to become more widely

known for my advocacy. I became one of the go-to people for media seeking comment on the Uyghur crisis. Soon, I was only sleeping about four hours a night, often getting up at 5:00 a.m. to take calls from European broadcasters to do interviews. I was also working full-time at a busy white-shoe law firm, Covington & Burling, and carrying out my duties at UHRP. And I was taking frequent meetings on the Hill—whereas once I had gone there as a student to meet with staffers over coffee, I was now being invited by senators, senior administration officials and House members—and trying to raise funds to support Uyghurs who had escaped to America, such as Zumrat and Mihrigul, who were struggling to get by.

It was exhausting. I'd get home late at night and my son would already be asleep, then I'd be up the next day before dawn again. I was carrying three cell phones to try to keep the various strands of my life separate, and to ward off Chinese hacks. In August of 2018, I was heading off to pay my respects at the funeral of the late John McCain, whose maxim that "hope is the best weapon against oppression" had kept me going in the darkest times, when my media phone rang. It was France 24, wanting an interview. I hurried to their offices instead, aware the pragmatic former navy pilot would have understood.

I was working to build a bipartisan consensus in the most divided political atmosphere that anyone could remember. Some on the left criticized me for working with the Trump administration, and it was true I had some strange bedfellows, people whose values differed from my own on so many other issues. Other people would try to twist my words from the BBC show to make it look like I was a separatist or an apologist for violence. Some hardline Uyghur activists have criticized me, even to this day, for not using my public persona and media appearances to advocate for East Turkistan independence. Someone even made a clip out of my 2018 interview with Matt Frei on Britain's Channel 4 and criticized me for my using the term "political autonomy" to describe the Uyghur grievances and demands in China. It is flattering that Uyghurs pay such close attention to my public remarks, but the Uyghur nation's future will not be decided by a TV interview. Regardless, I know that some will be unhappy with my work and my public remarks no matter what I say or do. So I have kept my focus and energy on pushing for robust policy responses to stop the Uyghur genocide.

The stress and worry often show when I do interviews and public speaking: I am not ashamed of being vulnerable or emotional. Sometimes I have been moved to tears when recounting what has happened to my people, and I am not alone in that. I have seen a number of men and women, academics and hardened journalists, tear up in public forums on the Uyghur genocide. It is simply a human response to the horror.

It also became a factor shaping the world's response to what is happening in the Uyghur lands. When Secretary of State Mike Pompeo made an official visit to Kazakhstan in early 2020, my friend Mary Kissel was with him as he met for more than an hour—a huge amount of time for an official at that level—with people whose relatives had been herded into camps across the border. Mary later told me Pompeo was visibly moved by their stories and called on the Kazakh government to help anyone who managed to escape across the border. Two months later, he personally presented Sayragul Sauytbay, the ethnic Kazakh woman who had provided the world with its first eyewitness account of the camps, with an International Women of Courage Award.

Mihrigul's awful tale of being jailed and abused, and losing one of her babies, made it to Matt Pottinger even before she left Egypt. He heard from colleagues in the State Department of efforts to get her out of Cairo, and when she arrived in Washington he invited her to the White House to hear her account firsthand. He showed her around the West Wing and they talked for a long time in Chinese. Matt made sure she had access to adequate health care to help her recovery, and then wrote up her account to show the administration that what they had suspected was, in fact, true.

"Her story became important because I shared it with a lot of people, people at the highest levels," Matt later told me. "It was emblematic of a crisis and exposed the true nature of the regime."

It later struck me as fitting that such simple things—the power of people to connect with each other on a deep emotional level, and to touch others' lives with their story—should be the key to combating a regime where AI algorithms order thousands of people locked up, and where apparatchiks and prisoners alike are forced to swallow the meaningless jargon of a party machine.

In his office at home, Matt Pottinger has a single photo on his wall. It was taken in the Oval Office on October 7, 2019, and shows him and Mike Pompeo talking to President Trump, explaining the need to impose sanctions on China, which the president signed off on for the first time. Robert Lighthizer, the US trade representative, and Karen Dunn Kelley, the deputy secretary of commerce, are also there, selling the argument to Trump. By that point, the two countries were already locked in a war over tariffs, but this was different: these sanctions were being imposed for Beijing's appalling actions toward the Uyghurs.

Some critics of the Trump administration claim this was a calculated political move to weaken China's hand in the trade war, a geostrategic sucker punch in support of US foreign policy. But it wasn't: most of the key people in the Oval Office that day involved in this felt the very human need to act against this atrocity, and their job that day was to convince the president.

Now, Trump may not have cared for the Uyghur Muslims, and he may even have said, as Bolton claims, that Xi was right to lock them up. But early in his presidency, he had ordered missile strikes against Syria for the use of chemical weapons against civilians, including children: if he felt something with his gut, he could act. I don't know whether Matt discussed Mihrigul's story that day in the Oval Office—that was after all a confidential conversation—but it was the sort of tale that would likely have moved the president to action. The assembled officials told him that imposing sanctions would both have a concrete impact on China's economy and deal a hugely symbolic blow to China's carefully honed self-image, showing the true nature of the party-state.

And it worked. Trump signed the decree adding twenty-eight companies to the so-called "entity list," banning US firms from doing business with them without permission from the government. Among them were two of the world's largest manufacturers of video surveillance products, Hikvision and Dahua Technology. Significantly, the list included literally every police department in the region, including the one credited in Disney's controversial movie *Mulan*. The list also included many artificial intelligence companies that were developing the technology used to persecute and exploit the Uyghurs, such as voice and facial recognition software used by the Xinjiang police. It was gratifying to see these historic and unprecedented policy responses by the US government.

The battle had truly begun at that point. Despite all the earlier trade spats and tariff disputes, this was the first time that the Communist Party had really started to froth at the mouth. This, after all, wasn't the action of an enlightened leadership trying to combat Western imperialism or to lift up the downtrodden: this was the appalling handiwork of a ruthless dictatorship.

And it was just the start. Soon, European and Asian countries would start following the American lead, debating the concentration camps and forced labor sites in parliaments around the world. China was livid, and started retaliating with its own sanctions, on individuals like Adrian Zenz and, eventually, on senior officials like Matt Pottinger and Mike Pompeo. And these people would pay a price: Pompeo might have expected to leave the State Department and walk into a lucrative board position on Wall Street and make millions. Instead, no finance company would touch him for fear of falling afoul of China. While just about everyone now understands that China's Communist Party is a monster that should be shunned, Wall Street is still dazzled by the size of its market, and refuses to take any real steps to prod the dragon.

That first raft of human rights–related sanctions was a great start, and was followed by a series of new strictures against trade with China. That same year, 2019, I was called again to testify before Congress in hearings that produced the Uyghur Forced Labor Prevention Act, punishing Chinese companies that used my fellow countrymen as slaves. That has inflicted even more pain.

But we were still lacking one key element to fight back, and that was a decision over what to call the atrocities China was perpetrating in Xinjiang. Names matter, especially in law and in international relations: concentration camps aren't "vocational training facilities," and locking up millions of people, sterilizing them, taking away their children and trying to strip them of their cultural identity while reducing them to sub-Chinese drones to be put to work in forced labor camps isn't just a crime against humanity. It is genocide.

There are four legal categories of large-scale human rights atrocities: ethnic cleansing, war crimes, crimes against humanity and genocide. Lawyers for the US State Department will tell you that there is no hierarchy among them, and that crimes against humanity are just as bad as genocide. But "crimes against humanity" is an expression that lacks the sheer power that the word "genocide" holds in the collective imagination. Genocide has become widely conflated with the physical killing of large numbers of people, largely because of the Holocaust and the horrors of Rwanda. But under the Genocide Convention, of which the United States is a signatory, the definition is much broader and does not in fact have to include actual extermination.

Article 2 of the convention states that "acts committed with intent to destroy, in whole or in part, a national, ethnic, racial or religious group" can be construed as genocide, and include acts such as "causing serious bodily or mental harm to members of the group; deliberately inflicting on the group conditions of life calculated to bring about its physical destruction in whole or in part; imposing measures intended to prevent births within the group; forcibly transferring children of the group to another group."

These acts are essentially the same as for crimes against humanity. The difference is that with genocide, it is a specific group—either ethnic, national or religious—that is being targeted.

It quickly became clear as news broke of mass detentions, beatings, torture and rape that crimes against humanity were being committed in Xinjiang. Friends inside the administration let me know that the National Security Council was pushing for a genocide designation, but that many inside the State Department were wary—historically, State has not labeled acts as genocide if they do not involve mass killings, and there was no evidence that China had moved to that stage yet, even if the Uyghur population was shrinking at an alarming rate.

Within the State Department, it is the Office of Global Criminal Justice that handles accountability for mass atrocities by other countries. It used to be called the Office of War Crimes, but war crimes can obviously only be committed during a period of conflict, and plenty of countries indulge in crimes against humanity during periods of peace.

There are three elements that go into a genocide designation: the evidence itself, which was becoming more damning with every Uyghur who managed to escape and tell their tale. Then there is the legal analysis of the evidence and how the law interprets it. Finally, since this is the State Department and not a court of law, there is the policy justification, which makes recommendations to the secretary of state in a memo. That is because something has to be done once genocide has been officially determined: the United States is a signatory of the Genocide Convention (as is China, incidentally) and Article 1 states that signatories must "undertake to prevent and to punish" the heinous act. So you cannot just call something genocide: you are obliged to act on that designation.

Many department lawyers—and even many in the media, such as *The Economist*—were reluctant to label what was happening a genocide, so the office came up with a so-called "split memo," providing the cases for and against and essentially leaving it up to the secretary—in this case Mike Pompeo, himself a trained lawyer—to make the final call. Atrocity determination is the secretary of state's prerogative.

What swayed some of the more influential voices in State to call it a genocide was Adrian Zenz's report on forced sterilizations in the spring of 2020. There were also reports that as many as eight hundred thousand Uyghur children had been taken away from their parents. Some inside the administration wrote to Pompeo, arguing that these facts were game-changers if they could be verified.

Pompeo's job had, ironically, become easier since the outbreak of the COVID pandemic in early 2020. Until then, Trump had been reluctant to go all out against his old "friend" Xi. But when the virus that originated in Wuhan triggered an implosion of the US economy and undermined his chances of being reelected, he listened far less to Steve Mnuchin and his Treasury officials and was much more receptive to the hardliners.

"The handcuffs had been taken off after the pandemic," one senior administration insider told me.

As Pompeo weighed the evidence and the legal considerations, the sanctions started to pile up against officials and organizations in Xinjiang. Chinese companies were added to the entity list, sanctions were slapped on Chen Quanguo and Zhu Hailun, and US Customs began seizing goods suspected of being made with forced labor. In fact, Chen was quietly replaced as Xinjiang party secretary just a few months later, as pressure started to pile up on Beijing in the run-up to its hosting of the Winter Olympics.

Pompeo was also trying to enlist other countries into backing the US change of attitude toward Beijing: many were reluctant because of China's economic and political heft, but many leaders in Asia were reacting positively, asking why the hell it had taken Washington so long to wake up to what was happening.

At the same time, the pro-democracy demonstrations that had brought Hong Kong to a standstill were being brutally crushed, and China rammed through a national security law that allowed leaders of the demonstrations—and any journalists who supported the cause of democracy—to be jailed simply for speaking out. The world looked on in shock: Xi's government had shown that it was willing to slaughter the goose that laid the golden eggs in order to impose the order of the Communist Party.

"Hong Kong was part of the free world. And the free world lost a city to its enemy," said my old friend Wu'er Kaixi, the Tiananmen Square protest leader who supported my asylum application in the United States.

Even the China hawks in the Trump administration knew there was little they could do to stop what was happening in Hong Kong. Instead, they decided to hold it up as a sobering example to the world of the true face of China, which had previously committed to a "one country, two systems" agreement to allow the territory to carry on its own way of life for decades to come. The administration launched what it called a "broken promises" campaign to expose the CCP's lies. It started treating China and Hong Kong as one country now, revoking the extradition treaty with Hong Kong and refusing to sell it any more dual-use technology. That campaign was rolled into efforts to alert the world about what was happening in Xinjiang: there was a very definite pattern here. The way Pompeo framed it was not in terms of a power struggle between the dominant US and the rising superpower of China, but as the free world versus authoritarianism.

It shouldn't take a genocide of the Uyghurs and the crushing of Hong Kong's democracy and rule of law for the international community to see the true colors of the CCP and its leaders. Alas, though, that is precisely what it has taken.

But Washington still had not decided on whether to call the crisis in Xinjiang a genocide.

Different countries declare genocide in different ways: some countries wait for their courts to make a ruling; in others an attorney general might make a legal case. But in this instance, it was the secretary of state making a policy designation. The argument in favor was that, if you look at the totality of all the actions that were being carried out, it was clear that Xinjiang's Turkic Muslim minority was being targeted by specific policies that would qualify under the Genocide Convention: the sterilizations, mass detentions without trial, separation of children from parents, destruction of cultural heritage and the denial of the right to practice their religion. The intent was clear, especially when combined with the language about "excising tumors" and "killing all the weeds."

It was enough to prove intent in the eyes of many State Department lawyers, though not all. But the final decision came down to Pompeo: according to people close to the secretary, he went through huge stacks of legal papers and documentation, reviewing much of it all himself.

In November of 2020, as Trump was furiously denying his loss in the election, there was another hopeful sign from the State Department. Pompeo dropped the so-called East Turkistan Islamic Movement from the US list of designated terrorist organizations. For years, I had been criticizing first the Bush administration and then all of its successors for the strategic blunder of agreeing to designate this obscure group as terrorists, which had given the CCP a pretext for today's nightmare.

Whether the group had ever really existed is difficult to say. Hardly anyone had even heard of it after the Chinese authorities managed to get the US to declare it a terrorist organization twenty years earlier. Most of the "attacks" ascribed to it turned out to be spontaneous outbursts of anger by individuals or small groups, which the Chinese regime portrayed as evidence for its assertions. And the Uyghur language itself has no word for "terrorism" or "terrorist."

Chinese authorities were furious at Pompeo's move. "The United States should immediately correct its mistakes, refrain from whitewashing terrorist organizations, and stop reversing the course of international counter-terrorism cooperation," a Chinese Foreign Ministry spokesman said.

Meanwhile, the Trump administration was sliding into its final frenzy of chaos and, ultimately, insurrection. Trump's claims that he had won the election were tearing at the foundations of US democracy. Eventually, the outgoing president whipped up a mob which stormed the US Capitol building on January 6 to try to stop the legal certification of the results. I started to wonder whether Pompeo had left it too late. I was worried about the Trump administration kicking the can down the road in light of the post-election chaos.

I had spent a lot of time advocating for a genocide designation from the beginning: in May of 2020, I had been appointed by Nancy Pelosi to the US Commission on International Religious Freedom. I was the first Uyghur to hold political office in the United States, and this gives Uyghurs around the world, myself included, much-needed hope and inspiration. The appointment—backed by Trump administration officials, despite their antipathy toward the Speaker of the House—was seen as a bipartisan rebuke to Beijing, and gave me an even broader platform to alert the world about the persecution of the Uyghurs.

I quickly mobilized my fellow USCIRF commissioners to send Pompeo a letter asking to review and determine if the Chinese atrocities in Xinjiang amount to genocide.

Then, on January 19, literally the last full day of the Trump administration, Pompeo had to make his decision, or else leave office with a vital piece of the fight unfinished.

All that morning, I had been frantically texting my White House and State Department colleagues to see if there would be a last-minute decision. I was told to stand by for an announcement that would be going out at noon. I was desperately anxious and couldn't stop checking my phone.

Then my phone pinged. A text from a National Security Council colleague. "It is out."

"Genocide or Crimes Against Humanity?" I instantly wrote back.

"Both," came the answer.

A flood of relief swept over me.

The United States of America was officially recognizing that what the Chinese Communist Party was doing to the Uyghurs and other Turkic minorities in Xinjiang was genocide. Biden and his incoming team quickly agreed with the determination.

There was no going back now to the old "business as usual" approach with the CCP, either for US leaders or multinational businesses. It was now a genocidal regime, and who can afford to do business or trade deals with that?

EPILOGUE

Shortly after I was appointed to the US Commission on International Religious Freedom in May 2020, *Time* magazine named me on its list of the one hundred most influential people in the world in 2020.

Such recognition was a huge honor for me, and reminded me of just how far I had come, from a Uyghur kid born in a Maoist prison camp in Kashgar to being a US government official. I had mixed feelings when I heard the news, however. Excitement for the honor, but sadness that it had to come off the back of such a tragic situation back in my homeland.

It was bittersweet for another reason, too: also on the list was Xi Jinping, and there is no doubt that his malign influence is far greater than anything I can muster.

Yet I live in hope that things are changing, and faster than I could have hoped even a few years ago, and that we may yet act in time to save the Uyghur people and their culture.

I spend many of my days in the halls of the greatest superpower in the world, trying to plant the seeds that will shape the future for the better. Most recently, I have been trying to persuade the world to boycott the Winter Olympics in Beijing, comparing them to the 1936 games held in Berlin, that odious showcase for Hitler's power. I am shocked that the world might be about to make the same mistake again, even though many countries are coming to support the US designation of genocide. Luckily, an increasing number of states are following the US lead of a diplomatic boycott at the very least.

I was worried about the Biden administration dropping the terms "genocide" and "crimes against humanity" in official statements. I aired my frustration with administration officials in the summer of 2021 when this trend was glaringly apparent, right about the time that the United States was withdrawing from Afghanistan. I was pleased that the White House resumed using these terms when it announced the diplomatic boycott of the Olympics in December 2021. Words matter and are incredibly consequential in a situation like the Uyghur crisis where phrases such as "human rights violations or abuses" and "mistreatment" are bandied about by governments and the media but do not carry the same weight as "genocide." Human beings can be abused without genocide having occurred, and accountability for the very real horrors of genocidal crimes must start with the proper language. I was also concerned that the business lobby and climate activists would kill the Uyghur Forced Labor Prevention Act, which would let Beijing continue its enslavement of Uyghurs and continue to pollute the global supply chain with the goods produced by slave labor.

The diplomatic boycott, which I had been pushing since May 2019, was a big victory, but one that was more symbolic than practical. A much more palpable move against China was when President Biden signed the Uyghur Forced Labor Prevention Act into law two days before Christmas 2021: that put around one hundred Chinese companies on the entities list for their links to the oppression of the Uyghurs.

Crucially, it also provided a framework for other countries, including European powers, to base their own sanctions on, since this really is a global supply chain problem and demands a worldwide response.

In retaliation, China sanctioned me and three other members of the US Commission on International Religious Freedom, cutting me off from my family and trying to hurt me financially.

But at night, I go home and spend long, sleepless nights fretting about my family, about all the people I know who are in the concentration camps or whose relatives have disappeared. I am haunted by the memory of that little Uyghur child sitting on the knees of a Chinese police officer, playing with the cop as her heartbroken and ignored parents look on from thousands of miles away through the tiny screen of their cell phone.

When I manage to talk with my old and frail parents, missing their children and scarcely even knowing their grandchildren, the pain is almost too much to bear. My father looks so weak these days, but I can't reach out and hold him; I can't even tell him how sad I feel because that would be a victory for Chinese police listening in. It would show them just how much they are hurting us, and that would give them the power to do even worse. So I stay strong for as long as I can, then cry alone afterward.

I worry about my kid brother Mirsalih, too: prematurely aged and suffering hypertension, he has given up so much—including his PhD—to go back and take care of my parents in Xinjiang. But at least I can still *talk with* my parents. So many Uyghurs don't know where their mothers and fathers are, or if their children are being raised in an orphanage or by strangers, taught to disown their own people and heritage. They could well be dead, and no one would tell them. Now that I have been sanctioned, permanently banned from entering China, who will bury my father when he dies? Who will visit their graves in some nameless cemetery, their location known only to some faceless government bureaucrat?

At the height of the COVID-19 pandemic, disturbing videos popped up online of Uyghurs in prison uniforms being herded onto buses or trains, apparently being sent off to work in Chinese factories to keep the economy running when Han Chinese people were too afraid to return to work. What happened in the packed camps when the pandemic ripped through them? How did those undernourished prisoners, denied medication or sanitation, survive the disease that killed millions worldwide? Will we ever know the death toll, or will the CCP cover that up, too?

I remind myself of those words of the late Senator John McCain, that hope is the best weapon against oppression. But it is difficult to stay hopeful sometimes. The weapon gets blunted by pain and despair. True, the world is waking up, but how many Uyghurs will have been tortured or raped in the camps, or forced into slave labor in sweatshops, by the time sanctions start to take their toll on the Chinese economy?

Will it get worse before it gets better? The CCP has been crushing the independent spirit of Tibetans, Uyghurs and Hong Kongers: Will they try the same in Taiwan, which China considers an integral part of its territory? Could that trigger a new world war? There are worrying echoes of a resurgent Germany in the 1930s, when Hitler first reclaimed the Rhineland, then the Polish Corridor and Danzig, and was then handed Czechoslovakia's Sudetenland by Neville Chamberlain's shameful gesture of appeasement. A year later, an emboldened Hitler triggered WWII by invading Poland: it was during that world war that the concentration camps became extermination camps for Europe's Jews and Roma.

"If you're going through hell, keep going," Britain's wartime leader Winston Churchill once said.

But I also take solace from the fact that the Uyghurs are not the only ones walking a high wire. Xi Jinping is, too. His drive to crush China's minorities may come at a heavy price: If the economy stalls, will the Chinese people still be willing to put up with his souped-up Maoist tactics? He is engaged in a delicate tacking operation, like a sailor in a storm: he has to sail close enough to the free market winds to keep the economy growing before swinging about and heading back for centralized and repressive control, as he is now. Will there be enough wind in his sails from a free economy to power through another deadening period of repression? Will this become a new normal, that economically powerful regimes and global bullies like the CCP commit genocide with impunity? What if the international community caves in and ends up accepting the "Chinese governance model," as China's former ambassador to Washington, Cui Tiankai, called it? Remember, the impressive growth rate of China's economy is in part so staggering because the country was coming back from an economic collapse under Mao.

"There's no totalitarian system that allocates funds efficiently and has stable political machinations," a China expert friend reminded me recently. For all that Xi has been gathering power around himself, if the economy starts to sputter he could find himself in trouble with the party elite, many of whom have eyed his high-risk tactics with worried eyes.

And when the Chinese people learn what is being done in their name to millions of innocent people, will they still silently watch their video clips on TikTok and refuse to speak up? It is unlikely, and the Great Firewall of China, like its stone equivalent snaking across the land, is impenetrable.

Will what we have done be enough? It is a good start, that is for sure, and there is much more the world can do, starting with pressuring China to allow more access to Xinjiang by governmental entities, reporters, researchers and investigators. Can it save my elderly parents in time? I don't know, but I have learned this: I had feared that speaking up might condemn my parents to the camps. But in fact, speaking up has spared them. Those who do not give voice to their cause remain silenced.

And as the eighteenth-century English statesman Edmund Burke once observed, "The only thing necessary for the triumph of evil is for good men to do nothing."

That is why I will always speak up, even if it is through my own tears.

ENDNOTES

Introduction

18 ""Never Again?" It's already happening,'": Anne Applebaum, "'Never Again?' It's Already Happening," *Washington Post*,
February 15, 2019, https://www.washingtonpost.com/opinions/
global-opinions/the-west-ignored-crimes-against-humanity-
in-the-1930s-its-happening-again-now/2019/02/15/d17d4998-
3130-11e9-813a-0ab2f17e305b_story.html.

The Lawyer

69 "to a Chinese request to 'soften up' the detainees": Justin
Rood, "Report: U.S. Soldiers Did 'Dirty Work' for Chinese Interrogators," ABC News, July 17, 2009, https://abcnews.go.com/
Blotter/story?id=4894921&page=1#:~:text=May%2020%2C%20
2008%E2%80%94%20%2D%2D%20U.S.,in%20a%20new%20
government%20report.

How to Delete a Culture

192 "wrote in his final report, entitled 'Demolishing Faith.'": Bahram K. Sintash, *Demolishing Faith* (Uyghur Human Rights Project, 2019), 39, https://uhrp.org/report/demolishing-faith-destruction-and-desecration-uyghur-mosques-and-shrines-html/.

192 "or damaged as a result of government policies.": Nathan Rusera et al., *Cultural Erasure* (Australian Strategic Policy Institute, 2020), 5, https://www.aspi.org.au/report/cultural-erasure.

204 "'If Beijing can't bring the situation under control and continues to behave like a colonial power, we will continue to witness tragedies such as this one.'": Thomas Latschan, "Ilham Tohti—The Moderate Critic," Deutsche Welle, September 17, 2014, https://www.dw.com/en/ilham-tohti-the-moderate-critic/a-17928684.

204 "'I am not a terrorist!'": Joshua Lipes, "Popular Uyghur Singer's Whereabouts Unknown, Believed Detained in Xinjiang Re-Education Camp," Radio Free Asia, May 18, 2018, https://www.rfa.org/english/news/uyghur/singer-05182018131924.html.

205 "They can be tolerated 'as a necessary and temporary stage before their final integration,' according to Communist dogma.": Dongyan Ru Blachford, "Language Planning and Bilingual Education for Linguistic Minorities in China" (PhD diss., University of Toronto, 1999) 94, cited in Rustem Shur, *Resisting Chinese Linguistic Imperialism* (Uyghur Human Rights Project Report, 2019) 13, https://docs.uhrp.org/pdf/UHRP_Resisting_Chinese_Linguistic_Imperialism_May_2019.pdf.

211 "'I was turned into a diversion and was being played like a monkey in a circus. The monkeys that surrounded me were rid-

ing me one after another.'": Abduweli Ayup, "My First Cellmate in Kashgar," *PEN/Opp*, April 6, 2020, https://www.penopp.org/articles/my-first-cellmate-kashgar?language_content_entity=en.

The Reinvention of Genocide

228 "'no longer baby-making machines,'": Helen Davidson, "Twitter Removes China US Embassy Post Saying Uighur Women No Longer 'Baby-Making Machines,'" *The Guardian*, January 10, 2021, https://www.theguardian.com/world/2021/jan/10/twitter-removes-china-us-embassy-post-saying-uighur-women-no-longer-baby-making-machines.

228 "That is only a little over half the figure for 2017, when the birth rate was 15.88 births per 1,000 inhabitants.": Mo Yu, "Chinese Statistics Reveal Plummeting Births in Xinjiang During Crackdown on Uyghurs," Voice of America, March 27, 2021, https://www.voanews.com/a/east-asia-pacific_voa-news-china_chinese-statistics-reveal-plummeting-births-xinjiang-during/6203821.html#:~:text=According%20to%20the%20China%20Statistical,8.14%20births%20per%201%2C000%20people.&text=And%20there%20are%20signs%20that,south%20where%20Uyghurs%20are%20concentrated.

229 "'Target 2: [target] population for sterilizations 14,872 people'": Adrian Zenz, "China's Own Documents Show Potentially Genocidal Sterilization Plans in Xinjiang," *Foreign Policy*, July 1, 2020, https://foreignpolicy.com/2020/07/01/china-documents-uighur-genocidal-sterilization-xinjiang/.

230 "'more than double the rate of decline in Cambodia at the height of the Khmer Rouge genocide (1975–79).'": Nathan Ruser and Dr. James Leibold, *Family De-Planning* (Australian Strategic Policy Institute, 2021), https://www.aspi.org.au/report/family-deplanning-birthrates-xinjiang.

230 "a hotbed of poverty and fanaticism which could 'heighten political risk.'": Associated Press, "China Cuts Births with IUDS, Abortion, Sterilization," AP News, June 29, 2020, https://apnews.com/article/ap-top-news-international-news-weekend-reads-china-health-269b3de1af34e17c1941a514f78d764c.

232 "'It will make them easier to assimilate into the mainstream Chinese population.'": Ibid.

235 "'suspected to be made with human hair today that originated in Xinjiang, China, indicating potential human right abuses of forced child labor and imprisonment.'": CBP Public Affairs, "CBP Detains Chinese Shipment of Suspected Forced Labor Products Made with Human Hair," US Customs and Border Protection press release, July 1, 2020, https://www.cbp.gov/newsroom/national-media-release/cbp-detains-chinese-shipment-suspected-forced-labor-products-made.

236 "an ingredient of the Zyklon B gas used to kill Jewish prisoners.": "Did German Firm Schaeffler Process Hair from Auschwitz?" Spiegel International, March 3, 2009, https://www.spiegel.de/international/germany/claim-by-polish-researcher-did-german-firm-schaeffler-process-hair-from-auschwitz-a-610786.html.

240 "'We want those sons-of-turtles to wriggle out and sing and fart,' he said. 'That way we can catch them.'": Matthew White, *Atrocitology* (New York: Canongate, 2011), 431.

A Message from a Slave

256 "'Tell them it has been two years, [I have] not been released.'": Sophie McNeill et al., "Cotton On and Target Investigate Suppliers after Forced Labor of Uyghurs Exposed in China's

Xinjiang," ABC News, July 16, 2019, https://www.abc.net.au/news/2019-07-15/uyghur-forced-labour-xinjiang-china/11298750?nw=0&r=HtmlFragment.

257 "'seamless link between learning in school and employment in society.'": Laura Murphy and Nyrola Elima, *In Broad Daylight* (Sheffield Hallam University Helena Kennedy Centre for International Justice, 2021) 10, https://media.business-humanrights.org/media/documents/In_Broad_Daylight_Uyghur_Forced_Labour_and_Global_Solar_Supply_Chains.pdf.

257 "they live under what is called 'military-style management.'": Vicki Xiuzhong Xu et al., *Uyghurs for Sale* (Australian Strategic Policy Institute, 2020) 8, https://www.aspi.org.au/report/uyghurs-sale.

262 "The market grew by more than 250 percent between April 2019 and April 2020, and includes many industries such as clothes, footwear, hair products, metals and plastic.": Amy K. Lehr, *Addressing Forced Labor in the Xinjiang Uyghur Autonomous Region* (Center for Strategic and International Studies, 2020), https://www.csis.org/analysis/addressing-forced-labor-xinjiang-uyghur-autonomous-region-toward-shared-agenda.

262 "Britain was even hungrier for Xinjiang's products, with imports up by 192 percent for the same period.": Finbarr Bermingham, "Xinjiang's Exports to the EU Boom, Despite Political Concerns over Forced Labor," *South China Morning Post*, July 25, 2021, https://www.scmp.com/news/china/diplomacy/article/3142389/xinjiangs-exports-eu-boom-despite-political-concerns-over.

264 "The list also featured Adidas, Calvin Klein, Campbell Soup Company, Costco, H&M, Patagonia, Tommy Hilfiger

and others.": *Global Supply Chains, Forced Labor, and the Xinjiang Uyghur Autonomous Region*, staff research report prepared by the Congressional-Executive Committee on China (2020), 6, https://www.cecc.gov/sites/chinacommission.house.gov/files/documents/CECC%20Staff%20Report%20March%202020%20-%20Global%20Supply%20Chains%2C%20Forced%20Labor%2C%20and%20the%20Xinjiang%20Uyghur%20Autonomous%20Region.pdf.

265 "H&M, the second-largest clothing retailer in the world, was gone.": Stu Woo, "China Disappeared H&M from Its Internet, Splitting Fashion Industry Group, *Wall Street Journal*, May 22, 2021, https://www.wsj.com/articles/chinas-campaign-against-h-m-divides-fashion-industry-group-11621686650#:~:text=Following%20the%20online%20blocking%20of,by%20forced%20labor%20in%20Xinjiang.

257 "'Xinjiang long-stapled cotton is one of the best in the world. We believe top quality raw materials will definitely show its value. We will continue to buy and support Xinjiang cotton.'": "Hugo Boss, Asics Will Continue Buying Xinjiang Cotton," La Prensa Latina Media, March 26, 2021, https://www.laprensalatina.com/hugo-boss-asics-will-continue-buying-xinjiang-cotton/, cited in "China: Hugo Boss and Asics Say They Would Continue to Source Cotton from XinJian," Centre de Ressources sur les Entreprises et les Droits de l'Homme, March 26, 2021, https://www.business-humanrights.org/fr/derni%C3%A8res-actualit%C3%A9s/china-hugo-boss-and-asics-say-they-would-continue-to-source-cotton-from-xinjiang/.

266 "they were reportedly lobbying to have some of its provisions watered down, arguing that the measures would overcomplicate their supply chain.": Ana Swanson, "Nike and Coca-Cola

Lobby against Xinjiang Forced Labor Bill," *New York Times*, November 29, 2020, https://www.nytimes.com/2020/11/29/business/economy/nike-coca-cola-xinjiang-forced-labor-bill.html.

273 *"'But the prospect of shifting to better, cheaper PV products with the potential for even greater emissions reductions over the long run, has been deferred or even lost.'"*: Izabella Kaminska, "Is Solar Manufacturing a Highly Automated Business?," *Financial Times*, May 18, 2021, https://www.ft.com/content/8614fdca-dd80-4d1f-8b01-8d9c9538ac69.

267 "The letter begged whoever might find it, out there in the free world, to alert governments and human rights organizations to the plight of the prisoners, jailed because they adhered to an organized spiritual group that the paranoid Communist Party had branded a threat to its security.": Amelia Pang, *Made in China* (Chapel Hill: Algonquin, 2022), 1.

The Digital Dictatorship

285 "the *People's Daily*, claimed the country's facial recognition system was capable of scanning the faces of all of China's 1.4 billion citizens in just one second.": People's Daily, China (@ PDChina), "'Sky Net', a facial recognition system that can scan China's population," Twitter, March 26, 2018, https://twitter.com/pdchina/status/978444380066390016.

286 "Western-inspired ideas of an independent media or of civic participation, and any criticism of the party's oppressive history.": Chris Buckley, "China Takes Aim at Western Ideas," *New York Times*, August 19, 2013, https://www.nytimes.com/2013/08/20/world/asia/chinas-new-leadership-takes-hard-line-in-secret-memo.html.

291 "For example, Chinese security is reportedly testing on Uyghurs an app that purports to be able to detect a person's emotional state.": Jane Wakefield, "AI Emotion-Detection Software Tested on Uyghurs," BBC News, May 26, 2021, https://www.bbc.com/news/technology-57101248.

293 "According to the Carnegie Endowment for Global Peace, at least seventy-five out of 176 countries are already actively using AI surveillance technology.": Steven Feldstein, *The Global Expansion of AI Surveillance* (Carnegie Endowment for International Peace, 2019), https://carnegieendowment.org/2019/09/17/global-expansion-of-ai-surveillance-pub-79847.

294 "It was later discovered it had built into the sleek design a number of hacks to allow it access to what was being discussed inside the headquarters.": Ghalia Kadiri and Joan Tilouine, "A Addis-Abeba, le Siège de l'Union Africaine Espionné par Pékin," *Le Monde*, January 26, 2018, https://www.lemonde.fr/afrique/article/2018/01/26/a-addis-abeba-le-siege-de-l-union-africaine-espionne-par-les-chinois_5247521_3212.html.

294 "'or engineered pathogens to target the U.S. population or food supply,' the report quoted experts as saying.": Kirsty Needham and Clare Baldwin, "China's Gene Giant Harvests Data from Millions of Women," Reuters, July 7, 2021, https://www.reuters.com/investigates/special-report/health-china-bgi-dna/#:~:text=Reuters%20has%20found%20that%20BGI's,and%20altitude%20sickness%20in%20soldiers.

294 "Eric Schmidt, the cofounder of Google, said in September 2018.": Aaron Holmes, "Tech Leaders Have Long Predicted a 'Splinternet' Future Where the Web Is Divided between US and China," *Business Insider*, August 6, 2020, https://www.busi-

nessinsider.com/splinternet-us-china-internet-trump-pompeo-firewall-2020-8.

295 "the biggest shipping hub in the Mediterranean, a bridgehead into Europe": Silvia Amaro, "China Bought Most of Greece's Main Port and Now It Wants to Make It the Biggest in Europe," CNBC, November 15, 2019, https://www.cnbc.com/2019/11/15/china-wants-to-turn-greece-piraeus-port-into-europe-biggest.html.

295 "a serious blow to Montenegro's sovereignty.": Rob Schmitz, "How a Chinese-Built Highway Drove Montenegro Deep into Debt," NPR, June 29, 2021, https://www.npr.org/2021/06/28/1010832606/road-deal-with-china-is-blamed-for-catapulting-montenegro-into-historic-debt.

295 "Gwadar, at the entrance of the Persian Gulf, another vital shipping route.": Philip Reeves, "In a Remote Seaside Town, China Envisions a New 'Silk Road,'" WFDD, October 20, 2015, https://www.wfdd.org/story/remote-seaside-town-china-envisions-new-silk-road.

296 "'with censorship, controls, etc.,' Google boss Eric Schmidt has warned.": Lora Kolodny, "Former Google CEO Predicts Internet Will Split in Two—and One Part Will Be Led by China," CNBC, September 20, 2018, https://www.cnbc.com/2018/09/20/eric-schmidt-ex-google-ceo-predicts-internet-split-china.html.

297 "lost some fifty thousand people to the disease by that point, diplomats told the Associated Press.": Jamey Keaten, "AP Exclusive: Diplomats Say China Puts Squeeze on Ukraine," AP News, June 25, 2021, https://apnews.com/article/united-nations-china-europe-ukraine-health-a0a5ae8f735b92e39c623e453529cbb9.

298 "a clear washing of his hands of the Uyghurs and the other Muslims of Xinjiang.": Mohammed bin Salman, "Saudi Crown Prince Defends China's Right to Fight 'Terrorism,'" Al Jazeera, February 23, 2019, https://www.aljazeera.com/news/2019/2/23/saudi-crown-prince-defends-chinas-right-to-fight-terrorism.

298 "'China is buying Muslim leaders' silence on the Uyghurs.'": Alex Ward, "China Is Buying Muslim Leaders' Silence on the Uyghurs," *Vox*, June 23, 2021, https://www.vox.com/2021/6/23/22545232/axios-pakistan-khan-china-uyghurs-belt-road.

298 "like Algeria, Congo, Eritrea, Ethiopia, Gambon, Ghana, Libya, Zimbabwe and Zambia, but the list also included wealthy Muslim states like Saudi Arabia, Iran and the UAE.": ET Bureau, "South Asian Nations Back China's Take on Human Rights in Xinjiang," *Economic Times*, October 23, 2021, https://economic-times.indiatimes.com/news/international/world-news/south-asian-nations-back-chinas-take-on-human-rights-in-xinjiang/articleshow/87217828.cms?from=mdr.

298 "He even went as far as saying that if the government didn't do so, his flagship company would consider leaving Sweden itself.": Monica Alleven, "Ericsson CEO Lobbied Swedish Minister over Huawei Ban—Report," *Fierce Wireless*, January 4, 2021, https://www.fiercewireless.com/wireless/ericsson-ceo-lobbied-swedish-minister-over-huawei-ban-report.

299 "to transparency 'very impressive, and beyond words.'": Associated Press, "How China Blocked WHO and Chinese Scientists Early in Coronavirus Outbreak," NBC News, June 2, 2020, https://www.nbcnews.com/health/health-news/how-china-blocked-who-chinese-scientists-early-coronavirus-outbreak-n1222246.

292 "When Vice Premier Sun Chunlan visited Wuhan, residents dared to shout out, 'Fake, everything is fake!'": Lily Kuo, "'Fake, Fake': Senior Chinese Leader Heckled by Residents on Visit to Coronavirus City, *The Guardian*, March 2, 2020, https://www.theguardian.com/world/2020/mar/06/fake-fake-senior-chinese-leader-heckled-by-residents-on-visit-to-coronavirus-epicentre.

300 "'by its own strength alone, staunchly held off the novel coronavirus epidemic for a very long time.'": Oiwan Lam, "Campaign Urging Wuhan Residents to Show Gratitude to the Communist Party Leadership in Fighting COVID-19 Backfires," *Global Voices*, March 9, 2020, https://globalvoices.org/2020/03/09/campaign-urging-wuhan-residents-to-show-gratitude-to-the-communist-party-leadership-in-fighting-covid-19-backfires/.

Fighting Back

305 "'Living in China is confusing now, because it can feel like being in North Korea and the United States at the same time.'": Jeffrey Wasserstrom, "Why Are There No Biographies of Xi Jinping?" *The Atlantic*, January 30, 2021, https://www.theatlantic.com/international/archive/2021/01/xi-jinping-china-biography/617852/.

307 "'ready to develop relations with China based on the principle of no conflict, no confrontation, mutual respect, and win-win cooperation.'": Hannah Beech, "Rex Tillerson's Deferential Visit to China," *New Yorker*, March 21, 2017, https://www.newyorker.com/news/news-desk/rex-tillersons-deferential-visit-to-china.

318 "'had to tell the Chinese community in Australia that Labor did not support the relationship between Australia and China.'":

John Garnaut, "How China Interferes in Australia," *Foreign Affairs*, March 9, 2018, https://www.foreignaffairs.com/articles/china/2018-03-09/how-china-interferes-australia.

325 "and even many in the media, such as *The Economist*": "'Genocide' Is the Wrong Word for the Horrors of Xinjiang," *The Economist*, February 13, 2021, https://www.economist.com/leaders/2021/02/13/genocide-is-the-wrong-word-for-the-horrors-of-xinjiang.

328 "'and stop reversing the course of international counterterrorism cooperation,' a Chinese Foreign Ministry spokesman said.": Ayaz Gul, "US Removes Anti-China Militant Group from Terror List," Voice of America, November 6, 2020, https://www.voanews.com/a/east-asia-pacific_us-removes-anti-china-militant-group-terror-list/6198046.html.

325 "in Chinese factories to keep the economy running when Han Chinese people were too afraid to return to work.": Joshua Lipes, "Xinjiang Authorities Sending Uyghurs to Work in China's Factories, despite Coronavirus Risks," Radio Free Asia, February 27, 2020, https://www.rfa.org/english/news/uyghur/work-02272020160853.html.